EASTERN EUROPEAN THEATER
AFTER THE IRON CURTAIN

Edited by

Kalina Stefanova

English Style Editor

Ann Waugh

harwood academic publishers
Australia • Canada • France • Germany • India
Japan • Luxembourg • Malaysia • The Netherlands
Russia • Singapore • Switzerland

Amsteldijk 166
1st Floor
1079 LH Amsterdam
The Netherlands

British Library Cataloguing in Publication Data

Eastern European theater after the iron curtain
   1. Theater – Europe, Eastern   2. Theater – Economic aspects –
   Europe, Eastern   3. Theater and state – Europe, Eastern
   I. Stefanova, Kalina
   792'.0947'09049

   ISBN 90-5755-054-7

Cover illustration: Muvesz Theater, Hungary. *Uncle's Dream*, directed by Vassiliev. Photo: Peter Korniss

To the theater-makers of Eastern Europe
who work under very difficult economic conditions
and still work wonders

CONTENTS

Acknowledgments   xi

List of Plates   xiii

Introduction *by John Elsom*   1

Albanian Theater

First Foreword
Ismail Kadare   5

Second Foreword
Teodor Laco   7

Introducing Albanian Theater to the World
Kudret Velca   9

Bulgarian Theater

First Foreword
Anton Donchev   21

Second Foreword
Krassimir Spassov   23

Economic Downfall and Artistic Boom:
The Paradox of Bulgarian Theater
Kalina Stefanova   25

Czech Theater

Foreword
Václav Havel   39

Czech Theater from 1989 to 1996: Discovering Terra Incognita
Jana Machalicka   43

Hungarian Theater

Foreword
Árpád Göncz   61

Hungarian Theater: In Search of an Identity
Krisztina Galgoczi   63

Latvian Theater

Foreword
Raimond Pauls   79

The Ecology of Theater in Post-Soviet Latvia
Valda Carace   81

Lithuanian Theater

Foreword
Eimuntas Nekrosius   101

New Seasons of Hope and Crisis
Ramune Marcinkeviciute   103

Moldovan Theater

Foreword
Mihai Chimpoi   153

At the Crossroads: Moldovan Theater in the Year of Liberalization
Leonid Chemortan   155

Polish Theater

Foreword
Zofia Kalinska   169

Contemporary Polish Theater: A Hamletesque "Body of Time"
Tomasz Kitlinski   171

Romanian Theater

First Foreword
Andrei Serban   181

Second Foreword
Nicolae Manolescu   183

Once upon a Time in Romania …
Five Years of Post-Communist Romanian Theater
Marina Constantinescu   185

Russian Theater

Foreword: An Interview with Yury Lyubimov
Nina Velekhova   201

The State of Russian Theater in the 1990s
Nina Velekhova   203

Slovak Theater

Foreword
Darina Karova   215

Closer to the "Sewer"... A View of Slovak Theater
Anna Gruskova   217

Ukrainian Theater

Foreword
Les Tanyuk   229

Ukrainian Theater: On an Uneasy Path to Self-Awareness
Anna Lypkivska   231

Notes on Contributors   245

Index   251

ACKNOWLEDGMENTS

This book was conceived in Chicago, one October evening in 1994, at a Young Critics Seminar of the International Association of Theater Critics. Representatives from six Eastern European countries were in attendance. Anna Gruskova, a Slovak critic, suggested that we should compile a book about theater criticism in Eastern Europe after the political changes. I suggested instead that we should create a book not only about theater criticism but about the whole theatrical process in Eastern Europe following the lifting of the Iron Curtain. So, my thanks first to Anna whose idea served as a springboard for this book.

The consequent problem of funding was resolved by a kind of deus ex machina. From Bulgaria I had made numerous applications abroad and had received exclusively negative responses when suddenly a new figure – truly a benevolent one – entered my life. My dear friend Snejina Tankovska, a Bulgarian theater director, introduced me to Douglas Funk, the SOLON Foundation's representative in Bulgaria. So, my thanks next to Douglas for his understanding and interest in my project, and to the SOLON Foundation whose grant made possible the editorial work on this book.

Many thanks also to my friends Ewa Staweska, Nikita Pokrovsky, Ruta Rubina, and Taras Filenko, whom I met at the Salzburg Seminar and who helped me enlarge the network of contributors through Eastern Europe. Unfortunately theater in Estonia and Belarus is not included here. Due to communication problems I was unable to maintain contact with the contributors from these two countries, which I much regret.

Finally, I would especially like to acknowledge the crucial contribution of Ann Waugh, an American set designer, whose dedicated and professional work has enhanced the style of this book.

Kalina Stefanova

LIST OF PLATES

(Between pages 115 and 149)

1 Alternativa 2000 Theater, Albania, *Nightmare Pains* (*Exodus*) by Kudret Velca and Elona Velca, directed by Elona Velca.

2 Alternativa 2000 Theater, Albania, *Nightmare Pains* (*Exodus*) by Kudret Velca and Elona Velca, directed by Elona Velca.

3 Midjeni Theater, Shkoder, Albania, *No Exit* by Jean-Paul Sartre, directed by Dominique Dolmieu, with B. Shiroka, R. Marku and S. Garrusi.

4 Bulgarian Army Theater, *Waiting for Godot* by Samuel Beckett, directed by Leon Daniel, with I. Surchadjiev and I. Hristov.

5 Theater of Satire, Bulgaria, *Leonce and Lena* by Büchner, directed by Galin Stoev.

6 The Bulgarian National Theater, Sofia, *Lorenzaccio* by Alfred de Musset, directed by Margarita Mladenova, with M. Kavardjikova and St. Danailov.

7 Theater Na Zabradli, Czech Republic, *The Seagull* by Chekhov, directed by Petr Lebl.

8 Theater Labyrinth, Czech Republic, *Dada Opera* by K. Kriz, V. Gallerova and J. Gerha, directed by Karel Kriz.

9 Theater Comedy, Czech Republic, *Hamlet* by Shakespeare, directed by Jan Nebesky.

10 Hungary, independent production of *Midsummer Night's Dream* by Shakespeare, directed by Janos Csanyi, with D. Udvaros.

11 Asroth Utca Theater, Hungary, *Leonce and Lena* by Büchner, directed by Eniko Eszenyi, with V. Papp and A. Kaszas.

12 Muvesz Theater, Hungary, *Uncle's Dream*, directed by Vassiliev.

13 The New Riga Theater, Latvia, *The Portrait of Dorian Gray* by Oscar Wilde, directed by Alvis Hermanis.

14 The Latvian National Theater, Riga, *The Tailor's Days in Silmaci*, directed by Edmunds Freibergs.

15 The Daugavpils Theater, Latvia, *The Sound and the Fury*, based on William Faulkner, directed by Peteris Krilovs. Photo: The Daugavpils Theater.

16 Lithuanian International Theater Festival, Vilnius, *Three Sisters* by Chekhov, directed by Eimuntas Nekrosius, with D. Micheleviciute, A. Bendoriute and V. Kuodyte.

17 Lithuanian State Academic Drama Theater, *The Old Woman* by Danil Kharms, directed by Oskaras Korsunovas.

18 Lithuanian State Academic Drama Theater, *There To Be Here* by Danil Kharms, directed by Oskaras Korsunovas.

19 Eugène Ionesco Theater, Chisinau, Moldova, *The Bald Prima Donna* by E. Ionesco, with N. Kozaru and B. Kremen.

20 Gugutza Puppet Theater, Moldova, *Hirzobul*, directed by Victor Stefanine.

21 Karman Theater, Moldova, *One Hundred Years of Solitude* by G. G. Marquez.

22 Grupa Chwilowa Theater Company, Poland, *A Stop in the Desert* with A. Zaitsev.

23 Academia Theater Company, Poland, *A Meek Girl*, based on Dostoyevsky.

24 Grupa Chwilowa and Z. Lublina, Poland, *A Home by the Sea*, with E. Bojanowska.

25 The Romanian National Theater, Bucharest, *The Ancient Trilogy* (*Medea, Electra* and *The Trojan Women*), directed by Andrei Sherban.

26 Lucia Sturza Bulandra Theater, Romania, *The Winter's Tale* by Shakespeare, directed by Alexandru Darie, with D. Astilean and S. Cellea.

27 Puppet Theater of Arad, Romania, *Trufaldino*, directed by Ion Minzatu.

28 The Young Spectator's Theater, Perm, Russia, *Candide* by Voltaire.

29 Saint Petersburg's Puppet Theater, Russia, *Hantor's Secret* by L. Sevbeau, with A. Mitrohin.

30 The Russian Army Theater, *The Oresteia* by Aeschylus, with E. Mironov.

31 The Slovak National Theater, Bratislava, *Karate Billy is Coming Home* by Klaus Pohl, directed by Vladimir Strmisko with J. Kroner, E. Horrath and M. Labuda.

32 The Slovak National Uprising Theater, Martin, *Decease of Palo Rocko*, written and directed by Matus Olha with F. Virostko and J. Olhova.

33 Stoka Theater, Bratislava, Slovakia, *Komora*, directed by Blaho Uhlar.

34 Suzirya Theater, Kiev, Ukraine, *Radiation of Fatherhood* by Karol Wojtyła (Pope John Paul II), with L. Kadyrova and S. Djugurdya.

35 I. Franko Theater, Kiev, Ukraine, *Tevie-Tevel* by Grigori Gorin, based on Sholom Aleichem, with B. Stupka.

36 Zankovetska Academy Theater, Lvov, Ukraine, *Marusya Churay* by L. Kostenko.

INTRODUCTION

I started to discover the theaters of Eastern Europe in 1977, when I went to the *Meetings* Festival in Warsaw "to learn", as I wrote in my column for the BBC's weekly magazine, *The Listener*, "a language which was not Polish". I had in mind the richly allusive language of the Polish theater, in which the text, stage imagery and music all seemed to play equal parts. There had been some memorable examples during Peter Daubeny's World Theatre Seasons at London's Aldwych Theatre, such as Andrzej Wajda's *The Possessed* and Konrad Swinarski's *Forefathers' Eve* both from the Stary Theater in Cracow; and I had seen Jerzy Grotowski's *The Constant Prince* and Jozef Szajna's *Replica* in Edinburgh. One particular production drew me eastward, the oddest of all, staged in an Edinburgh charnel house, Tadeusz Kantor's version of Witkiewicz's dadaesque *The Water Hen*.

It was clear to me then, as it still is, that nobody who loves the theater could afford to ignore what was happening in Poland, but the *Meetings* Festival raised more questions than it answered. It took place in late November, as the snow was framing the too-cute shop signs of the reconstructed old town, producing a silent and ghostly calm, smothering the tensions of the alleyways, the political dramas off and on the stages. The festival was organized along the principle of the German *Theatertreffen*: the best regional productions were invited to the capital for wider national coverage. It was clear even to an ignorant outsider that Polish theater had the capacity to absorb many traditions without ceasing to be Polish. Some were familiar to me, influences from Stanislavsky and Tairov, from Reinhardt and Brecht, but others were exotic and strange. I wanted to follow the sources wherever they could be found, in Lithuania, Latvia and Belarus, and over the next few years, whenever time, money and the invitations allowed, I returned to the homelands of the nations lost in the Cold War, trying to piece together for my own satisfaction a European heritage fragmented by a century of suffering and human dispersals.

With each visit, more surprises and more vistas came into view, "far beyond far", to use the haunting Russian phrase. It came as a startling shock to encounter the Rustaveli company in Tbilisi for the first time, the Bulandra Theater in Romania and the extraordinary Tashkent Theater Festival, where Asian and European audiences met without seeming to exchange a word except to their tribal cousins. In 1983 I went to Moscow and Novosibirsk for the BBC, believing that the only company in the Soviet Union allowed to be dissident was the Taganka under its charismatic director, Yury Lyubimov, but I found out that there was a whole continent of them, sometimes speaking in Shakespearian parables, sometimes in plain Russian. The most savage attack on communist bureaucracy which I have ever seen came from the Maly Theater in Leningrad (now St. Petersburg), *Brothers and Sisters* adapted and directed from Fyodr Abramov's novel by Lev Dodin in 1985.

Apart from these brave groups, there were conformist and positively reactionary theaters, whose habits did not seem to have changed since the mid-nineteenth century. The political pressures were sometimes intensely repressive, at other times led more to a managerial sloppiness. I came to appreciate the discipline and efficiency of British actors, who would never turn up drunk to a morning rehearsal or allow themselves to be bullied by a Master Puppeteer of a director. But there was one non-Western quality which seemed to be widely present across these different and changing countries, a Slavic trait perhaps but more social than racial, a non-intellectual seriousness, an almost mystical commitment to the service of their Art. I was told the story of how Kantor, a Jew, kept on working in his Cracow studio throughout the Second World War, without seeking to hide or escape. He may have led a charmed life, but he had more important things on his mind.

This stubborn refusal to take refuge from the storm, such inner strength, was needed then – and is necessary now, as this collection of testaments from the theaters of Eastern Europe, ably compiled and edited by Kalina Stefanova, reveals. It tells a common story of the battle against the new poverty, of once lavishly funded theaters reduced to penury, of artists surviving against the odds, and fighting back. As a historical account, it is invaluable for all students of the theater. As a record of human determination, it will inspire everyone.

John Elsom
Honorary President
International Association of Theater Critics

ALBANIAN THEATER

FIRST FOREWORD

Ismail Kadare

Albania lies in that part of Europe where ruins of ancient theaters abound. For centuries on end, these ruins of antiquity have loomed in silent reproach of this area of the Balkans where theater was born and then died. Culture was wiped out in this entire region and countries such as Greece and Albania were to lose their theater for centuries.

It was a misfortune of history that theater was not only forbidden but forgotten in this part of the world. The sad paradox is that theater died precisely where it had been born. However, as often happens when cultural values risk extinction in one sphere, they find refuge elsewhere. Struck by disaster, theater fled the stage and reemerged in the life of the ancient Balkan peoples as rich social ceremony, assuming a splendour and dramatic character unseen in other parts of the world. Apparently, theater had found its way back to its origins.

For over a century now, theater has been revived in the Balkans. But memories of antiquity, when theater flourished, died, and was reborn, have certainly made a special impact on the artistic life of these countries.

SECOND FOREWORD

Teodor Laco

The Albanian theater is now experiencing the most interesting period in its history. Under the communist regime, theater was the most censored art form. In those days, a dictum existed that paved the way toward mediocrity. According to this dictum, in any controversy regarding the Party line, a communist was the specialist to be consulted for the ultimate decision. I cannot forget my experience with a member of the nomenclatura of the so-called Trade Union at one of the provincial theaters. In regard to every play he would remark, "The play is not bad, but a worker character should be added in order to bring in the spirit of the working class." Nowadays, this mediocrity seems grotesque, but then it was painful.

Nevertheless, art has hundreds of ways of deceiving censorship, and many good artists were able to write realistic works that will remain in the repertoire of Albanian theater forever. What was lacking, was the "unknown", that is to say, modernism. The Albanian theater longed for the innovations of the twentieth century. It is this present day search that is so beautiful and so difficult. Beautiful, as is anything that strives to be new; difficult, as is any venture into the unknown where not everything that glitters is gold. The thirst for the new and modern is great, and artists are trying to quench this thirst with the works of Beckett, Ionesco, Pirandello, Lorca and Arthur Miller. They are the famous ones – tried and true. But there is no knowledge of the drama of the last twenty or thirty years. Young playwrights are trying "modern" experiments with what they have learned by reading. Although some have achieved inter-esting results, everything is in a state of fermentation. Time is needed yet before good wine can be had. Having found the crucial element of free-dom of expression that it had been lacking for so long, Albanian theater is still searching for its contemporary identity.

INTRODUCING ALBANIAN THEATER TO THE WORLD

Kudret Velca

The world knows nothing or next to nothing about the Albanian theater for two reasons. First, Albanians, subjected to a policy of self-isolationism under a totalitarian regime, were not allowed normal relations with the rest of the world, especially in the domains of cultural affairs, literature, and art. This isolationism was especially marked in the field of theater, which would normally have been gathering artistic experience through direct contacts and exchanges with outside influences. For fifty long years, such exchanges were impossible in both thought and deed, and Albanian artists' great desire to experience and profit from world theater remained only a dream. It is only through the establishment of such cultural contacts and exchanges that other countries will come to know the Albanian theater in a comprehensive way.

Second, foreign critics must be able to come to Albania freely in order to familiarize themselves with Albanian culture, especially theater. Through their studies, they can introduce this theater to the rest of the world. Following the overthrow of the totalitarian dictatorship and thanks to recent democratic developments, Albanians are now able to learn about world art, and conversely, the world now has the opportunity to learn about theirs.

A Short History

In order to better understand Albanian theater in the 90s, it is necessary to know something about its early history, traditions, and development. Theatrical traditions in Albania date back to the time of the Illyrians in the fourth century BC. Archeological excavations have uncovered a number of ancient theatrical buildings throughout the country. While the subsequent development of the theater was interrupted due to continual foreign invasions and occupation, theatrical traditions were preserved by the people and passed on from generation to generation. During the Albanian National Renaissance of the late 19th/early 20th century, a national drama began to develop and theatrical performances were staged by amateur groups. Through their treatment of the great political and social issues of the time, these theater companies contributed significantly to the awakening of the national consciousness. By giving voice to the national cause and by expressing the interests of the nation, the theater became an integral part of the moral, political, and cultural life of the country and has remained so to date.

The theater also played an important patriotic role from 1912 to 1939. Sokrat Mio had an important place in the amateur theater during these years. A graduate of the Paris Conservatory, he began his career as a director in 1934 and is considered the pioneer of Albanian theater for his efforts in raising it to international standards. During the National Liberation and Antifascist War (1941–1944), amateur theater groups were organized amidst the ranks of the freedom fighters. They gave improvised patriotic performances intended to educate people about the struggle against the Fascist-Nazi invaders. In 1944, Albania was liberated from foreign oppression and a new period began for the theater: the era of the professional theater.

The Professional Theater

The first professional theater, the Central Theater, was created in the town of Perment in May, 1944, on the eve of the Albanian liberation. The company was composed of actors who had been performing in the amateur theater for many years. The Drama School was founded on November 21, 1944 in Tirana, headed by Sokrat Mio. On May 25, 1945, the State Theater was inaugurated. Later called the Peoples' Theater and today known as the National Theater, its creation marked the beginning of professional theater life in Albania. Theaters were soon established in other major cities, bringing the total number of professional companies to ten. The first professional puppet theater was established in Tirana in 1950. The largest puppet theater, it is one of twenty-five in the country, over half of which are professional companies.

The Alexander Moisiu Drama School played an important role in the training of professional actors. Founded in 1959, it merged with the Music Conservatory and the School of Figurative Art in 1966 to create the High Institute of Arts, known today as the Academy of Fine Arts. The drama school is now known as the Academy of Theater Arts and is composed of three departments: acting, production, and theater management.

During the 1950s, Albanian theaters and drama schools were influenced considerably by the Russians, who introduced high theoretical and practical professional standards, based primarily on the Stanislavsky's method. This professionalism would develop further in the following years under the influence of actors and directors trained not only in Russia, but in the Czech Republic, Hungary, and Albania itself.

The creation and nurturing of a professional theater was the greatest legacy of the forty-five year totalitarian regime. In all other respects, the government was a destructive force – turning the theater into a kind of daily Party/State newspaper. Mediocre plays were staged as a means of divulging decisions made in Party sessions. The stage became nothing more than a podium for the dissemination of political propaganda, subject to extreme censorship, and under the control not of artistic leaders, but of Party members. From 1960 on, when the policy of isolationism began, control and censorship became especially harsh. The movement was accompanied by an unprecedented xenophobia, which people in artistic circles were never able to accept. This marked the beginning of a silent conflict between the State and theater artists, which was manifested in the plays of anti-conformist and dissident authors. In the early 1960s, a new generation of foreign trained producers aspired to stage contemporary, internationally known plays by authors such as Arthur Miller, Tennessee Williams, Mayakovsky, Koch, and Sartre. They were met with extreme opposition by the authorities, and their performances were banned because they were considered to be "decadent" and out of line with the principles of socialism and Marxist ideology. Only certain "classic plays" could be staged, and even these were categorically banned from 1973 to 1985. Tragic also was the fate of the dissident, anti-conformist plays and their authors, who were imprisoned, exiled, or forbidden to publish. In 1969, the Korca Theater staged a play by Minush Jero, directed by Mihail Luarasi, one of Albania's most gifted artists. The play took a critical stand against socialist society, attacking contemporary morality, which, it claimed, was degenerating into self-interest, moving society away from the bright ideals of a free and democratic Albania which had originally inspired the National Liberation movement. The play won first prize at the theater festival that year and was lauded by public, critics, and artists alike. But the joy of victory lasted only twenty-four hours. The next day, head of state Enver Hodga attended the performance and condemned the play because it was negative and did not reflect socialist reality. The production was subsequently banned and its producers were persecuted. The author and director were imprisoned for five years, which effectively destroyed not only their artistic careers but their private lives. As the critic who had praised the play, I myself was forbidden to publish for ten years.

Nevertheless, despite these suffocating circumstances, the Albanian theater developed rich traditions in acting, directing, and scenography, creating a number of fine productions of high, artistic value which have provided a powerful base for future growth. The difficult conditions under which the theater was forced to function caused most artists to view democracy as the sole system under which they could realize their aspirations. Only a democratic system could provide the conditions necessary for creative freedom and contact with contemporary theater abroad from which it had been isolated for over fifty years.

Democratic Transformations and the Theater

Thanks to recent democratic developments in Albania and to growing freedom and independence, the theater is able to return to its original identity as an integral part of the life of the nation. In fact, a primary duty of the theater is to help radically eliminate the totalitarian culture, and to replace it with a democratic culture. Now that they have won creative freedom, one of the main responsibilities facing theater artists is that of learning and applying those new methods and trends that characterize all aspects of contemporary theater.

During the initial years of the effort to establish democracy, life in Albania (as in other Eastern European countries) was characterized by great economic difficulties. This economic crisis was reflected in all areas of culture, including theater. During those years, only two or three of the ten theaters in the country remained open, and even those were confined to very limited activity. As a result, many actors and directors (especially young ones) emigrated to other countries as refugees, taking ordinary jobs and abandoning their profession. Today, this dilemma is even greater for students and recent graduates of the Theater Academy who are faced with no employment opportunities and feel they have to emigrate. In discussing this problem with students, they all say, "We are going to emigrate." It is truly painful to see the young minds that could have injected new, creative energy into our theater leave their country and forsake their art. It seems that this phase of transition economy paralyses art. In an attempt to alleviate these problems, the democratic government instigated a number of theatrical reforms, which have brought about a relative improvement in the overall situation and standards. On the basis of these reforms, all ten of the state subsidized dramatic theaters were saved, although staff sizes were reduced. Only the most talented employees with proven abilities were kept on. As a result, some artists were forced to retire, others now receive welfare payments. At present, 113 people (actors, directors, and designers) are employed full-time in theater, 33 of whom are employed by the National Theater. At other theaters, the number of artists employed varies from twelve to six. Artists' salaries are divided into five categories with monthly incomes varying from US$40.00 to US$80.00. It is difficult to make a living on such a relatively low salary. However, supplementary pay does exist for actors, directors, and designers. According to current regulations, ninety percent of the profit from a performance must be distributed among the realizers. The way in which the revenues are distributed is determined by a "point system" set up by the Artistic Council of each theater. Points are awarded to artists based on merit. The more points one is awarded, the larger the share of the revenues one is entitled to receive. Eagerness to profit fully from this system has resulted in the staging of plays with relatively few characters and artists' salaries can now vary as much as ten to fifteen percent.

In addition to dramatic theaters, puppet theaters exist through-out Albania. They too are subsidized by the State, although not by the Ministry of Culture (as are the drama theaters), but by the municipalities. In 1994, 26 puppet theaters were in operation, with combined audience capacity of 2,711 seats. 1,123 performances were given (46 premieres) with a combined audience attendance of 84,800, bringing in combined profits of 276,900 Leks (nearly US$3,000.00). At the nine district drama-tic theaters, combined audience capacity is 3,628 seats. 262 performances (27 openings) were given to combined audiences of 48,000, bringing in profits of 549,500 Leks (approximately US$5,000.00). In 1993, the 600 seat National Theater held four openings and gave 100 performances at a profit of 428,000 Leks (or US$4,500.00). In 1994, it held 6 openings, and gave 140 performances for audiences totaling 33,295, all of which brought in profits of 1,664,800 Leks (nearly US$13,000.00). In accordance with the point system, ninety percent of this money was distributed to artists as supplementary income. It should be kept in mind that the price of a the-ater ticket in 1994 ranged from 30 to 50 Leks (approximately US$0.50).

It should be pointed out that the Albanian theater has been going through an artistic crisis as well as an economic one. Democratic trans-formations are to blame, because the plays inherited from the past are no longer relevant to today's audiences. Those plays, which were intended to serve the Party agenda, reduced the theater to a mere political tool. Nothing has been carried over from the prior drama of the national revival period. What does remain satisfies neither actor, nor director, nor audience member. Playwrights today are in a difficult position. It is understandable that they need a period of time in which to reflect and change their artistic values. A vivid debate on this problem ensued in the literary press early in 1994, instigated by the fact that only one Albanian play was included at the 1993 Theater Festival. Seemingly as a result of this debate, mainly Albanian plays were presented at the 1994 festival. Over the last few years, one might have expected dramatists to have made real progress in overcoming the decades-long backwardness of the communist era, and, in fact, there was clear evidence of this happening at the 1994 Theater Festival. However, the overall quality of the work left much to be desired.

Due to the lack of good Albanian plays, theater artists quite naturally focused their attention on foreign drama. The current desire to stage foreign plays is justifiable. The fifty year period of isolation that had stifled creativity and disconnected Albania from the best achievements of international theater, created a desire to "taste the forbidden fruit." This longing was satisfied over the last few years by staging plays that had previously been banned. However, by staging these works, it became apparent that despite some successes, our actors and directors lacked the artistic experience demanded by the plays.

Professional Theater Festivals

National theater festivals were organized in 1993 and 1994 in order to help the theater overcome the crises and chaos. At the 1993 festival, the general tone was set by absurdist theater, which was staged for the first time. This marked an important turning point for the Albanian theater. This trend towards absurdist theater was supported primarily by young artists. In 1994, the National Theater presented Arrabal's *Fando and Lis*, directed by Agim Qirjaqi. This director, who is also one of the best actors at the National Theater, has been directing for ten to fifteen years. His abilities, however, have truly become apparent within the last three or four years with his stagings of absurdist plays. After *Fando and Lis* (for which he won Best Director that year), he went on to stage Ionesco's *The Bald Prima Donna*, which was presented at the Kichinev Ionesco Festival in Moldova. Qirjaqi is also respected for his 1992 production of Shakespeare's *Richard III*, and his 1995 staging of the Albanian comedy, *The Craziness of Grandeur*. In examining his artistic activity over the last few years, it is apparent that his main concern is with his country's problems, past and present. He says, " ... at the beginning of the changeover to democracy, I was overwhelmed by the terrible impressions left by the totalitarian era. The themes of crime, blood, violence, and power were the inspiration behind the adventure of *Richard III*". In this production, the director attempted to show the inhumanity of taking and keeping power through violence, treading on the bodies of innocent people – all in reference to the communist regime. He aimed to convey the message that every epoch, every system, and every method of taking power should be lawful. As a result, Qirjaqi's perception of real-life events changed. He says, "The renaissance of the nation and of the deformed spirit of fifty years will take a long time. Thus optimism will eventually give way to pessimism, to lost hopes, and to chaotic emotional and mental states. In this sense, appreciation of the absurd takes on an important role in life." Many artists saw absurdism as a means of rebelling against socialist realism. "Involvement with the absurdist theater," says Qirjaqi, "has appealed to me since the very beginning of my career."

Another director of absurdist drama is Arben Kumbaro, whose staging of Beckett's *Waiting for Godot* won Best Production at the 1993 Theater Festival. Like Qirjaqi, Kumbaro found a perfect outlet in absurdist plays, especially those of Beckett. Not only did they allow him to express his rebellious point of view, but also to demand the opening of new artistic paths along which to lead the Albanian theater to modernity. The new content and form of Beckett's drama challenged the director and actors to make new creative and aesthetic choices, which they did quite successfully. Agim Qirjaqi, in the role of Vladimir, discussed the part as follows: "My dream was to stage *Godot*, but I hesitated about starting off with the "advanced mathematics" of absurdist drama, and turned instead to Arrabal's *Fando and Lis*." He added that he had realized his dream in an excellent way by playing the part of Vladimir. Asked what he could find in the role, he replied, "Myself. The role was within me, but at the same time, it portrays the psychological state of artists in general, of the Albanian intellectual actually, who is waiting for something better. His waiting is fatal. He knows that Godot will not come, but encourages Estragon who keeps the hope of his coming alive. Through Vladimir, I wanted to portray the position of some intellectuals who cannot aspire to greater things, but who should do so."

The design for *Godot*, realized by the well-known painter Edi Hila, played an important role in the production. The stage, although closed in, gave the impression of endless space, establishing an ironic contrast between the endless universe and the microscopic individual. The abstract scenery of *Godot* and the cubist/surrealist design by Agim Zajmi for *The Bald Prima Donna*, mark an important turning point in Albanian scenography by their departure from realistic design.

A number of Albanian plays presented at the 1994 Theater Festival are worthy of note: especially *Three Minds on Auction*, a comedy by Ferdinand Hysi, directed by Armando Bora and performed by the Theater of Vlora; and *Cmurosja*, written and directed by Serafin Fanko, and performed by the Migeni Theater of Shkodra. In *Three Minds on Auction*, the author attempts to abandon theatrical cliches of the past and to experiment with new forms of contemporary drama. The play is a cross between comedy and drama, interweaving tragedy and humor, the grotesque and the absurd, in a harmonious way, resulting in a unique point of view. The use of symbols and allegory give the play a philosophical nature. Serafin Fanko, on the other hand, with his play based on the legends of sacrificing people by building them into the foundations of walls, conveys the timely and important message that Albanians should be shocked by their past (they have been "walled-up" in their past) in order to move forward.

Gezim Kame's production of Eduardo de Filippo's comedy *The Great Wonder* was also presented at the festival of 1994. In his own creative way, Kame remained faithful to his realistic style with this play, as he did with Dürrenmatt's *The Visit* and *Fernando Krofti Wrote Me This Letter* in which he criticized society. Alfred Trebicka's production of *Papyrus '94*, by the Youth Studio, was a special one, as it marked the first experimentation in Albania with the "Theater of Movement".

In 1994, a young French director, Dominique Dolmieu, staged a successful production of Sartre's *No Exit* at the Migjeni Theater of Shkodra. In the same year, this theater staged Ferdinand Radi's play *8 Persons Plus*, directed by Anton Qesari. A truly brilliant play, this comedy is characterized by spontaneous humor, clever dialogue and very comical situations.

Developments in 1995

In 1995, Arben Kumbaro staged a controversial production of Ionesco's *Victims of Duty* with students from the Academy of Fine Arts. Critical and public opinion of the staging was divided. Poor editing was accused of changing the actual content of the play. The director was accused of focusing on formal aspects of the staging at the expense of the under-lying themes of hostile relations between individuals and authorities, themes of extraordinary importance to Albanians. Nude scenes and scenes of rape, on stage for the first time in Albania, shocked audiences. Had they been introduced in order to serve the play, or to elicit applause from young audiences? In response to the criticism, the director stated, "They are simply artistic elements necessary to the spectacle as a whole. This is not exhibitionism." This declaration began a heated debate in the press. Painter and designer Edi Hila commented, "I don't like the fact that the discussion about the play is centering on the scenes of nudity and rape ... . It would be better if the discussion could focus on the value of the work." The theater critic Z. Kutaj pointed out the shortcomings in the director's ability and desire to communicate the aesthetic message of the play to the audience when he wrote, "... [This communication] is realized in part, perhaps to the extent necessary for the creative team, but not for the audience ... . As far as the nude scenes and scenes of rape are concerned – as it is unclear how they serve the function of the play, we may arrive at the conclusion that they do not." This debate illustrated not only the creative freedom of the theater, but also the freedom of the critic, which, in turn, illustrates the emancipation of the society in general.

1995 marked another significant event in the development of the Albanian theater: the creation of private theaters. The first private the-ater, Cafe Theater 1, opened on May 8, 1995 with a production of Dritero Akolli's *Zylo Kamberi*, based on his novel, *The Rise and Fall of Comrade Zylo*. A 60-seat, black box type theater, it is expected to expand to 100 seats in the future. The decor makes use of typical Albanian ele-ments, such as wooden furniture and cane dividers, reminiscent of Myzeqe in central Albania. The founder of this theater is a former actor from the National Theater, Petraq Xhillari. His passion for theater made him open this theater, and his humanity allows actors and directors to use the space for their productions free of charge. "I do not profit. All the proceeds from performances go to the actors and directors. I shall have the satisfaction, which gives me hope for the future," Xhillari says.

Another private theater staging quality productions is the Alternativa 2000 Theater. Created in October, 1994, it has only two productions in its repertory due to financial difficulties: *Judith*, by Eugenio Barba and Roberta Carreri, directed by Elona Velca; and the performance piece *Nightmare Pains (Exodus)*, which combines elements of "Theater of Movement" and dance. This second production took part in the Brouhaha International Festival of Street Theater in Liverpool in August, 1995 where it was met with great success. Hopefully, the creation of small private theaters will allow for the kind of artistic experimentation not possible at the large, state-run theaters.

It is important to emphasize that not only is Albanian theater overcoming the crises and chaos of the last five years, but it is entering a phase of rebirth-opening new paths and experimenting with new creative forms.

1995

BULGARIAN THEATER

FIRST FOREWORD

Anton Donchev

Today the Balkans – the cradle of the ancient theater – are turned into a gigantic scene on which one of the oddest and the most fearful dramas written by History itself takes place. This is a real stage – the word meaning a "tent" – which swings and flaps its tarpaulin as a bird ready to take off and fall apart into feathers and down. The Balkan peoples enter the stage as the choruses – the overlords of the ancient drama. As of yet there are no personalities to lead the choruses and to embody the tragedy and the strength of the epoch. Tens of millions of human beings, "hypnotized" hitherto and deprived for decades of the right to exercise their own will, awake from the sleep of communist illusions.

Theater has never existed apart from its time and its audience. The Bulgarian theater too reflects the problems and the diseases of the Bulgarian society as well as the hopes for its recovery. It's not a full reflection though, because the Bulgarian theater is actually better off and healthier than the ill Bulgarian culture. Born from the ancient mysteries, the Bulgarian theater is still mysterious. The theater temples are not full but they are never empty as well, the actor-priests are exhausted, but they still enter on stage, the theater religion is not a creed of millions, but it still has faithful followers.

The truth is that the Balkans of today resemble the Augean stables in which the people were tied to cribs and fed with the dry straw of illusions. Hercules diverted the waters of Alfea and Pellea in order to clean the Augean stables. Now streams and deluges are flooding Bulgaria. Native springs and foreign rivers wash and carry away the monstrous layers of chewed straw, and the water is turbid not only because of the decades-old filth but also because the water that floods Bulgaria is not the clean water of Hercules. Most of the rivers that pour into our lakes today are dirty and muddy already before they enter Bulgaria. Filthy literature poisons the consciousness of the readers, trite movies blind the eyes of the audience, violence and injustice suffocate human souls.

However the scene-tent of the Bulgarian theater shines in the darkness heavy with fear and hope. Turbid waters flow from the stables where the Pegasuses of the Bulgarian writers used to live. Let alone the cinema. Whereas in the current that flows away from the theater there is already the first fish. Foreign deceitful words printed on the unanimated paper overwhelm Bulgarian books. For the white sheet of the movie screen it doesn't make any difference who rolls in it. Whereas it's Bulgarian actors who act in the Bulgarian theaters, their words are not dubbed, and their speech comes out of their hearts and their bitten lips. Enriched by foreign wisdom, the Bulgarian theater survived because it remained Bulgarian.

SECOND FOREWORD

Krassimir Spassov

What happened was entirely improbable! Suddenly, without any conceptual insights, omens, or presentiments whatsoever, the Bulgarian theater found itself involved headlong in the realization of an ancient goal. I don't mean anything like the long cherished classical Greek ideal of a symmetrical culture confined in its own wisdom. A different ancient culture is a more appropriate analogy in at least partially explaining what happened to the Bulgarian theater: Babylonia – not as symbolized by the tower of Babel, but as the epitome of many deities, many languages, and many passions existing simultaneously in the same place, Babylonia as the epitome of freedom.

In Bulgaria, newly discovered freedom combined with typical Balkan fury turned into an "anything goes" state of mind. Theater as an institution, which for decades had molded reality, problems, aesthetics, and methodology, ceased to exist and was quickly forgotten. It moved over and took its proper place as a chapter in the annals of Bulgarian theater history. Whether or not this was a positive event remains to be seen.

As it concerns the "Babylonian model" of the contemporary Bulgarian theater, it is visibly getting tired of its own furious self-satisfaction with freedom. It is obviously getting fed up with its whirlwind rush to explore all possible routes. From an enterprise of passion, the Bulgarian theater is becoming more and more an enterprise of spirit. It is in the process of creating a completely new history of its own. Now, its speech is freer, more natural, and more theatrical. The Bulgarian theater today has both the experience and the energy necessary to reach its cultural maturity and to discover its own identity. It has a real chance of taking its proper place in the common theater history of Europe and this already is a good twist of fate.

ECONOMIC DOWNFALL AND ARTISTIC BOOM: THE PARADOX OF BULGARIAN THEATER

Kalina Stefanova

Communism, Free Market Economy, and Lots of Basic Theatrical Figures

Don't think that communism was entirely evil! Being brought up under communism meant, among other things, being raised to believe that you could, and even should, work for nothing. There could hardly have been any better psychological preparation for Bulgarian theater-makers (or for the rest of the intelligentsia for that matter) in coping with the free market economy of today. Consider the following facts: the average monthly salary for an actor during the 1994/1995 season was the equivalent of US$60.00, the maximum salary – US$90.00. The average director's salary was US$90.00. You have to be a magician to make ends meet on such money, and there are fewer and fewer venues for earning more. The formerly booming film industry is now non-existent. TV and radio commercials are a fledgling business. Only dubbing films for TV is a sure, albeit limited source of additional income. Money, however, is not the only problem. Under communism, to be an artist meant to be at the top of the social ladder. Now, it means being on the bottom rung.

The paradox is that in spite of the dismal psychological and financial state of affairs of Bulgarian theater-makers, they are producing better and better theater. For the last three years, the theater scene in Bulgaria's capital, Sofia, is brimming with brilliant productions. As Dimitar Gotchev (a Bulgarian director working for years in Germany) put it recently, "in Germany, one needs to travel all over the country to see as many good shows as one can see in one week on one street in Sofia." Furthermore, after two years (1991, 1992) of desperately empty theaters, the audience is back. At the end of the twentieth century, theater in Bulgaria is a lively and sought-out art form.

Bulgarian theater-goers (the country's population totals 8 million) have quite a choice of theaters. Fifty-four state-owned (35 dramatic and 19 puppet theaters), four municipality-owned, one dramatic theater belonging to an institution (the Bulgarian army), and approximately ten private theaters. Seventeen theaters are located in the capital, the rest are in big towns throughout the country. Attendance at the different theaters varies, of course. For instance, during the 1994/1995 season, some 80,000 people attended the Bulgarian Army Theater, one of the most popular theaters. The same season, the maximum ticket price reached the equivalent of US$1.50 (at the National Theater), the minimum price being US$0.40. These figures may seem funny, but given an average monthly salary of less than US$50.00, they are not insignificant. As Valentin Stoichev (the head of Theater 199) put it, "Keeping in mind the poverty of the majority of the people, they still pay a lot of money for theater." Revenues from ticket sales at the three best-attended theaters of the 1993/1994 season were as follows: the National Theater brought in the equivalent of US$30,769.00; Theater 199 – US$24,614.00; the Theater of Satire – US$15,385.00. In 1995, a sold-out show at the National Theater brought in revenues of approximately US$950.00 a night.

All Bulgarian theaters are repertory companies. They maintain a constant repertoire of plays and present different plays every night. Approximately 670 plays are performed annually on all stages across the country, 270 of which are premieres of new productions. The cost of a new production in 1994 equaled US$13,447.00, seventy-two percent of which was allotted to salaries and fees. Most theaters have permanent companies consisting of actors, directors, designers, dramaturgs, etc. 3700 people were employed in theater full-time during the 1994/1995 season, 1200 of whom were artistic personnel. There is a constant give-and-take between the subsidized theaters and the private ones. All theater buildings are owned either by the state or the municipalities, which means that theater companies do not pay rent and, in a way, are in the position of property owners as they can sublease parts of their buildings to third parties. All theaters are equipped with their own workshops for the production of costumes, sets, and props.

Unlike formerly state-owned sectors that have been privatized, such as publishing, book distribution, and the film industry, theater as an institution still depends mainly on government funding. Twenty-five percent of the Ministry of Culture's budget is allotted to theater subsidies. In 1994, a total of approximately 3.8 million dollars were given to theaters by the state. The National Center for Theater, an affiliate of the Ministry of Culture, is in charge of the distribution and the transfer of these funds. Yet this money is not sufficient, and theaters must rely on private and institutional sponsorship as well. Unfortunately, cultural sponsorship isn't really encouraged under the law: currently, only 3% of the taxable profit of state-owned companies can be donated tax-free, and a maximum of 5% for private companies.

Telephone Death Threats, Changes in Company Size, and Other Structural Reforms

In 1990 and 1991, the theater director Plamen Markov, then serving a second year term as head of the Theater of Satire in Sofia, had a very difficult time: he received anonymous death threats by phone, in the mornings he regularly found the tires of his car punctured, there was a huge uproar about him in the media. "I could write a book about that time," he says. The plot of the book would be how he reduced the company's staff by half: from 88 down to 44. "For instance, there was a group of actresses who hadn't been on the stage for ten years and whose husbands were employees of the Ministry," he says, pointing at the building of the Ministry of Internal Affairs, across the street from his window. "On the other hand, all the best actors and actresses of the company were resolutely behind me and backed me up in all difficult situations."

Some years before 1989, people from the theater guild began talking about the need for a general change in the system of employment. It was evident that a reduction in the inflated size of theater companies was overdue. Substitution of the established actors-on-payroll system with an actors-on-short-term-contracts one was considered a certain way of improving the theaters. But it was only after the political changes that something of the kind started to happen.

Before 1989, there was only one example (a very successful example!) of a theater functioning without a permanent company of actors and hiring actors only for specific roles: Theater 199, so named after the number of its seats. Yet establishment of a contract system has been a very painful and controversial issue for the majority of theater-makers since, for decades, employment in theater has meant life-long financial and social security.

The dwindling of the state budget for culture since 1989 has meant a dwindling in theater subsidies, which in turn has reduced salaries of theater professionals to the level of a welfare payment. Nevertheless, most actors prefer the security of that dismal payroll and have resisted becoming freelancers. "From a social point of view, this is understandable," says Yavor Koinakov, deputy head of the National Center for Theater at the Ministry of Culture. "But from the point of view of the art, this is fatal because it doesn't stimulate any inner development of the theater system. It puts it on the defensive, and makes theater heads juggle the subsidy funds so that they can pay salaries rather than concentrate on the theater process for which the society intends the money." This is so because for years, the amount of subsidy a theater received was based primarily on the size of the theater's staff. The subsidy covered salaries and the cost of mounting new productions.

Now, with the reduction in subsidies, the money covers mainly salaries, and very little is left for anything else. "This kind of automatic theater subsidizing, which we are trying to change, has meant equalizing the wages of, say, the National Theater and a small theater in the country – something which doesn't stimulate theatrical activity," says Koinakov. "On the contrary, it encourages actors to become clerks. If they left the staff and signed one-role or one-year contracts, they would earn much more money because their fee would be dependent on the success of their work."

After the political changes, a huge reform in theater subsidization and employment was planned. Its ultimate goal was the formation of a free actors' "stock exchange" and a subsidy combining state and municipal money. As Valentin Stoichev puts it: "The state of affairs of the Bulgarian theater will only change when actors are prepared to sell their professionalism. Only then will the theater system start functioning in a brand new way." The reform was not carried out entirely though, due to general resistance from the majority of theater-makers.

Most actors do now sign contracts with the theaters they work at, but these are generally one to three year contracts and not role specific ones. In the end, this kind of actor–theater relationship does not differ much from the old system of wage employment. There is only one theater in Sofia where the new contract system really works: the National Theater. For the last three years, it has reduced and overhauled its company, constantly hiring new actors for roles in almost every new production, thus being constantly dynamic. The result has been that from an archaic, boring, academic theater, the National Theater has truly become the leading theatrical institution in the country, turning out some of the best shows in Bulgaria.

Another argument in favor of an overall reform is the fact that the best actors were the first to leave theater staffs once they were able to do so and now they are the best paid members of the theater union.

The two central aspects of the planned general reform are being experimented with at 21 theaters around the country. 16 theaters are being subsidized jointly by the state and the municipalities, and five others (two drama theaters and three puppet theaters) have been designated "open stages", retaining only an administrative staff that hires actors on role-specific contracts.

In the Fledgling Private Theater Sector, the Formula is *Zeal, Zeal, Zeal*!

On May 31, 1989, five months before the change of the political system in Bulgaria, the first opening of the first private theater, Dialogue, took place. The theater was not yet registered at the time. The authorities hadn't agreed to give it the permit necessary in order to function as an independent legitimate theater. The founding members later appealed to the supreme court, and on January 4, 1990 they finally received their license. Boiko Iliev, the founder and current head of the theater, says, "For three years, Dialogue existed completely on its own. It wasn't subsidized by anyone. The term 'sponsor' was still something very vague at the time. We worked for next to nothing. Friends from other theaters and from the film studio lent us costumes, sets, and props for free. Everything we did was based on sheer enthusiasm for creating something nobody had done before. I was summoned to many places. The Party structure was still very strong and I had to explain to all levels of the Party what we were doing at the theater."

Now, after having changed homes several times, Dialogue is the only private theater lucky enough to be located in one of the best areas of Sofia: on the theater street itself – Rakovsky, the Bulgarian equivalent to Broadway. It occupies a 180-seat hall where it performs four times a week. There are eight plays on its playbill. Tickets cost the equivalent of 90 cents. All 25 actors working there also work elsewhere, as it's impossible to live on the very low fees they receive (US$4.00) per performance. Sometimes they rehearse at night – the only time everyone is available.

Money-wise, the situation is quite similar at almost all other private theaters. "We have been in the preposterous position of paying our conductor (who is a performer as well) ten cents per show," says Vesselin Kalanovski, head of the Free Theater, founded in 1991. "But if an actor is in most of the shows at our theater, his total fee could equal the average actor's salary at the state-owned theaters."

Besides the lack of money, the private theaters all have many other things in common. For example, the youth of the actors and the fact that they are not confined to working only at the respective private theater (on the other hand, Kalanovski points out: "all Bulgarian actors are potential members of our theater."). Paradoxically, the repertoire of the new theaters consists mainly of very serious, usually classical plays. "We don't want to have any potboilers or variety shows on our playbill. There's enough of that around," says Boiko Iliev. The life of a show at the private theaters is twenty to thirty performances on average.

Theater 13 is a private theater of a different breed. Named after the number of actors in the company, its productions consist of shows based on music, dance, puppetry, and very little text. Thus not confined by language, Theater 13 is constantly on the road, and has already toured most of Europe, China, and Japan. Higher ticket prices abroad and full houses everywhere make Theater 13 somewhat less concerned with money problems.

Another theater in a similarly privileged financial situation is the Barbukov Theater, named after its sponsor. Founded in 1994, it is one of the youngest private theaters, but it has on its payroll mainly elderly actors. It has five of the best senior Bulgarian actors on staff. When additional actors are needed, the theater hires mainly well-known actors on role-specific contracts. The theater doesn't have its own home and functions as a touring company. Their sponsor pays the salaries of the actors and the administrative staff. Additional funds necessary for rent, electricity, accommodation, transportation, etc. come from box-office revenues.

The Barbukov Theater's huge success is rivaled only by that of some of the shows at the La Strada Theater. "There are people who buy tickets for our shows one month in advance," boasts theater head Nikolai Dodov, quite rightfully too, as such practice is not at all common in Bulgaria. "We have performed some of our shows more than forty times already, and we always sell at least twenty standing room tickets a night."

How do theater-makers at the private theaters feel in the bittersweet atmosphere of their everyday life? Vaselin Kalanovski says: "Quite comfortable at times, because you know that everything from A to Z is born from your hands, heart, and soul. At other times, when we are heading toward financial ruin, I feel like jumping through the window. But somehow we always manage to find money … It's like being on the stage – you can "take off" only once, but it's enough for ten times." Nikolai Dodov says: "The main formula is zeal, zeal, zeal! For instance, there was a period of three years in my life when I had to leave the theater to solve my financial problems. I sold cans then. Now, if it's necessary, I'll do it again."

La Strada is sponsored by a famous businessman. In Bulgaria today, rumors of money laundering surround every nouveau-riche businessman. I asked Nikolai Dodov whether they were concerned about their sponsor in this regard. "Do you call $23,000 money?" he asked in turn, citing the amount of their latest donation. "If our sponsor were laundering money, he would own at least five Mercedes and wouldn't care about the theater. Look at the banks! They don't sponsor any theaters. And if some of them would only order their employees to drive their Mercedes slower, in one day they would save enough money to sponsor a theater. I would most happily embrace a sponsor who's laundering money, but unfortunately, there are no such sponsors anymore."

The Love–Hate–Love Relationship Between the Audience, the Theater, and Politics

Before 1989, the audience loved the theater because it was one of the very few social outlets. Things were said on stage that couldn't be heard anywhere else but at home and between close friends. Of course, these things were not said directly. The Aesopian language of the theater attained perfection during those years, but everyone knew what the hints meant, what was hidden behind the puns – including the authorities.

As was everything else, the theater was strictly censored, yet it was kind of tacitly endorsed by the authorities, achieving the "honorary" status of an outlet for social tensions. The audience loved the "openly hidden" state of conspiracy between itself and the theater, and packed the houses, whether in organized groups from the workplaces or on their own. Then came the political changes of November, 1989, and everything in the routine, 45-year-old theater–audience relationship turned upside down.

Politics took to the streets and became itself theater – new and much more interesting in its unprecedented openness and directness than the old one. There were no more taboos and no more need for Aesopian language. The audience left the theaters and moved into the open air of the street spectacle, or stayed glued to televisions and radios, watching or listening to the theater taking place in Parliament. Along came other temptations too: the market was inundated with videos; satellite TV channels began broadcasting overwhelming numbers of programs. On top of all that, skyrocketing inflation took its toll and money for entertainment became too scarce. Every rise in prices was followed by a conspicuous exodus from the theater. The theater resorted to the help of potboiler plays, quite a novelty to the Bulgarian stage. Sometimes this "weapon" worked, but not always. Then, sometime in 1992, when the situation already seemed desperately black, the theater of politics loosened its grip on the public. Fed up with the easy talk and quarrels of the politicians, the public turned back to the legitimate theaters. There it found entertainment of very high quality and at relatively very low prices, especially in comparison to restaurants. "Over the last couple of years there has been such an unusual boom in our theater," says playwright Stanislav Stratiev. "It's like a strange blossoming on this dunghill that our country has become at the moment. To me, the explanation lies mainly in the general breakthrough made in directorial thinking. Directors have begun to express themselves thoroughly, as never before, without any limitations. On the other hand, there are no more forbidden names, themes, or plays. So, although it's late, directors have obtained free access to all the great names of world drama and are turning out some very good shows."

In spite of the audience's return to the theater, old attendance records are still only wishful thinking these days. Before, a show was considered a huge success if it had 400 to 500 hundred performances. Now, 50 performances is considered impressive. Since one show can be expected to run for a shorter time than before, more shows are being mounted. Prior to 1989, three to four new productions would open at each theater per season. Now, many more open. Among the exceptions are some shows that survived the 1989 changes: Brecht's *Herr Puntila and His Servant Matti* ran from 1987 to 1994; and *Zoo Story*, by Edward Albee, ran from 1984 to 1994. Two Bulgarian plays – *The Last Night of Socrates*, by

Stefan Tzanev and *How Pisar Tricho Didn't Marry Princess Kita*, by Nikola Russev are among the longest running recent shows. The first one ran from 1986 to 1994, and the second, which opened in 1990, is still running. But, the unbeatable record is held by *Waiting for Godot* which opened in 1988 and is still running.

Let's Stage *Waiting For Godot* at Last! ... At Least It Will Be on Record That We Were the Last Ones To Do So!

It is joked that this was said by Leon Daniel, the director of the play at the Bulgarian Army Theater, when he was preparing to stage it. This highly successful production was the harbinger for the influx of absurdist plays that have flooded the Bulgarian stage since 1989. There is hardly any play by Beckett or Ionesco that hasn't already been produced. However, the abolishment of the decades-long taboo on absurdist drama has been a double edged sword. On the one hand, directors and actors have at last been able to try their hand at some of the greatest plays of world drama of the 1950s and 1960s and the audience has finally been given the long overdue chance to enjoy them. On the other hand, these productions have been guilty of condescending to the mass audience while at the same time claiming to be the hottest theater commodity of the day. Here are two commentaries on this post-totalitarian trend in Bulgarian theater:

Director Plamen Markov says, "Bulgarian theater is living through something like puberty – as if it wants to make up for all the things it should have been doing over the last 45 years, but couldn't. Some great shows have come to life as a result. But, at the same time, this trend is like someone deciding that since they never read the novels of Mayne Reid as a teenager, now all of a sudden as an adult they have to do it. We're always late and then, at some point, we want to catch up very quickly with all the things we lost in the meantime."

Director Zdravko Mitkov says, "All these absurdist plays are really great, but they have already played their role in time and world theater has advanced a long way since then. Unfortunately, we are again lagging far behind the rest of the theater world and are far from being modern. Moreover, in this absurdist euphoria, our theater is in the naive position of perceiving itself as an experimenter without any experimentation actually being carried out."

"Neither Godot Nor Beckett will Solve the Problems of Bulgarian Drama!"

So says Stefan Tzanev, one of the best and most popular Bulgarian playwrights. The foremost problem facing Bulgarian drama over the last seven years has been the almost complete lack of new Bulgarian plays. In factual terms, that means that foreign plays form 90 percent of the repertoire now, while Bulgarian plays account for only the remaining ten percent. In comparison, prior to 1989, some 50 percent of plays being performed were Bulgarian, 15 percent were Russian, 20 percent were classical plays, and 15 percent were foreign. This ratio was not a mandatory rule, but rather a tacit requirement that theaters had to abide by. In order to do so, theaters had to stage some very mediocre Bulgarian plays. According to some, it was exactly this decades-long forced priority of Bulgarian drama over everything else that has driven the repertoire to the opposite extreme today. Others think that the reason for the current crisis in Bulgarian drama stems from the fact that young directors don't take any interest in new Bulgarian plays, and in general, don't want to make any commitment to the playwrights of their generation. Tzanev says, "At the Bulgarian Army Theater, we had the idea of designating our small stage for plays by young Bulgarian playwrights staged by young directors. We received some good plays, but no directors were interested in staging them. They probably have plans to conquer world drama first?! OK, let's forget about us, the elderly playwrights, but who's going to nurture the young ones?"

Tzanev's colleague, the playwright Stanislav Stratiev, finds this quite understandable. "It's not only the young playwrights' plays that directors are unwilling to take on, it's ours also. To me, it's a normal reaction. After being forced to 'help' so many imperfect, mediocre Bulgarian plays, now they simply want to direct only very good plays with international reputations so that they can best express themselves."

The tally of active Bulgarian playwrights is really dismal. There are less than ten living playwrights – all in their fifties and sixties. Less than five are somewhat active. "If it goes on like this, in 20, 30 years, there won't be any Bulgarian drama," says Valentin Stoichev, the head of Theater 199. "It's natural that in these economically precarious times theaters prefer to play it safe and stage already famous plays. Actually, there isn't any motivation to do otherwise. Our theater for instance, is a perfect place to stage new, low-budget Bulgarian plays, but we are not encouraged in any way to do so. The problem, it seems to me, stems from the anti-cultural politics of the 1980s. Then there were no real competitions for new plays, only commissions. This was a very comfortable way for playwrights with already established reputations to make money. That's why there are very few good plays written by them. Now, again on a national level, there is no better political policy toward theater."

There is yet another explanation of the current crisis in Bulgarian drama. Zdravko Mitkov says, "The current generation of Bulgarian playwrights was under governmental and self-control for so long, that they were never really able to develop and perfect their skills. They had to make political calculations all the time, and they became experts at getting a play past the censors rather than at writing plays. So now, when there isn't any censorship, it turns out there are very few playwrights out there with fresh ideas."

In the first half of the century, there had been a special law for encouraging Bulgarian drama. The National Theater had taken this on as one of its missions as well. For years, it maintained the tradition of opening every new season with a Bulgarian play. Now, such an attitude toward theater on a governmental level is long overdue. Moreover, throughout the years, before and after 1989, Bulgarian plays have proved to be among the best attended. A wave of revivals of plays by Yordan Radichkov – considered by many to be the greatest Bulgarian playwright – have been hugely successful over the last few years. Several festivals of Bulgarian plays (both new and classical) sprang to life in the first half of 1995. Hopefully, this is a harbinger of the future recovery of Bulgarian drama.

Why Chekhov?

Chekhov's plays have always been present in the repertoire of the Bulgarian theater but they have never been audience favorites. The ordinary explanation for this has been that since his plays are rather monotonous and slow-paced, Chekhov is not quite fit for the Bulgarian temperament. After 1989, and especially over the last three years, there has been an outburst of Chekhov's plays on the Bulgarian theater stages. *The Cherry Orchard*, directed by Krikor Azarian at the Bulgarian Army Theater, *Three Sisters* directed by Margarita Mladenova at SFUMATO, and especially *The Seagull* directed by Krassimir Spassov at the National Theater have become real theater events.

Why such a surprising turn in the theater fashion? My explanation is that it's right now when Chekhov turns out to be a kindred soul to the Bulgarian audiences because his characters have one very important and topical thing in common with the ordinary theater-goer, that is their attitude toward the change – in society, family, love relationships, economic and social status, etc. Similar to the Bulgarians of the mid 1990s, the Chekhovian characters feel a desperate need for a change in their lives but they don't know how to achieve it, how to fight about it, and may be, who knows?, deep down they may not be ready for a change, so for now they can only talk about, and sigh for, a coveted change.

Art, Commercialism, Spectacle: Bulgarian Theater in Search of Its New Face

Art or commercialism? Never throughout its 150-year history has Bulgarian theater ever faced such a dilemma. Born out of the Bulgarian peoples' struggle for national identity and for liberation from the five-century long Turkish occupation, Bulgarian theater is at its very core highly moralistic and didactic. The concept of theater as "a teacher" charged with conveying some kind of a moral (no matter what genre is being conveyed on stage) was deeply ingrained in the audience's consciousness and perception during the first decades of the Bulgarian theater's history. Later, the theater was highly influenced by Russian psychological drama and the Stanislavky's Method. Then came 45 communist years of highly political theater, subjugated to the dogma of Socialist Realism. The on-stage presence of a "positive hero" (that is, an ideal character) was a must, as was an accompanying politically correct moral. This was a futile process that amounted to *Waiting For Godot* in real life. Anyway, it helped reaffirm the predominant inclination of audiences and critics alike to disregard shows that are sheer entertainment.

After 1989, in the middle of their worst audience crisis, theaters tried to lure people back to their halls with frivolous, escapist shows – the equivalent of the romance novels and other escapist literature that inundated the book market at the same time. Unlike publishing, this tactic succeeded in the theaters for only a short while. The need for grand, lavish spectacle – as a novelty – was obvious, yet it was not a demand for spectacle for its own sake. Over the last couple of years, a new generation of actors and directors have finally hit on the needed formula: spectacle plus philosophy or politics.

Don Quixote at the National Theater – the ultimate example of this formula to date – became the hit of the 1993/1994 season. It combines drama, puppetry, ballet, spectacular sets, farce, and poetry. Its effect on the audience has been as captivating as the fall of the chandelier in the *Phantom of the Opera*. Riveted to their chairs by the magic of the show, audiences have loved it so much that it is still the hottest ticket at the National Theater.

Don Quixote is directed by Alexander Morfov, a graduate of the puppet theater department at the National Academy for Theater Arts and Film in Sofia. Other graduates of this program include the lead actor of the show and several other young theater-makers, such as the directors and actors of the La Strada Theater and Theater 13, as well as the creators of the most watched satirical political TV show, *Ku-Ku*. All have become extremely popular over the last few years. With their diverse talents and ability to combine different media within their shows, they have become the Bulgarian theater's answer to the audiences dream of a new type of theater-maker.

The middle generation of directors – Ivan Dobchev, Plamen Markov, Zdravko Mitkov, Margarita Mladenova, Krasimir Spasov, Snejina Tankovska, etc. – have responded to this challenge in their own way, creating highly imaginative and sensual productions.

The audience has been looking for spectacle not only in the lavish shows on the big stages of the big theaters, but also on the small stages of the studio theaters. Some of the most successful responses of the smaller theaters in this respect have been through the plays of Eric Bogosian. *Sex, Drugs, and Rock 'n Roll*, for instance, has set a new precedent by playing to sold-out houses in three different theaters in Sofia simultaneously – an unheard of phenomenon in the Bulgarian theater.

Vasil Stefanov, critic and head of the National Theater since 1990 says, "Before 1989, theater was a shadow of reality. Now it either tends to escape from reality or create a new one. Before, the audience came to enter into a conspiracy with the theater regarding the reality they lived in. Now, it comes in search of entertainment and a new reality different from their own. In other words, the Bulgarian theater is in the process of reclaiming its right to be a second reality – the reality of Art."

1995

CZECH THEATER

FOREWORD

Václav Havel

For the first time in the history of man, the planet he inhabits is encompassed by a single global civilization. Because of this, anything that happens anywhere has consequences, both good and ill, for everyone everywhere. This civilization, however, is composed of an enormous number of peoples or ethnic groups with widely diverse customs and traditions, and of many cultures, or cultural spheres, both large and small, many religious worlds, and many different kinds of political culture.

It seems that the more tightly this variegated community is crowded together by contemporary civilization and compelled to accept common values and modes of behavior, the more powerfully will different groups feel the need to defend their national, racial, and cultural autonomy and identity. Many dangerous conflicts in the world today can be explained by the simple fact that the closer we are to one another, the more we notice our differences.

Moreover, we are living at a time when various artificial orders have collapsed, whether these orders have been formed by the colonial system, or the bipolar system dominated by two superpowers. The world is becoming genuinely multicultural and multipolar and is only now beginning to seek a new, genuinely just order, one that meets the needs of the present.

All of this makes the modern world an especially dramatic place, with so many people in so many places resisting coexistence with each other. And yet its only chance for survival lies precisely in such coexistence.

It is not true that because of television, film, video, and the other great achievements of this era, theater is dwindling in importance. I would say that exactly the opposite is true, that the theater is better suited than any other medium to reveal, in genuinely compelling and challenging ways, not only all the dark forces that are dragging the world down, but also everything bright and luminous, in which its hopes are contained.

In today's dehumanizing technological civilization, theater is one of the important islands of human authenticity. That is, it is precisely what – if this world is not to end up badly – must be protected and cultivated. After all, the return of the irreplaceable human subjectivity, the concrete human personality and its concrete human conscience, is precisely what this world of mega-machinery and anonymous mega-bureaucracies needs. Only man is capable of confronting all the dangers that face the world, confronting it with his renewed responsibility, his awareness of connections – in other words, precisely with something within him which not even the best network of modern computers can replace. The hope of the world lies in the rehabilitation of the living human being.

Yes, theater is not just another genre, one among many. It is the only genre in which, today and every day, now and always, living human beings address and speak to other human beings. Because of that, theater is more than just the performance of stories or tales. It is a place for human encounter, a space for authentic human existence, above all the kind of existence that transcends itself in order to give an account of the world and of itself. It is a place of living, specific, inimitable conversation about society and its tragedies, about man, his love and anger and hatred. Theater is a point at which the intellectual and spiritual life of the human community crystallizes. It is a space in which it can exercise its freedom and come to understanding.

In the global technical civilization created by so many autonomous cultures and threatened by conflicts between them, theater is – I firmly believe – a telescope into the future and a means of giving a concrete shape to our hope. Not because its purpose is to describe a world better than the one that exists, or to construct a vision of a better future, but because it embodies the main hope of humanity today, which is the rebirth of a living humanity. For, if theater is free conversation, free dialogue, among free people about the mysteries of the world, then it is precisely what will show humankind the way toward tolerance, mutual respect, respect for the miracle of Being.

I appeal to you all, people of the theater, to remember your colleagues in Sarajevo. They have been doing precisely what I have been talking about. Through the exercise of freedom of the spirit, through the cultivation of dialogue and the creation of a space for real human communication, they are confronting the terrible war in their country. Ethnic fanatics and thugs are casting the world back into its darkest past. People of the theater who engage their audiences in a dialogue about the dramas of the world of today and the dramas of the human spirit point the way to the future.

There is another war going on in Sarajevo beside the one we see on television. It is an unarmed conflict between those who hate and kill others only because they are different, and people of the theater who bring the uniqueness of human beings alive and make dialogue possible. In this war, the people of the theater must win. It is they who point toward the future as a peaceful conversation between all human beings and societies about the mysteries of the world and Being.

These people of the theater are serving peace, and they remind us that theater still has meaning.

Prague, March 27, 1994
International Day of Theater
Reprinted by permission of Václav Havel's press office

CZECH THEATER FROM 1989 TO 1996: DISCOVERING TERRA INCOGNITA

Jana Machalicka

Prelude

In order to portray the Czech theater after 1989, it is necessary to make some mention of the period which directly proceeded the political changes. The events which took place on November 17 1989 on *Narodni Trida*, the major opposing reaction, the theater strike announced the following day at the Realistic Theater – all were essentially only the culmination of the systematic erosion of the former regime. The role that theater played in this destruction was substantial. The main currents of opposition, which united to form Civic Forum, also came together in the theater at a meeting on November 19 at the Chinohcrni Klub. The theater was transformed into a place for political discussion and debate. From a historical viewpoint, theater had once again played an important role in the awakening of national consciousness and, in its own way, this process culminated in the events of 1989.

In the late 1980s, many theater people had tried to find a certain modus vivendi, formulating their protest against the political regime. In some ways, the studio theaters had an easier time in this regard as they were better able to manouvre while escaping ideological supervision. Of course, even the official so-called "stone theater" did not remain unaffected by these trends as shown by the progressive work of the time at the Realistic Theater (now the Labyrinth Theater), the work of director Evald Schorm at the Theater Na Zabradli, Kacer's productions at the Theater Na Vinohradech and the Ostrava State Theater, Ivan Rajmont's work at the Chinoherni Studio, etc.

During the season immediately preceding the fall of the totalitarian regime, it was not accidental that there were a number of exceptional productions that in their own way anticipated and accelerated the subsequent socio-political changes. For example, the plays of Josef Topol, which had been banned for years, were staged again. The theatrical "collage", *Res Publica I & II*, at the Realistic Theater signaled a loosening up of cultural life. Staged on the 70th anniversary of the founding of the Czech Republic (October 28th, 1988) *Res Publica I* attempted to evoke feelings of the inter-war period, an era of youthful democracy that had been intentionally erased from public memory. *Res Publica II* took place virtually on the eve of the November revolution (October 28th, 1989) and was a daring call back to the 1960s. For the first time, names which had been banned for years rang out from the stage. The audience could not believe their ears when they heard lines from Havel's *Garden Party*. The initiator of this project, director Karel Kriz, commented, "We had no idea whether or not we would be able to perform these pieces again. The respective offices would rather have banned everything, but they didn't really want to get that involved. So they put heavy pressure on us, they wanted us to ban the production ourselves, which did not happen."

The event of the 1988/89 season however, was, without a doubt, Jan Grossman's production of Molière's *Don Juan* at the Theater Na Zabradli. Jan Grossman (1925–1993) was among the major figures of Czech theater. In the 1960s, he showcased mainly Absurdist drama at the Theater Na Zabradli, including works by Václav Havel. During the period of normalization, he was unable to work in the capital and withdrew to the asylum of theaters outside Prague. In 1982, he was allowed to return to Prague and take an engagement at the S. K. Neumann Theater in Liben. After his return to the Theater Na Zabradli in the late 1980s, he created several key productions during this critical period of change.

A Wave of Banned Plays

After the dramatic November intermezzo, theatrical activity gradually returned to normal. The remainder of the 1989/90 season was characterized by a wave of productions of banned plays, especially plays by Václav Havel. Plays by Pavel Landovsky, Pavel Kohout, Milan Uhde, Karol Sidon, Ludvik Askenazy, and others were also revived. Many plays by foreign playwrights like Dürrenmatt, Mrozek, Rozewicz, Stoppard, and Pinter among others, which for one reason or another had been objectionable to the former regime, were staged again. Among the most extraordinary productions of Havel's plays were: *Largo Desolato*, directed by Jan Grossman at the Theater Na Zabradli; *Beggar's Opera*, directed by Jirji Menzel at the Chinoherni Klub; *Garden Party*, directed by Vladimir Strnisek at the National Theater; *The Redevelopment*, directed by Karel Kriz at the Realistic Theater/Labyrinth; and *Temptation*, directed by Jan Burian at the J. K. Tyl Theater in Pilzen. Most of these productions were enormously popular. For example, *The Redevelopment* at the Realistic Theater had over one hundred performances. Havel's *Largo Desolato*, the story of a dissident who cannot bear his responsibility, is a highly stylized piece and Jan Grossman staged the play as an angst ridden dream, enclosed in trap-like apartment walls. The all-pervasive absurdity became a means for portraying the tragic frailties of the individual. Along with his special sense of irony Grossman strengthened the farcical nature of the play and thereby maintained the balance between the tragic and the comic. Jan Burian staged *Temptation* at the J. K. Tyl Theater in

Pilzen setting it in a framework similar of the folklore marrionette plays about Faust, which altered the interpretation of individual characters.

Homecomings and Goodbyes

During the 1989/90 season, a number of personnel changes took place: theater managers and artistic directors were changed, there were migrations of actors and transformations of acting companies. Even greater changes took place during the following season. Original heads or co-founders of legendary Prague stages of the sixties, renowned even abroad, as well as other figures who had been repressed under the communist regime returned to the Czech Republic. Among them were Jan Grossman who returned to the Theater Na Zabradli and Jaroslav Vostry who returned to the Chinoherni Klub.

A special aspect of the post-November evolution of the Czech theater is the renewal of the Theater Za Branou and its short five-year history. Otomar Krejca reopened the theater bringing back the original actors and artistic staff – dramaturg Karel Kraus and director Helena Glancova. He filled in the company with young people, and attempted to pick up where they had left off with the works which had been forcefully disrupted in 1972. For example, he staged Chekhov's *Cherry Orchard*, Nestroy's *String with One End*, and *The Difficult Man* by Hugo von Hofmannstahl. These productions did not reach the level of Krejca's period in the 1960s and audience response was also substantially less enthusiastic, but they certainly were the confirmation of a personal poetry and the ability to exhibit precisely composed stage forms. Critical reaction however was for the most part negative, and the theater had a very low attendence rate. At the beginning of 1995, the Ministry of Culture decided that it would not establish any new theaters, nor would it continue to finance any theater to the present extent, with the exception of the Prague National Theater. Otomar Krejca resigned as manager and artistic director. The company with its new management continued to exist for nearly half a year as the Theater Za Branou III, but from the beginning it was evident that the era of this theater was drawing to a close. Krejca's last production at this theater was Pirandello's *Mountain Giants*, which the director interpreted as a depiction of the fate of his theater and the current state of society. Together with designer Josef Svoboda, he reworked the basic conflict of the play. His staging was primarily a glum kind of reverie, oscillating between dream and reality. Theater theoretician Jindrich Cerny characterized the demise of the Theater Za Branou quite concisely: "In spite of all reservations, none of the ten productions of this theater entitled anyone to sweep them aside like that".

The entire affair around Theater Za Branou and Otomar Krejca is above all a sad example of one typical characteristic of the Czech nation: to bury their great personalities alive and then to build glorious monuments to them after their death.

The fate of the Semafor Theater, the most progressive of the "small form theaters" of the sixties with its distinctive poetry was similar. The theater was founded by Jiri Suchy and Jiri Slitr. After Slitr's death during the years of normalization, Suchy was quietly pushed out not only by the political power, but also by his colleagues, who turned his Semafor into a socialist tabloid theater. After November 1989, Suchy attempted to revive Semafor's good name. Restaging of old productions were unconvincing, and did not contribute to the revitalization of the Semafor's magic. The eviction notice Jiri Suchy received from the new owner of the building in which the Semafor was located was just another unhappy chapter in the history of the past five years. Now slot machines reign in the theater and like toadstools after the rain, all kinds of shops of questionable repute have sprung up in the vicinity. Yet on the walls of the abandoned stage one can still see the autographs of famous visitors and collaborators of the theater beginning with Václav Havel and ending with Milos Forman. Jiri Suchy and his troupe may have been granted sanctuary at the Prague City Theater and at Studio Karlinek, but this is in fact the swan song of a once popular company.

Restitution and Financial Dictates

The situation at many Czech theaters since 1990 has been characterized by internal conflicts within companies caused in part by new artistic management often running up against run-down systems of operation. In addition there were also property disputes as a result of restitution. One of the first conflicts of this kind was the affair surrounding the Realistic/Labyrinth Theater. Originally a property of the Svanda family, this extensive complex of theatrical buildings was nationalized after the communists came to power in 1948. Over the years, the theater was reconstructed at considerable cost and when the family made a claim for the property to be restituted, an investment of millions was at stake. The theater management, which had formed a center of intellectual resistance to the regime before November 1989, refused to take responsibility for giving away such valued property, although they did not doubt the claim for the return of the building. The building was then devalued by the Ministry of Privatization. The entire affair became a juicy tidbit for the press. At the moment there is no legislation which would protect cultural institutions in buildings which have been returned through restitution. A ten-year-protective period (until 2001) has been passed, but it is a temporary proposal which solves nothing. The case of the Labyrinth Theater is in this regard a cautionary precedent. The new owners, who clearly had no interest in maintaining the theater, in turn sold the property to a film production firm, which from the very beginning had vehemently attempted to close down the theater as it had a clear conception of the potential commercial uses of the building. The state more or less watched these procedings without any interest in supporting the endeavors to create an interesting theater center.

Other theaters located in privately owned buildings find themselves in similar situations, even if mutual relations between owner and tenant have not disintegrated as much as in the Labyrinth Theater case. Many theaters are in tight situations especially where funding for regular maintenance is concerned. The municipality has no money and the private owners don't want to give any, and are eagerly waiting for the possible condemnation of the premises when they will finally have an empty building which can be rented to more lucrative tenants. It can be expected that as soon as the protective deadline is up, there will be a number of disputes. Provided, of course, that the state does not find some legal manner to sort out the relations between the owners and the tenants of similar cultural institutions.

Since 1992, according to the law on municipalities, theaters fall under city administration which does not have sufficient resources. As a result of this senseless cultural policy there is permanent tension between theaters and their owners. No steps have been taken to resolve this situation and theater managers call in vain for some legal grounds which would make multi-purpose funding possible. All these negative facts have caused a syndrome, which over the last five years has entered the public's consciousness as "theater causes". These disputes in individual theaters or conflicts between the theaters and the city magistrates have become an integrated part of domestic folklore. In essence, this is constantly the same dispute, which cyclically appears in various forms.

Czech theaters are almost exclusively repertoire theaters, based on the Central European model with a tradition dating back to the last century. The current network of professional theaters was formed after the Second World War, and consolidated in the beginning of the 1960s. With the fundamental changes in the socio-political situation and the transition to a free market, this system has begun to crumble. It's gradually been directed towards the English-American and financially more profitable method of theater production. All of this stems from the theory thesis that culture can make money on itself. Of course, propagating such opinions in a country where as of yet no legal possibilities for multi-source fundings for culture exist could have unpleasant consequences. Aside from this, the repertoire format has its indisputable advantages: above all it offers the opportunity of continual work in the sense of creating style and poetry. The Czech theatergoer is not used to long-running productions, with the exception of large musical projects, and even in this case certain limitations exist. The wave of disputes between city offices with the management of theaters stems from the continual lack of funding. The cities are then faced with absurd decisions – they must prioritize the allocation of funds to theaters, hospitals, and public transport, for example. Added to this is the evident incompetence of the magistrate officials, who take into account only the factor of attendence, and are not capable of assessing the artistic aspect of the theater. During the course of the last five to six years, there is not a single theater which has not had some dispute with its owner. The tendency to whittle down or break up permanent companies is common and apparent. In this period for example, theater companies which have been broken up include the City Stage in Kolin, the E. F. Burian Theater in Prague, The Evening Theater in Brno, the Krusnohorsky Theater in Teplice, and Theater Za Branou II.

The operation of the traditional four company model of the repertoire theater (drama, opera, operetta, and ballet) is extremely demanding financially and a number of theaters have resolved this situation by fusing together individual companies. In recent times, a resolution is finally taking shape: multi-source funding is being considered for theaters operating beyond the regional level. The 1994/95 season was the first time in the republic that the theory of multiplying effects was applied to the area of culture. The sociological poll which was carried out in two cities in the Northern Moravia region (in cooperation with theaters in Ostrava and Olomouc) brought interesting results. It was observed that within the context of wider economic factors, the subsidies for theater operations show higher returns to the city budget and subsequently to the state budget than were expected. This fact fundamentally changes the view of the socio-economic function of theaters and casts doubts on the generally accepted opinion that the economic contributions of theaters cannot be numerically expressed.

Reconstruction and New Theater Buildings

The reconstruction and renovation of theater buildings is another delicate problem. The previous regime built theater buildings of mastodon proportions in certain cities as display cases for their care of socialist culture (Most, Ostrava – J. Myron Theater), but many theaters did not have the resources for even basic maintenance. This unfortunate heritage essentially continues to persist. Basic reconstruction has taken place at the Horacky Theater in Jihlava and the Silesia Theater in Opava. Partial reconstruction has taken place at the F. X. Shalda Theater in Liberec. In many cases, renovations have been carried by the managers of individual theaters, who have not hesitated to beg for finances from the highest representatives of the government. After several years of reconstruction, the unique rotating open-air stage is once again in operation at the castle park in Chesky Krumlov. There are even plans to renovate the Chesky Krumlov castle theater, an important Baroque landmark. In Prague, a major work was the expensive renovation of the historic Estates Theater, where Mozart's *Don Giovanni* had its premiere.

The single example of a multi-purpose, newly constructed theater space is the Archa Theater in Prague, which arose from the reconstruction of the former E. F. Burian Theater. It has operated since 1993 and serves primarily as a venue for foreign and Czech theater groups. Most recently it has shared in the productions of various theatrical and musical projects. Of course, not even this theater, which had originally been conceived of as self-supporting, can survive without municipal funding. In 1992, partial reconstruction was carried out at the Labyrinth Theater, thus creating a theater complex with two stages.

A number of Prague theaters however are still waiting for funding for necessary renovation. The former Chamber Theater, which was associated with productions directed by the important Czech director Alfred Radok met a lamentable fare. And the Tyl Theater in Nustle, home to much-loved folk operettas, is also in desolate condition.

New Companies and Shifts

In spite of the constant economic pressure during the course of the last five years, new theaters have been formed. Often the new formations are a result of the regrouping of defunct companies. For example, the City Theater in Mlade Boleslav, which was formed during the split up of the Central Bohemian Theater, is the only case in which a city has shown an interest in its theater. The absence of a permanent city theater in this city of automobile manufacturing created favorable conditions for the theater's reopening. The first season (1994/95) may not have brought astounding results, but a sober estimate of the theater's own resources led to a solid beginning.

Another shift in the theater network was the move of the entire graduating class of the DAMU Acting Studio, including two directors and dramatists, to the Chinoherni Studio in Usti nad Labem during the 1992/93 season. Meanwhile the original company left for Prague to the Theater Rokoko, which is one of the Prague City Theaters. A group of graduates from the alternative and marionette theater department of DAMU formed the Dejvice Theater.

Another young group, which may be labelled as representative of this generation is the Kaspar Company of directors Jakub Spalek and Michal Docekal. In the beginning it existed as a part of the Prague City Theaters, but since the 1992/93 season it has freed itself from this association and now functions under the protective wing of the Theater Institute at the Celetna Theater, which is practically the only professional private theater legally shielded under the heading of a social organization and with no small financial problems. One of the first productions of this company was Rostand's *Cyrano*, a classic title which director Jakub Spalek freed from its pathos and from the sediment of convention, staging the work from a contemporary perspective. The dramatization of Daniel Keys' tale *Flowers for Algernon* directed by Jakub Spalek addressed basic moral values in an unostentatious manner. Goethe's *Clavigo* in its provocatively post-modern garb however pointed out a number of the young company's problems especially due to a lack of professional acting tools. In the 1994/95 season, Michal Docekal left the theater with his group for the Theater Komedie, which is part of the Prague City Theaters.

Aside from these companies, a number of small theater groups have come into being. In Prague, for example, they include the Theater Ungelt, the Theater Uhasicu, the Theater Bez Zabradli, the Black Sketched Theater of Frantisek Kratochvil, etc. They produce an entertaining repertoire of a sometimes questionable level of quality. A clear tendency towards commerciality is even shown by the newly formed Theater of Boleslav Polivka in Brno. There are also a number of agency groups which concentrate on one-time, primarily commercial projects.

Shooting at a Moving Target

Let me return, however, to the dramatic production situation on the Czech scene. After the wave of banned plays, the play selection of Czech theaters was reminiscent of shooting at a moving target, since the major problem of the post-November 89 theater was the drop in attendance caused by a number of factors. A large portion of the population threw itself into private enterprise and actually began to work, and the popular habit of socialist week-ends beginning in the middle of the week passed away. Borders opened and all kinds of commercial pap came pouring into the country, from film productions to laser shoot-em-ups, and a nation for whom commercial culture had for years been limited, if not directly prohibited, could not get enough. Also, socio-political life had become much more active. With such competition, theater could not hold its ground and naturally fell by the wayside. In addition, it stopped functioning as a means of political protest.

Playwrights tried the possible and the impossible to coax their audiences back into empty theaters, until they finally more or less gave in to the enormous tide of entertainment. It is certainly not by chance that the only playwright to remain in circulation is Pavel Kohout, whose plays show considerable dexterity and a certain tendency towards superficiality. His plays, such as *Poor Murderer* or *August, August, August* continue to be successfull at the box-office.

One of the many efforts to stimulate contemporary playwrights is the contest for the Alfred Radok Foundation prize for the best original Czech play written since 1992, which is sponsored by the literary and theatrical agency Auro-pont and the professional theater magazine *World and Theater*. At the time when this competition was founded, it seemed that the original Czech play was dying out and the playwrights of the middle generation who had been active during the period of totalitarianism, had gone silent – Karel Steigerwald, for example. Some of the winning plays from the first two years have gradually found their way to the stage, but in practice only one has enjoyed positive reviews from the critics – *Little Room* by J. A. Pitinsky directed by Petr Lebl at the Theater Na Zabradli. In the third year of the contest, there was a change. A number of the plays given awards were produced on stage. The common denominator of these plays, which is clearly the dramatic style of the nineties, is "a grotesque vision". A distinctive characteristic of these plays is playfulness with form, the mixing of genres, inspiration through low brow forms, but also through a number of artistic styles such as surrealism and dadaism. The age of the winning playwrights is nearly without exception 26, so their plays are also an expression of a single generation. These playwrights perceive the surrounding world as an impersonal, uniform world of programmed careers and they often attempt to satirically reflect upon the problems of post-communist society. Despite the significance of these first fruits, in many aspects they suffer from introspective infantilism.

As I've already mentioned, problems with attendence do not plague those theaters which count on a line-up of entertaining fare. Among the Prague theaters, the ABC Theater, which is a Prague City Theater stage, began producing comedies immediately after the November 89 revolution. This stance was not entirely by chance: the artistic director of ABC, director Milos Horansky and the manager of the City Theaters, Jan Vedral, were following in the footsteps of their predecessors – the Liberated Theater and Jan Werich. The theater's program of "good entertainment" however, was vague. Moreover, the incompatible notions of the members of the comedy team were projected into conceptionless stagecraft. Aside from the ambitious attempts of Milos Horansky, the main staple of the theater were the reliable, conversational detective shows of director Lida Engelova and other tabloid comedies. The convulsive attempt to entertain climaxed with a musical based on *L' Ecume des Jours* by Boris Vian, which financially wiped out the theater. For a number of other reasons as well, the theater management was forced to resign. From the ensuing competition for the management position, a new creative team emerged with a fundamentally more sensible idea of running an entertainment line-up. The artistic director Milan Schejbal manages this without great innovation, but with a feeling for the needs of a wider audience. He also tries to draw upon the domestic tradition of musical comedies and classic musicals.

With regard to the genre of comedy, it is necessary to at least mention the phenomenon of the Theater of Jara Cimrman, which is a specifically Czech comic affair. A circle of quick-witted humorists created the character of a fictitious Czech Jack-of-all-trades, Jara Cimrman, who purportedly has influenced all types of human activity. The Cimrman plays have reached an unbelievable number of performances and not even the post-November 89 decline in theater audience has affected this theater. The plays exude fresh intellectual humor which, for the foreign viewer however, is untranslatable and really incomprehensible.

Directors and Their Theaters

In Prague there are distinct creative theater groups with characteristically artistic playbills. Among them is the Labyrinth Theater. Its repertoire is formed of Czech and foreign contemporary plays and less frequently produced classics. This is the result of years of cooperation between its creators Karel Kriz and Vlasta Gallerova, director Jiri Frehar, and composer Jiri Cerha. The artistic director Karel Kriz belongs to the generation that was influenced by the extremely theatrical work of the major Czech director, Alfred Radok. Decisive elements of Kriz's directing style are a playful feeling for the situation and the ability to pictorially present the stage metaphors. Now the Labyrinth Theater has two theater spaces – a studio and a main stage. At the same time, the theater serves as a cultural center, offering opportunities to related artistic forms and to educational activities like the Children's Studio. Directly after November 89, two striking productions were put on at the Labyrinth Theater – Stoppard's *Travesties* directed by Karel Kriz as a post-modern jig-saw puzzle of styles, which humorously reflected Czech experiences with various ideologies; and Tabori's *Mein Kampf* directed by Jiri Frehar, who read the text as a grotesque and absurd farce with emphasis on the comic counter-point.

The Labyrinth Theater Studio, which opened as an entirely new theater space, quite quickly became known to audiences. Its artistic profile is developing simultaneously along two lines. Part of the studio's productions are highly composed musical dramas. These are primarily author's projects: the *Dada Opera* stage collage, the rock opera based on the life of St. Adalbert, Shakespeare's *Sonnets* directed by Karel Kriz, and Claudel's *Proteus*, directed by Jiri Frehar. The other part of the Studio's production are chamber productions dealing with the problems of human identity (Ionesco's *Delirium for Two*, Dostoyevsky's *Tender Women*, Pinter's *Moonlight*.) One of the Studio's most recent shows is a play by

the Danish playwright Astrid Saalbach directed by Karel Kriz. The director utilizes an interesting principle of communication to set the individual scenes: the audience peers into the special world of women – the
inner workings of a ballet lesson, as if behind a non-existent mirror.
Productions running on the main stage include a show based on the
tragedies of Euripides and a satirical drama called *The Tamers of Troy*,
again directed by Karel Kriz. The production was a contemporary parable about the flux of life constructed as a series of tragic stories inter-
spersed with grotesquely comic scenes.

Labyrinth Theater has also offered space to a number of young
talented directors, namely Hana Buresova, whose production of
Grabbe's *Don Juan* and *Faust* won the Alfred Radok Foundation prize.
Audiences also responded well to Buresova's production of Rossini's
Barber of Seville, which parodied more than just operatic conventions.

Another interesting Prague theater, which has revived itself
within the last five years is the Theater Pod Palmovkou (previously the
S. K. Neumann Theater in Liben), headed by Petr Kracik. This theater in
the Prague suburbs enjoyed successful period under Vaclav Lohnicky in
the 1960s, but stagnated during the normalization period, even if it did
offer a haven for two "undesirable" and important directors – Otomar
Krejca and Jan Grossman, who staged several noteworthy productions
here. Kracik should be appreciated for staging a more demanding repertoire, without losing perspective on the theater location. After his arrival,
an interesting version of Martin Sperr's play *Hunting Scenes from Lower
Bavaria* was put on. Next were productions based primarily on the great
classics: *Peer Gynt*, Shakespeare's *Hamlet*, Dostoyevsky's *The Idiot*, Lorca's
The House of Bernarda Alba, and Calderón's *Life is a Dream*. Kracik also
brought back Bertold Brecht to the Czech post-November 89 stage with
the production of his play *Herr Puntila and His Servant Matti*. Brecht's
plays were produced often during the communist years. Oh, to what
ends has Brecht not been used and abused! Kracik's production of Brecht
bears the markings of his directing style – a distinct and uncomplicated
rendering of a basic fable, a production free of ideological accents, free of
gross farce.

At the Theater Na Zabradli, the death of Jan Grossman (Feb.
10th, 1993) brought about the end of an entire period of this theater. The
Grossman's last production was *Kafka's Dick* by Alan Bennett. He transformed this entirely banal text into a timeless testimony of life and death.
By pushing the limits and balancing on the sharp edge of grotesque
irony, he addressed the basic idea of the play: it is not important what
Kafka suffered or enjoyed, his work remains and will continue to inspire.
In the 1993/94 season, the young director Petr Lebl became the artistic
director of this theater. He is a graduate of a graphic arts middle school
and his directing style is characterized by a feeling for visual art

combined with a post-modern approach with a certain tendency towards self-irony. In his opening season at the Theater Na Zabradli, he directed Genet's *The Maids*. Here, he took the central conflict of two women who poison their master to be a psychodrama framed into the story of two inmates. A number of critics criticize Lebl, sometimes justly so, for his forceful treatment of texts and free-handed destruction of them. These reproaches cannot be entirely ignored. Lebl's post-modern arsenal is not inexhaustable, some of his productions have a uniform character. Nonetheless, his provocations are not lacking in distinctive expression or invention in searching out the substance and the original. His production of Chekhov's *Seagull* was again very controversially received, but was awarded the critic's prize for 1994. The grotesque situation of the play here slips into a whirlwind of feverish dreams, many situations move on the verge of the unexpressable. Ironic humor connects reality and poetry. However the revellry of form and meaning in Lebl's directing sometimes comes up empty. His last productions – an adaptation of the musical *Cabaret* and Gogol's *Government Inspector* – hide this danger within themselves. In spite of all reservations, Lebl is among the most distinctive 30-year-old directors.

A poetic style similar to the one of Lebl can be seen in the work of Vladimir Moravek, who worked for several years in the Brno theater, Goose On a String, and is now engaged at the Klicpera Theater in Hradec Kralove. Recently he has devoted himself primarily to adaptations of classic village drama. His post-modern remelting of classic elements is often done through a mere chain of associations or constructions which practically lack any logical support in the text. The result tends to be a strange cross-breed, a mish-mash of genres and a series of infantile satirical references.

Another director of this generation is Michal Docekal, who after amateur beginnings at Prague's Rubin and A-studio, formed a directing duo with Jakub Spalek in the Kaspar Theater group. He called attention to himself with an interesting production of Joyce's *The Exiles* on the studio stage of Prague's National Theater, at the Kolowrat Palace.

A somewhat solitary position in this generation is held by two other directors – J. A. Pitinsky and Jan Nebesky. Pitinsky is an intuitive and imaginative director and playwright. His productions are distinguished by strong poetic stylization. So far, his most extensive project took place at the City Theater of Zlin, which was an adaptation of Federico Fellini's film *Eight and a Half* performed under the title *Eight and a Half (and a half)*. In this production he fused the world of Fellini's poetry with his own motifs, emotions and associations. Impulsive Jan Nebesky has for years been interested primarily in works by northern playwrights – Ibsen and Strindberg – which he stages with a raw, expressive approach.

The National Theater

Recent stylistic changes are also reflected at the leading Czech stage, the Prague National Theater and its three departments – drama, opera, and ballet. Aside from the historic building on Narodni Trida, the National Theater is also composed of the Estates Theater and the Kolowrat Palace. After November 89, Ivan Rajmont became the new artistic director of the drama department. Since he has worked for years on studio stages, the first thing he did at the National Theater was to engage a number of studio-stage actors – a current, which to this day many theater experts and theoreticians have not stomached. During the course of the last five years, Rajmont has had his fair share of criticism: the alteration of poetry in his own productions, inappropriate play selection, too many guest directors, few titles by contemporary world playwrights, the absence of original Czech plays in the repertoire. It is interesting, through, that even radical critics of the plight of the National Theater do not have a clear idea of the ideal form for this leading stage.

Even in spite of evident failures, the National Theater can boast of several interesting drama productions: Paul Claudel's *The Satin Slipper* directed by Roman Polak, the village chronicle *Year In the Village* directed by Miroslav Krobot and the original Czech play *Nobel* by Steigerwald directed by Ivan Rajmont. The critics en masse labelled the latter one a superficial reflection, of the current state of society and morality. After the death of one of the show's leading actors the production was reworked and now touches audiences as a "requiem for the Czech middle generation".

The other two National Theaters in Ostrava and Brno are far from being at the center of critical attention. The constant staple of their stagecraft are titles from foreign and Czech classics. Among the successful productions at the Brno National Theater have been Claudel's *The Tidings Brought to Mary* and Camus' adaptation of Dostoyevsky's *The Possessed*, both directed by Zdenek Kaloc.

Musical Fever

The general tendency towards entertainment in recent seasons has passed. Theaters rely heavily on the classics, and the most frequently produced classic author is none other than Shakespeare. The rage for comedy, however, has been replaced by musical fever, which in various forms has strengthened the Czech theater. The majority of these musicals are Anglo-American ones, but they represent an entirely specific domestic form of the musical theater genre. The standard method of presenting world musicals has hit the Czech stage with a considerable time lag. Large musicals such as *Les Miserables* and *Jesus Christ Superstar* have had great audience response. The home grown production copying these models are substantially weaker than the originals despite the fact that there are now a number of talented performers. The major musical team of Zdenek Merta and Stanislav Mosa creates so-called pseudo-philisophical musicals like A *Midsummer's Night Dream* by Shakespeare, and *The Illegitimate Daughter* by Goethe. One of the most recent pop hits of the genre is *Dracula*, a primitive patchwork on the given theme, unfortunately directed by renowned director Jozef Bednarika. Far more interesting are the productions which pay homage to the domestic traditions of the genre (the Liberated Theater of Voskovec and Werich, the small forum theaters of the 1960s, the studio creations of the last twenty years). Among them is the successful production of *Stars On the Willow* by Karel David at Ha-Theater from Brno. The entire project was born from a concert of 1960s retro rock and was a wonderfully nostalgic reminder of these years. This reminder was complete with a chill to the spine as the somewhat Formanesque story ends with the arrival of tanks in 1968.

Conclusion

Since November 89, the Czech theater has been missing a central platform in the sense of a country-wide review of its production. Previously, this function was filled by the bi-annual meeting, which was organized by the City Theater in Zlin. Now a selection of Czech productions is presented at the International Theater Festival which has been taking place since 1993 in Pilzen. In the last season however, there has been a boom of festivals and reviews of various theatrical genres, artistic associations etc.

In the period of the last five to six years, the Czech theater has undergone a series of artistical and institutional changes. It is paradoxical, however, that the values which were created during the previous regime are today trivialized and underestimated. Also not too encouraging is the state of theater criticism and theory. After November 89, a new generation of theater theoreticians began writing criticism. For many of them it is as if theater first began to bear fruit as they entered the field. Distortion of memory has become a common phenomenon, as well as the creation of myths about theater-makers often lacking full maturity. These critics don't have a logical value system. As it concerns professional theater literature very little has been published on important personalities of the Czech theater and on companies that have influenced the evolution of post-war theater. Partially, this is also because there are very few financial resources. All of these factors attest to the fact that in the life style of today's post-communist society, culture and theater occupy one of the least important positions. The average viewer easily succumbs to the flood of simple-minded commercial imports and their domestic counterparts. After the fall of the ideological barrier, the Czech theater has entered the age of financial dictates, thus landing on the banks of an uncharted shore – terra incognita, and the state, as the only possible protector of cultural values, is for the time being letting it blunder across the new continent. In the quick transformation of the economy there is no time left to devote to cultural policy. Let us hope that by the time someone is willing to deal with these issues, it will not be too late.

1996

HUNGARIAN THEATER

FOREWORD

Árpád Göncz*

The following chapter on the Hungarian theater deals with the condition of theater arts in a land laboring under the stress of transformation. A land where the better part of state subsidies for the arts have been taken over by society, where theaters have fought daily for survival, where in spite of it all the number of theaters has recently increased, where promising new talents – actors, directors, playwrights – undertake exciting artistic experiments.

Please, acquaint yourselves with our worries and joys, keeping in mind that nothing is more serious than playing, and that theater is the most serious kind of playing: the most resonant mirror for reality ever.

* Translated by Istvan Totfalusi.

HUNGARIAN THEATER:
IN SEARCH OF AN IDENTITY

Krisztina Galgoczi

Still Waters Run Deep ...

Changes rarely occur from one day to the next. It was only in mid 1995 that the time arrived for real structural change in Hungary's theatrical world. The alternative to the threat of theaters going bankrupt by refusing to cater to commercial tastes was that an institutional framework be created jointly by the state, local governments, and the theatrical bodies themselves, and this indeed seems to have taken place.

The last five or six years have brought with them increasing insecurity, but despite the repeatedly voiced fears of cultural patrons upon seeing the proliferation of McDonald's franchises and Hollywood action films, one must admit that countless positive tendencies can be found in contemporary Hungarian theater. As in other countries in this region, the political changes of 1989 created a vacuum in theatrical life. All that had previously made Eastern European (and Hungarian) theater exciting had suddenly become unnecessary. In spite of an all-encompassing internal and external censorship, until the late 1980s the theater was one of the few places where free vent could be given to social and political feelings and emotions, where social angst and woes – of which one could hardly have spoken without some kind of consequences – could be expressed through finely polished artistic means. This, then, was a theater predominantly political in nature and one could go as far as to say that no major performance could avoid being vested with some political meaning – occasionally, perhaps even against the intentions of its creators. Coupled with constant self-reflection, this critical, political undertone remained characteristic of the Hungarian theater despite the gradual decentralization of the theaters, which began in the 1960s and which resulted in the centrally controlled programming in the 1980s. Thus, in contrast to the press, television, and publishing, whose state control remained in effect, theater came to play a special role in public life because tone, emphasis, gesture, interpretation, and a living bond with the audience could never be as effectively controlled as the written word.

This type of socially sensitive theater could boast of great achievements, but mostly within the confines of psychoanalytical realism. It was less receptive to the aesthetics of art for art's sake. At the same time, a very sophisticated, ironic mode of expression evolved which often leaned toward the absurd and the grotesque.

In the interval following the political changes, the big question was whether the Hungarian theater would be capable of renewal while preserving its past values: the repertoire system, permanent theater companies, social sensitivity, and a subsidy system. It had to meet the challenge made by market forces in the midst of a changing economic situation. Looking back on the last few years from this point of view, a distinctly positive picture emerges. Even though there is a certain amount of commercialization, marked by an increase in commercial and musical theaters, not one classical or art theater has been forced to close to date. At the most, a certain change in profile and/or of directors has occurred, and there has been a welcome increase in the number of smaller studio and chamber theaters. The repertory companies have survived and this has made possible the emergence of theatrical workshops such as the ones at Kaposvar, Szolnok, and at the deservedly renowned Katona Jozsef Theater of Budapest. Although constantly on the decrease, state subsidization has also been preserved. The number of so-called alternative theaters increased with the emergence of various foundations and competition systems, and this is undoubtedly a basic precondition for the infusion of new life into the Hungarian theater as it was often the experiments conducted in these workshops that broke the impasse in which some professional theaters found themselves.

Obviously, the situation is not as idyllic when viewed close up and we are now at a point when the survival of old structures definitely obstructs new developments, proving beneficial to only a handful of exceptionally well-subsidized theaters. The state is no longer capable of supporting all 46 of the formerly subsidized theaters and the only course of action left open to the state is to sacrifice some in order to save others. One of the most hotly debated issues over the last few years was the question of who was to decide which theaters were redundant and which factors should be considered in making this decision. Current cultural leadership is inclined to diminish the role of central decision-making in cultural life, hoping instead for an increase in grass-roots initiatives, which would ensure that any selection made would not be the result of instructions from above or the consequence of commercial values, but would stem from real artistic values in an organic manner. However, the emergence of this kind of pluralism, of a professional life that is indeed tolerant of others' "otherness" requires time and a real change in attitudes. The state did attempt to involve local governments in the subsidization of theaters in their jurisdictions through a plan to provide 50 percent of Budapest theaters' financing and 60 percent of theaters' financing outside of Budapest, the remaining costs to be covered by local governments and other sources of income. However, few, if any, local governments actually developed any sense of ownership in their theaters.

The artificial protection of theater companies has had a similarly detrimental effect. The introduction of the 1992 Law on Civil Servants has actually temporarily blocked the easy mobility of actors. Only in optimal cases has it been beneficial, tending in general to hinder rather than help reinvigorate companies. This seems to be a basic pitfall of any intention, no matter how good, coming from "above", whereas an approach which allows initiatives to mature will undoubtedly bear more fruit in the long run. The best solution would obviously be one in which each theater were allowed to chose the form best suited to its own needs.

Privatization was in fact delayed, because both cultural leaders and theater directors were, to some extent justifiably, reluctant to expose theaters to market conditions. Operation costs are, in general, incredibly high and most theaters have to operate under extremely bad technical and safety conditions: built around the turn of the century, most theaters are in need of major renovations. Some theaters have been renovated within the last few years, the most recent being the Comic Theater in Budapest, but the renovation program was discontinued in 1995. Production costs are also often very high as the market price must be paid for any necessary materials or equipment. In contrast, the current economic situation does not allow raising the price of tickets since most people can no longer afford an evening out at the theater as it is. Consequently, smaller theaters and provincial theaters (the latter often being the single cultural center of a large region) consciously try to keep ticket prices down. Under these conditions, most theaters are being forced to cut costs, for example through lowering actors' salaries, staging low-budget productions, and producing more popular plays that promise greater revenues instead of more sophisticated plays aimed at a more refined, if smaller, audience. Some, like the Katona Jozsef Theater, have been forced to stay dark three nights a week. Another problem is that theaters receive their subsidies not as a lump sum, but as a monthly allowance, and most theaters have run up sizable debts in order to remain in continuous operation.

A structural change is thus truly inevitable. Plans for partial privatization are aimed at transforming theaters into local government property, with the state covering operating costs and the theaters themselves raising the rest of the money they need. The state would help the theaters overcome the difficulties of the initial transitional period by providing production subsidies – awarded through a system of competition – with the hope that the theaters would in time be transformed into independent, non-profit organizations. Many reservations have been voiced about the proposed plans, the most frequently heard objection being that this system would be detrimental to both the theatrical company system and the drama theaters. This, perhaps, is the main reason that, to date, this system has not moved beyond the planning phase.

New Situation, New Possibilities

Following the political changes, two opposing tendencies could be observed in Hungary. On the one hand, the events offered up a wide range of hitherto unknown opportunities: countless emigrant artists returned home to work again in their mother tongue and several Hungarian artists who had earlier voluntarily withdrawn from the art scene returned to it. On the other hand, a certain vacuum was left. The creative individuals and the few theaters that had carved out niches for themselves found that their special metaphorical language had suddenly become obsolete and they began to feel perplexed and to question their identity. Some proved incapable of adapting, while others still need time to find their place in the current scheme of things. These two phenomena are obviously interrelated. In the early 1990s, theater work in Hungary was again considered exciting because experiments held out the hope that one could try anything, that all ideas would fall on fertile soil, and that the time had truly arrived for the reassessment of theater's *ars poetica*. It is precisely this reassessment that has enabled recent structural changes after the initial period of insecurity. The main reason to adhere irrationally and obstinately to the status quo has passed.

First to return to Hungary was Peter Halasz, who had emigrated together with his company in the early 1970s. He had been the leader of the well-known Squat Theater and, later, of the Love Theater in New York. He first staged one of his New York productions at the Petofi Csarnok, one of the new arts centers in Budapest which accommodated a number of Hungarian and foreign alternative theaters. Next, he staged the first and second parts of an earlier play of his, *The Chinese*, at the Kamra, the studio theater of the Katona Jozsef Theater. Halasz's production added a welcome new hue to the palette of theatrical life in Budapest, where professional theaters all offered diluted versions of acting based on Stanislavsky, albeit on differing levels of quality and intensity. Halasz did not engineer a reform, but he did try to develop new aspects and forms stemming primarily from the personalities and improvisational capabilities of his actors. The changeover was by no means smooth, but both actors and audiences gradually acquired a taste for this new style. Halasz staged his most exciting shows in 1993/94, when, in a return to a former practice of his, he created performances from news items and newspaper articles four times a week. The plays were written at night, rehearsed the next morning, and performed that evening. His theater thus became an exciting venue that attracted a regular audience. The performances were characterized by a light atmosphere in which people could relax and not have to stare at Art as some kind of oddity.

The fact that traditional theaters are inviting alternative artists to collaborate on certain projects has enabled interaction between the two theatrical spheres and this trend has gained momentum over the last few years. A number of good theaters have flung open their doors and have invited in their colleagues from outside the establishment. If anything, the blending of values of the professional and the alternative theaters has been the most welcome change of the past five or six years, for it has enabled Hungary to concentrate on drawing a distinction not between professional and alternative theater, but between good and bad theater.

Along with Halasz's performances, Andras Jeles's productions also made Hungarian theatrical life exciting for a short period of time. Jeles was *the* charismatic figure of the 1980s, known for his films *Small Valentino, The Dream, No Man's Land,* as well as for the unconventional and experimental productions of his company, Monteverdi Birkozokor. While Halasz's theater exuded cool, wry cynicism and was characterized by a loose performance style, Jeles's productions were distinguished by his actors' extremely intense and suggestive presence on stage, stylized and fragmented dialogue and music, and a strong political slant. The changes in both directors' work can be partly explained by the fact that they have recently begun to work with professional actors – a far cry from their earlier, isolated work that was accessible to only a very limited audience.

Jeles first staged his productions at the International Merlin Theater, which was founded by two Kaposvar actors, Tamas Jordan and Kati Lazar, in April, 1991 – the first ambitious attempt at creating a place in Budapest where one could meet with friends and linger on after a performance ended. The Merlin Theater has remained an intellectual and cultural center, creating its own company in the process. It now offers theatrical performances in the evenings and the profitable jazz concerts at night in its restaurant subsidize its other activities. It welcomes guest artists and guest performances, and in 1995, it opened its club theater, which offers a wide range of entertainment. During the summer, the Merlin Theater stages three to four productions, usually in English, for foreign visitors and tourists. Jeles's first production at the Merlin Theater was *Hello, Tolstoy,* based on the Soviet ballet dancer Nijinsky's diary, in which the entire theater was transformed into a stage set by Csaba Antal's imaginative design work. Antal created a series of 18th century aristocratic opera boxes, each of which seated only a single viewer who was thus virtually sitting in a peep-show. A star-shaped mirror lit the actors from below. The actors expressed all that was happening in contemporary culture with fragmented, distorted movements that were at the same time incredibly passionate. Jeles is the master of "inside–outside" effects. There is always at least one character in his work who links these two spheres together and who is central in turning the dramatic situation "inside out." Music, rhythm, movement, and recitation all play important roles in Jeles's work. A good example of this was his production of *Kleist's Death* with music composed by Laszly Melis, which reconstructed Heinrich von Kleist's death on the basis of surviving documents and excerpts from his diary.

Jeles's most recent production opened in the spring of 1995 at the Katona Jozsef Theater. Symbolically, it can be seen as the conclusion of a brief crisis in this theater's life. After a decade-long existence as a fantastic and truly enviable company, the Katona Jozsef Theater began a process of reorganization in the early 1990s that resulted in the founding of a new art theater, the New Theater, in 1994, under the direction of Gabor Szekely. While Budapest was thus enriched with a new theatrical workshop, the transitional period for the Katona Jozsef Theater was by no means a smooth one, as demonstrated by several productions which were not so well received. Jeles's production represented an arrival: his adaptation of Victor Hugo's *L'Homme Qui Rit* was an enormous success – a sophisticated performance of the kind one had come to expect from this company. The Katona Jozsef Theater's artistic director, Gabor Zsambeki, gathers young actors (mostly his own students) to the theater, encourages young playwrights, and invites inventive, alternative artists and productions to appear at the theater – such as the internationally acclaimed dancer-choreographer, Yvette Bozsik, who has in fact now become a full member of the company. Zsambeki's policy seems to have borne fruit: excellent productions of plays such as *Hamlet* and, at their smaller studio theater, the Kamra, Tom Stoppard's *Rosencrantz and Guildenstern Are Dead* and of two contemporary Hungarian plays, Akos Nemeth's *Muller's Dances* and Lajos Parti Nagy's *Mausoleum*. The Kamra Theater also hosts the Writer's Theater series, to which the best Hungarian writers and poets are invited to read their own work. The Katona Jozsef Theater is a member of the Union of European Theaters which held its second festival in Budapest in 1993.

Tamas Ascher directed Chekhov's *Three Sisters* at the Katona Jozsef Theater in 1991. It ran for many years and was also a huge success in Europe. He went on to direct productions of Chekhov's *Platonov* and Heinrich Boll's *The Lost Honor of Katharina Blum*, both of which won the Critics' Prize that year. Ascher staged an exciting version of Pirandello's *Tonight We Improvise* that preserved elements of improvisation throughout the performance while extending the acting area into the house, the lobby, and the entire theater. In both *Katharina Blum* and *Tonight We Improvise*, precise, skilled casts were combined with experimentation in a tasteful way. In *The Lost Honor of Katharina Blum*, audience members were handed headphones through which they could hear the telephone conversations on stage – a brilliant technical solution.

Ascher began his career at the Kaposvar Theater, which, far from the censorship in the capital, was the legendary theatrical workshop of the 1970s and 1980s. Theater lovers and other intellectuals packed the buses to Kaposvar in order to see each and every performance. Ascher continues to direct plays at Kaposvar. One of his most memorable productions was of Molière's *The Misanthrope*, based on a new translation by the poet Gyorgy Petri, thereby introducing Hungarian audiences to a new Molière. Fully aware of the advantages offered by the new translation, Ascher wiped centuries of dust off the play and created a production that spoke to modern audiences in contemporary language without perverting the text. Ascher is regularly invited to direct abroad and he recently staged Gombrowicz's *Ivona, Princess of Burgundia* with Anne Bennent in the lead role (taken over by the talented Hungarian actress Eszter Csakanyi in 1995).

The opening of the New Theater in September, 1994, which marked the beginning of a new chapter in the theatrical life of Budapest, was preceded by huge expectations because the artistic director, Gabor Szekely, had not directed a play in Hungary for about six years. His company was formed partly by students and partly by actors from the Katona Jozsef Theater. His stage manager was none other than Janos Acs, who had created memorable productions himself, including a 1989 version of Peter Weiss's *Marat/Sade*. Szekely also brought with him two directors who had only recently graduated, thereby indicating his intent to create a new company and a new style with young artists. The first production was directed by the exceptionally talented Eszter Novak. It was an adaptation of one of the great classics of 19th century Hungarian literature, Vorosmarty's *Csongor and Tunde*. The production had a tremendous impact and, although it elicited some rather extreme reviews due to the complete modernization of the classical text, all agreed that an imaginative and talented director had made her debut. The New Theater is not the kind of theater that bursts into theatrical life. It is more inclined to develop a new project slowly, which is in fact more in keeping with the values of traditional theaters than with those of other experimental theaters. Gabor Szekely made his directorial debut at his own theater with a production of *Don Juan* that had a strong, definite concept and, thanks to designer Csaba Antal, fantastic scenery. The lead character was typical of our time: a dyspeptic, full of doubts and disillusions, who would have gladly converted had he found a worthy opponent.

Although no established theaters have yet been forced to close down, one very important enterprise has failed. This shameful event was clearly the result of a paranoia that accompanied the structural changes outlined above. The actress Mari Torocsik (who, with countless film and stage roles behind her, could rightly claim the status of the nation's leading actress) and the director Janus Taub opened the Art Theater. Its very name, which referred to an earlier, legendary Budapest theater and its Moscow counterpart, indicated the kinds of traditions it wished to cultivate. Taub and Torocsik endeavored to hire the most renowned actors and actresses and, like the New Theater, they tried to ensure that their actors would be properly paid.

This was important because even a cursory glance at an actor's average day reveals how difficult it is to be creative under current circumstances. After rehearsals actors race to the radio station, from the radio station to the dubbing studio, back to rehearsals in the afternoon, and on to sometimes even two performances in the evening. Actors in the provinces have an even harder time making ends meet with a single pay check, and they tour the country, often performing twice or more (sometimes different productions) every day. The idea of creating at least a handful of theaters that would enable serious, creative work in an attempt to remedy this situation obviously required funding, but the only question is who should, or would, foot the bill? Sponsors want to get their money's worth and therefore tend to fund more popular productions. This leads to the ironic situation in which the strongest theater artistically, the Katona Joszef Theater, is the one most plagued by severe financial problems.

Unfortunately, the founders of the Art Theater did not receive the necessary support and patience from their colleagues in the profession, the authorities, or their audiences. They did however, stage a number of excellent productions, such as Beckett's *Waiting For Godot* and Moscow director Anatoly Vassiliev's *Uncle's Dream*, based on a short novel by Dostoyevsky. The latter, starring Mari Torocsik and Dezso Garas, was visually an incredibly strong performance, but was unfortunately produced at a time when public opinion had already turned against the theater and audiences were unable to appreciate this unusual, slow, contemplative performance that, in all truthfulness, did tax the viewer's patience. This led to the paradox that, if one looked at the indexes, the season's most outstanding performance had been a flop. The directors of the theater were soon forced to resign, partly for economic reasons and partly to set an example. Thus, we will never know whether they would have eventually been able to realize their ambitious plans. The theater has reverted to its old name, (the Talia Theater), and it is uncertain whether it can preserve its reputation as a drama theater.

Something Has Been Lost in the Process...

The Radnoti Theater with its balanced repertoire has played a highly progressive role in theatrical life since the political changes: during the period of political upheaval it regularly provided an opportunity for political and social round-table debates which were so popular that many would-be audience members were unable to get in. This indomitable enthusiasm seems to have disappeared from our cultural life over the last few years, due in part to the gradual liberalization of cultural life. At first, one was inclined to believe that interest in culture in general had died. The loss of culture's unique political role can also, in part, be attributed to an ever increasing availability of choices. Ten years ago, the National Book Week was a major cultural event as it offered the hope that, at least once a year, one might obtain a copy of a limited edition book that had just managed to evade the censors. In contrast, there are currently so many publishers that it is impossible to keep track of everything being published, and books that would have caused quite a stir a few years ago now pass into circulation almost unnoticed. Similarly, an international film week used to be a cultural treat. Now, hardly a week goes by without a festival of some kind or some country celebrating its national week. The average intellectual can hardly hope to attend them all. The same is true of the theater. A scramble for tickets takes place only on the opening nights of truly renowned guest performances and for premieres at the best theaters. Gone are the days when one had to keep one's fingers crossed in the hope of finding tickets left for a Saturday evening performance of *Marat/Sade* at a small town community center 30 kilometers outside Budapest. This nostalgia can be quite misleading. The romantic shortage-economy of Socialism has, at least in the cultural realm, disappeared for good, and the theater now plays the same role as it does anywhere else in the world. One minute we think that it will save mankind, the next we think gloomily that it has indeed died and that there is no hope of ever resurrecting it.

The Radnoti Theater's annual festival of chamber theater productions and its guest performances by provincial theater companies were always hugely successful. These performances, which at one time were combined with staged readings of contemporary Hungarian plays, became real social events. In selecting their repertoire they have tried to strike a balance between profitable (but good quality) productions and more experimental works. Their repertoire currently includes plays by classic authors (Ibsen, Strindberg, Gogol, and Schikaneder, as well as the Hungarian playwrights Sandor Marai and Milan Fust) that can be counted on to attract a regular audience. The Radnoti Theater also stages modern, innovative plays by contemporary playwrights. Two directors must be singled out: Janos Szikora, who in 1993 experimented with a studio theater in Pecs; and Sandor Zsyter, one of the most promising members of the younger generation of directors who works regularly outside of Budapest, primarily in Miskolc and Szolnok.

The Budapest Chamber Theater, with its four different locations in Budapest, defies categorization. This theater has tried to fulfill many

different roles: it operates a *Volkstheater* as well as two small studio theaters in the heart of the city where truly exciting productions are created,
albeit of varying quality. It also runs the Central European Dance Theater
and the Budapest Chamber Opera, both of which can boast of spectacular accomplishments, each having tried their utmost to modernize their
respective genres. One of the great surprises of the 1991 season was
Büchner's *Leonce and Lena*, directed by the singularly talented young
actress, Eniko Eszenyi, at one of the Chamber Theater's studio spaces,
the Asboth Street Theater. *Leonce and Lena* was one of the best examples
of how more and more young actors, by trying their hand at directing in
an attempt to revitalize attitudes and techniques, are creating ingenious
productions. Although, in all fairness, it must be admitted that a chronic
shortage of directors also exists. Consequently, many theaters like the
Budapest Chamber Theater are inviting film directors, actors, and writers
to stage certain productions. One excellent case in point was the
Chamber Theater's newly translated staging of Heinrich von Kleist's first
play, *The Schroffenstein Family*, under the title of *The Revenge*. With uncanny
sophistication, this rehash of the story of Romeo and Juliet portrayed the
two families' tangled relationships, which were based on an intricate
web of grievances, and the senseless, ridiculous sacrifices they cause.
Bearing in mind that the season's other most important performances
were *The Lost Honor of Katharina Blum, Godot, Platonov,* and *The
Misanthrope*, one begins to gain a fairly accurate, if somewhat rough, idea
of the average Hungarian's disposition – a disposition characterized by
both a degree of expectancy and of apathy.

The success of Gabor Mate's above-mentioned productions at
the Kamra Theater (*Muller's Dances, Rosencrantz and Guildenstern ...,
Mausoleum*) and that of one of the best productions of the 1995 season,
A Midsummer Night's Dream (an independent production staged by the
young actor Janos Csanyi), can be attributed to the actors' ambition
and enterprising spirit. Csanyi's *Midsummer Night's Dream* was the result
of over a year and a half of exacting, assiduous work by enthusiastic
young actors from many different theaters. This undoubtedly resulted
in an experience completely different from that which is normally had
in Hungarian theaters. The moving spiritual force behind the production
was a joint willpower that allowed the actors to motivate each other.
A number of ingenious ideas also contributed to the success of this
production, such as a stage set of a forest of swings, a set that blurred
the boundary between acting area and auditorium. The resulting
communal space, an exciting concept in and of itself, was filled with
highly enjoyable and concentrated acting. Despite the fact that the rather
longish performance began at 10:30 p.m., the theater was always packed.
Over the summer the production toured the country and it has since
received countless invitations to international festivals. Janos Csanyi

is currently creating his own theater in which to stage his independent productions.

Commercialism Gains Ground with Undiminished Energy

Budapest has also seen a proliferation of musical, and commercial theaters, showing continuous performances of *Cats, Dr. Herz,* and *Joseph and the Amazing Technicolor Dream Coat,* as well as of *Miss Saigon, Crazy For You,* and who knows what else, all designed to bring a metropolitan feeling to the city. Outstanding among these theaters is the 100-year-old Comic Theater. It could, thanks to its solid economic policy, freshly renovated building, and company of talented actors and dramaturgs, become a truly good theater, but instead seems to grapple with some insurmountable internal obstacles. They have mounted a handful of good productions such as *West Side Story* with its bewitching rythm and choreography, directed by Eniko Eszenyi, and a few exciting experiments at the chamber theater, the Pest Theater, where the younger generation stirs up the tepid water every now and then. The dramaturgy is the most progressive aspect of the Comic Theater under the leadership of two excellent dramaturgs who draw inspiration from both contemporary Hungarian and foreign drama.

The provincial theaters have been left for the end of this chapter, mostly because 50 percent of theatrical performances are held in Budapest. This imbalance can be attributed in part to the fact that, unlike their counterparts in the capital, provincial theaters cannot be turned into exclusively musical or art theaters. These theaters are now in a period of transition and are fighting for their very survival. As has been mentioned above, important work is being done in Kaposvar, Szolnok, Miskolc, and Zalaegerszeg. For over a decade now, Zalaegerszeg has hosted the Open Forum, an annual meeting of playwrights, dramaturgs, directors, and actors which involves lively discussion and the staging of new plays in an effort to encourage and provide new opportunities to young playwrights. A new generation at Kaposvar under the guidance of director Janos Mohacsi has staged remarkable plays, such as Goldoni's *La Bottega del Caffe* and Arthur Miller's *The Crucible,* which won the Critics' Prize in 1995.

While the so-called National Theater is virtually a non-entity as far as theatrical forums are concerned, national theaters are active in Szeged, Pecs, and Miskolc. Their situation is made that much more difficult by having to fill a number of roles: that of *Volkstheater,* music theater, children's theater, and art theater. Outside Budapest, there is no real alternative to repertory theaters and towns which formerly had no permanent theater are now trying to establish them. Of course, there is always the fear that a dilapidated old building might fall down, but this doesn't stand in the way of the creation of excellent productions. Conditions can be said to be more ideal in some towns and cities far away from the capital in the sense that there actors' lives are less disrupted and, in theory, a more intense community life can evolve. However, this is inevitably accompanied by financial difficulties, since provincial actors have few, if any, means of complementing their ridiculously low salaries. It follows that there are enormous differences between individual actors, since a reasonably good actor in Budapest can earn several times more than his colleague in the provinces (especially if he has a chance to work in film) regardless of the quality of their work.

What to Expect as a Foreigner?

According to a comparative survey conducted in June, 1995 (a task not easily undertaken as smaller alternative, amateur, or semi-amateur companies are constantly emerging and disappearing), 150 performances were held in London (population: 10 million) in one week, while 139 performances were held in Budapest (population: 2 million) at 48 different venues during the same week. These figures would suggest that despite a brief faltering, interest in the theater has not subsided.

Although interaction between professional and alternative theaters is more frequent, there has been a welcome exploitation of new possibilities over the past few years and increasingly more alternative companies have been formed and have created their own productions. They have also been able to articulate themselves as a community by organizing festivals. In the spring of 1995, there was a representative review of alternative theaters which presented a mixed picture strikingly similar to that of the professional theaters, but which revealed some excellent productions that would not fall short of international standards. Alternative theatrical life had always had two centers: the Szkene Theater, in the building of the Technical University in Budapest, and the University Stage, which was perhaps the most progressive theater in Budapest and which has again been evicted from its premises. These have recently been joined by the Mu Theater which has staged one festival after another with unflagging energy.

Two grandiose plans have been proposed to boost cultural life in the capital. The first suggests the creation of a contemporary arts center in a former power plant on Liliom Street (a fantastic space but badly in need of renovation), which would accommodate all the arts, from film to theater. The second is for the Ark, currently being organized by Janos Csanyi, to host other performances in addition to retaining its own small company. The Liliom Street Art Center would sponsor a festival of the best theatrical productions of Eastern Europe in the spring as a continuation of the Budapest Spring Festival. The Ark would invite the most important productions from the provincial theaters to perform in the capital. A National Theater Festival had formerly been held every year, but always in a different town, and thus theater lovers in Budapest often missed many especially good productions.

In addition to the internationally acclaimed Spring and Autumn Festivals, there are now also many smaller events. Two important summer events now liven up the off-season (most Hungarian theaters close over the summer, except for the Merlin Theater and the open-air theaters). One is the Kapolcs Art Weeks, held in western Transdanubia, where, for two to three weeks, a real festival atmosphere is created by a wide range of theatrical and musical productions, folk artists and performance artists in a beautiful countryside setting. The other event is a festival held in the opposite corner of the country in Kisvarda, a small town with a medieval castle near the borders of Slovakia, Romania, and Ukraine. Owing to the town's geographic location, minority issues are felt more keenly there. It was considered a huge political concession when, in 1989, the first Festival of Hungarian Theaters from Neighboring Countries was allowed to take place. It has since become a traditional event. Hungarian audiences were at last able to see the two hundred year old Hungarian Theater of Cluj Kolozsvar from Romania. Gabor Tompa directed its hugely successful version of Ionesco's *The Bald Prima Donna* which met with such great acclaim throughout Europe and which toured Great Britain for five weeks.

Important performances and companies (such as the Independent Theater of Budapest, which has created a number of fine performances on their own under extremely puritanical conditions) have inevitably been omitted from this brief survey. However, I hope that I have been able to offer an idea of the colorful and exciting theatrical life that has emerged in Hungary since the lifting of the restrictions: a life that boasts a plurality of styles and genres and an increase in international contacts.

1995

LATVIAN THEATER

FOREWORD

Raimonds Pauls

Theater is an integral part of Latvian culture. I don't think this has changed since the political changes. Actually, the attitude toward theater is very much the same as it was under the Soviet regime.

First, theatrical reform has not been carried out properly. Theaters nowadays cannot retain their existing structure of huge administrative staffs which devour subsidies. Subsidies are very small and theaters can hardly make ends meet. At the same time, theaters lack able managers who could help them improve their financial situation. After the political changes, I expected small private theaters to appear instead of these huge monsters whose administrative staffs outnumber the artistic personnel. However, small experimental theaters could not survive under the conditions of a free market economy.

Second, foreign plays dominate theater repertoires. What has been written by Latvian playwrights over the last few years? Now there is no censorship, playwrights are free to choose any theme they like, but it turns out they have nothing to say. They used to write under the Soviet regime. Where are the plays now?

Third, our theaters suffer from a lack of talented directors and professionally trained young actors. At the same time, many talented actors of the older generation have been neglected. I have worked on twenty some productions and I have seen how it is done. To be honest, no masterpieces have been created. Our productions cannot be compared to those of Nekrosius in Lithuania, for instance.

I think that diversity of form should be encouraged – experiments, musicals, commercial productions, everything. I wish Latvian theater would be full of life and vigor.

THE ECOLOGY OF THEATER IN POST-SOVIET LATVIA

Valda Cakare

The Political and Cultural Scene in Latvia

Latvia is a small state on the coast of the Baltic Sea. Four thousand years have passed since the tribes of Balts settled this territory. Lithuanian and Latvian are two of the most ancient Indo-European languages. However, except for 22 years of political independence between 1914 and 1940, the present territory of Latvia has been subject to foreign rule since the thirteenth century. The Germans, the Poles, the Swedes, and the Russians have all had their hand in shaping political life in Latvia. Until the first half of the nineteenth century, native Latvians were serfs. Western ideas of a "national awakening" (as the movement was called in Latvia) took hold around the middle of the nineteenth century, leading Latvian intellectuals to envision and create a modern nation with its own cultural, economic, and political institutions. The twentieth century has seen a lot of change. The period of independence was a brief interlude brought to an end by Soviet occupation in 1940, German occupation from 1941 to 1945, Soviet occupation again at the end of World War II, and 45 subsequent years of Sovietization. Still, during the 22 years of political independence the economy and culture flourished. Thus, not only was the invasion of culturally less developed Soviet troops in 1940 seen as a painful loss of freedom, but as a deep humiliation. On the night of June 14, 1941, Stalin began his deportations in which 16,000 Latvians were sent to Siberia. In total, 34,000 Latvians fell victim to mental and physical violence during the first year of Soviet power. Thus, in the autumn of 1944, as World War II and the German occupation were coming to an end, thousands of Latvians fled to the West, seeking refuge abroad. 70 percent of those who fled were intellectuals, including professional actors, directors, playwrights, designers, and composers. Another deportation took place in 1949.

In 1991 after 50 years of Soviet occupation, Latvia regained its independence. At present, this country is facing serious economic and social problems very similar to those of other former Soviet countries. Latvia's total population is 2.5 million and almost 40 percent live in Riga, the capital.

Theater in Latvia – From Its Beginnings to *Perestroika*

Latvian theater is relatively new. Its beginnings date back to the national revival movement of "Young Latvians" in 1868. Since the invasion of German crusaders in the twelfth century, the German nobility had retained cultural, economic, and political privileges in Latvia. The national liberation was simultaneously a rejection of German supremacy and an adaptation of many German cultural institutions, since most "young Latvians" had been educated in Germany. One institution that the Latvians adapted to their national ends was the theater. The stage became the visual vehicle for the creation of a national consciousness. Latvian theater did not develop out of its folklore. On the contrary, it was strongly influenced by Germany, from acting style to theater architecture. In 1772, the rich and influential patron of the arts, Baron Otto von Futtinghoff, took the first German theater company in Riga under his wing. Theatrical companies and individual performers from Germany regularly appeared in Riga as well. Thus Latvian theater was influenced by provincial German theater and adopted its principles of decaying classicism. Later on, naturalism took hold, as did the principles of Stanislavsky's system, since many Latvian performers spent World War I in Russia, acquainting themselves with Russian theater practices. But it was not until the 1920s that the braided stream of Latvian theater practices divided into two main currents. One was represented by the National Theater, which cultivated psychological realism supported by the graphic form and static techniques inherited from German theater and the sensuality and demand for psychological character motivation taken from the Russian theater. From 1932 to 1934, the ponderous realism of the National Theater was refined by Mikhail Chekhov and the Latvian actor/director Ernests Feldmanis, who had studied the performing arts at A. Adashev's drama school at the Moscow Art Theater with E. Vakhtangov. The other current was represented by the Art Theater, led by Eduards Smilgis, who "blew up" tradition and rejected scenic realism, offering instead a new, highly metaphoric mode of expression. Influenced predominantly by symbolism and expressionism, the Art Theater under Smilgis's direction bore a distant resemblance to the Moscow Kamerny Theater, founded by A. Tairov. Smilgis and Tairov had met in Moscow during World War I. Smilgis may be the only Latvian director to have impregnated inherited western traditions with his own poetic vision, thereby creating a unique theatrical model that has no parallel in Latvian culture.

Latvian theater was isolated from social, cultural, and aesthetic processes in the western world for 46 years under the Soviet regime, and was committed to the tight boundaries of socialist realism. The only correct and acceptable way of acting was to move and speak as in everyday life. Themes imposed by Soviet officials were industrial problems, labor's achievements, and the desired communist future. But that does not mean Latvian theater was lacking in creative energy, nor was it completely detached from life or western aesthetic influences. An awareness of existentialist ideas and the Theater of the Absurd, as well as psychoanalysis and the Theater of Cruelty, could be observed. Most importantly, for almost 50 years, the theater served as the peoples' "spiritual resistance movement". Theater was the only place people could identify themselves with their culture and national community. Very often, theaters sought refuge in the classics: Shakespeare, Dostoyevsky, Chekhov, Ibsen, Rainis (the most outstanding Latvian poet and playwright). Theater spoke the language of metaphor and symbol. It stayed away from everyday events, but the contemporary nature of the productions became more and more evident. Aesopian language was the only one in which the truth could be spoken. Theater took on the role of the Church and of the mass media. There was a strong similarity between theater and poetry in this respect, since at that time both were extremely popular at all levels of society. Directors who achieved the most encouraging results included Mara Kimele, Adolfs Sapiro, Arkadijs Kacs, Olgerts Kroders, Valentins Maculevics, and Valdis Lurins.

In Premonition of Change

The late 1980s brought *perestroika*, followed by dramatic changes in all spheres of life. Theater continued to be a loudspeaker of truth, but now it dropped its Aesopic language and spoke openly about hot topics like the threatening future, the freedom of the Latvian community, ecology, and possible paths for national, economic, and spiritual recovery. The solution to the problem was not an ideological one, it was mostly a romantic one. References to the past, productions of plays which had been banned for fifty years alternated with contemporary plays that truthfully commented on life and confirmed belief in the future of the nation. One of the most popular productions of that period of great expectations was A. Pumpurs's *Lacplesis*, a stage version of a Latvian epic, directed by the young, rebellious Valdis Lurins. It was staged as a rock opera, with a book by the popular poetess Mara Zalite and music by Zigmars Liepins. The premiere took place on August 23, the day the notorious Molotov-Riebentrop pact was signed nearly fifty years before. Lurins dealt with certain universal archetypes, for instance those of a cultural hero and treason. The resurrection of a national hero let loose a torrent of previously suppressed self-confidence and a sense of ethnic identity. *Lacplesis* was performed in a large sports hall and all twenty performances sold out. A total of 100,000 people saw the production. It was an exercise in sharpening the perception of the historical fate of the nation.

The late 1980s marked the return of plays written by Latvians living in exile. The production of R. Staprans's *Four Days in June*, directed by Karlis Auskaps and Varis Vetra, proved to be of considerable artistic and political importance. This documentary play deals with the most dramatic episode in the life of Karlis Ulmanis, the president of Latvia from 1934 to 1940, and it was performed in the Palace of Riga, the former presidential residence. In the play, as in real life, Ulmanis is given less than 24 hours in which to decide whether to permit 200,000 Soviet soldiers to move into Latvia or whether to offer resistance which would lead to bloodshed. How should he solve this dilemma? This is a question that continues to plague the Latvian community even now.

Latvian Theaters: Geography

The number of professional theater companies in existence has changed over the last five years. Most of them are concentrated in Riga. The National Theater, the Daile Theater, the New Riga Theater, the National Opera, and the Puppet Theater are subsidized by the government. Since nearly half the population of Riga is Russian, the Russian Drama Theater continues to attract large audiences and receives financial support from the government. In spite of the difficult economic situation and thanks to government subsidies, theaters still exist in the towns of Valmiera, Liepaja, and Daugavpils. All of the state theaters are repertory theaters, with the exception of the New Riga Theater, which was founded in 1992. It has adopted the western practice of inviting artists from other Latvian theaters and from abroad to work there on specific productions. Often, they perform one production as long as they can attract audience. Several independent theaters have appeared over the last few years, but only two have been able to survive: the Pocket Theater, led by a group of directors; and the Scene Studio-Theater.

Professional training in acting and directing is only available at the Latvian Academy of Culture. Latvia cannot boast of an indigenous school of stage directing. The most prominent directors were educated in Moscow, others began as actors and have no formal directorial training. However, Latvia can boast of a national school of stage designers. Ilmars Blumbergs, Andris Freibergs, Marts Kitajevs, and Gunars Zemgals created a truly Latvian school of design. Symbolist in nature, it was perfectly in tune with the Aesopian directorial language of the time. In 1991/92, a new program for theater criticism was started at the University of Latvia. The director of the program, Silvija Radzobe, is one of the most competent theater critics in Latvia. However, the students' futures are uncertain because opportunities to publish articles on theater have become very few. The weekly newspaper *Literature and Art*, has ceased to exist as has the yearbook *Theater and Life*, which dealt exclusively with issues of Latvian theater. The only publication that prints more in-depth articles on theater is currently *The Theater Herald*. Studies in the history of Latvian theater are conducted at the Institute of Literature, Folklore, and Art at the Latvian Academy of Science and Letters.

A Trip into the Past

Since the late 1980s, Latvian history has seemed to be an inexhaustible source of ideological and aesthetic ideas. *Lacplesis* was the manifestation of the spirit of the time that gained the most publicity. But it was not the only one. In fact, every theater incessantly alluded to the new-found sense of ethnic identity and paid homage to the nation's heroic past. In 1987, the Daile Theater staged A. Caks's *Touched By Immortality*, directed by Karlis Auskaps. Caks's 1940 epic about Latvian riflemen in World War I was never published under Soviet rule and could not even be referred to. However, in the Latvian consciousness, *Touched By Immortality* was perceived as the most beautiful poetic manifestation of patriotism. Consequently, Auskaps's production did not have to be good, it just had to *be*. The very act of staging this piece took on a symbolic meaning because an outstanding work of art was returned to Latvian culture. The audience used to stand during each performance and sing along with the Latvian national anthem, the tune of which was used in the music of the production.

The artistic director of the National Theater, Mihails Kublinskis, greeted the approaching political changes with three productions. Two of these were contemporary plays – *Once Upon a Time There Was a Rider ...* , by A. Geikins, and *Kronis*, by L. Stumbre. Geikins's play was based on historical facts about the first Latvian priest of the seventeenth century, Johans Reiters (or *Jatnieks*, which means "rider"). Stumbre gave a symbolic name to her protagonist – *Kronis*, or "crown". In this play, which takes place during the Stalinist deportations, Kronis, a wealthy and arrogant farmer, is deceived by his poor and treacherous neighbor. Kublinskis's third production was of Schiller's romantic tragedy, *Mary Stuart*. Kublinskis's intention was quite surprising: to show through the fate of the beautiful heroine how small nations fall victim to larger ones.

The productions mentioned above exemplify an affirmative and somewhat one-sided attitude towards history. They appeal in a romantic way to national self-awareness, revealing the antagonism between the oppressor and the oppressed, but disregarding the inner conflicts of the oppressed.

A more adequate evaluation of past events and future prospects was demonstrated by Valentins Maculevics, who staged Rainis's dramatic poem *The Daugava*. The Daugava is the largest river in Latvia. It is referred to as Mother Daugava in Latvian folklore. This production set forth not only the idea of freedom, but for the first time since the beginning of the Soviet regime, publicly announced the idea of an independent state. A sort of political-musical blended with elements of Latvian folk rituals, the narrative part of the piece centers around the presence of an invisible foreign power that causes fear and a lack of personal and national pride. However, the people on the shore of the Daugava are not only devastated by foreign powers. No less dangerous is the hostility that springs up between compatriots. The finale, in which Spelmanis (a musician and poet) utters a loud, unheard cry, was filled with mysterious premonition. "The prophecy that the future of the nation was in danger if compatriots with diverse convictions did not find a common language seemed too pessimistic for many patriotic people at that time – it seemed to disparage the spiritual powers of the Latvians. But the future proved that this point of view was quite realistic."[1]

V. Lurins, who had offered a popular and affirmative conception of a national hero in *Lacplesis*, gave a psychological and philosophical study of the relations between individual and political forces in a production of the historical tragedy *Mirabeau* by A. Upits. No doubt the French Revolution provided a means of discussing the political processes of contemporary Latvia. Mirabeau, in Lurins's production, was not only a vigorous, handsome, and admired leader, but also an extremely ambitious and self-assured man. Played by Rolands Zagorskis, Mirabeau foreshadowed the new ambivalent political leader of Latvia.

Caks's epic *Touched by Immortality* inspired another production entitled *Psychic Assault*, which differed significantly in its evaluation of history. Directed by the young Juris Rijnieks at the Liepaja Theater, it showed that the time when glorification of the past was a form of spiritual resistance had come to an end. Auskaps visualized the Latvian riflemen as heroes who filled the brightest pages of the nation's history, but he disregarded the fact that at the same time, they had been mere tools in the hands of different foreign political forces. Rijnieks focused on the contradictory role that the riflemen had played in the tragic and grotesque carnival of history.

However, the nation's historical past was not an inexhaustible source of inspiration, largely because the present could not be ignored as theaters were coming face to face with a time of crisis.

Crisis: Life Outrivals Theater

For 25 years, theaters had been sold out. People lined up long before box offices opened. Many sought spare tickets before performances.

---

[1] Silvija Radzobe, *The Valmiera Theater*, in S. Radzobe, E. Tisheizere, G. Zeltina, *Theater of Latvia. The Eighties*. Riga: Preses Nams, 1995, p. 344.

But between 1991 and 1993, theaters emptied. Even the National Theater and the Daile Theater were threatened by the loss of spectators. Perhaps one reason for the lack of interest in theater was that the "theater of life" had become more interesting and exciting than the performing arts. Public life, which used to be extremely bland under the Soviet regime, recovered its spice and vitality. Mass meetings were held, TV and radio broadcasted the 1st Congress of the Peoples' Front of Latvia, future prospects for the nation were discussed openly as was the suffering, indignity, deprivation, and hopelessness that had been endured for many years. Another reason for the empty theaters was the hardship caused by the economic transition. The central bank held the currency relatively stable and the buying power was short. Intellectuals and pensioners, who had traditionally constituted theater audiences, became lower income groups and could no longer afford tickets. The price of a theater ticket under the socialist system was between 0.50 and 1.50 Rubles (US$0.50 to US$1.50) or approximately one eightieth of an average monthly salary. Now, it had increased to 2.50 or 3.50 Lats (US$5.00 to US$7.00), roughly one fifteenth of an average monthly salary. Some opening night tickets even cost 10 to 15 Lats (US$20.00 to US$30.00).

Theaters were not prepared to face the situation and they tried to cope with it by looking back to the Great Depression of the 1930s which had caused very similar conditions. They tried to bring back their audiences by rapidly increasing the number of productions and by staging cheap comedies and melodramas, very often copying the 1930s repertoire. A common opinion was held that people were tired of the hardships of life and they needed relaxation. The repertoire became very shallow, the mode of expression primitive and archaic. The economic crisis was accompanied by a deep spiritual crisis. It was not easy to understand what was going on, to determine who was to blame for the unfavorable turn of events. Deep depression replaced romantic expectations. Artists felt confused and tried to conceal their confusion by becoming obsequious to crude taste.

Perhaps the most dramatic event of that period was the closing of the Youth Theater in 1992. It was a heavy loss for Latvian culture. For almost 30 years, Adolfs Sapiro, the only stage director in Latvia with an international reputation, had been developing the taste of his spectators and the professional skills of his actors. Under his guidance, the theater had changed from a place of amusement for children and teenagers into a theater with a broad and serious repertoire, performing classics by Ibsen, Chekhov, Rainis, as well as contemporary Latvian plays. Sapiro's productions were subjects of debate. The director's ability to unify diverse theatrical elements (commedia dell'arte, Meyerhold's scenic reconstructivism) with subtle psychology, references to everyday life with deep philosophical understanding, conjured up a new world – architectonic in shape and modern in expression. At the Baltic Spring Theater Festivals Sapiro was regularly among the honorees. However, in the late 1980s, the theater's work was declared unsatisfactory. The Ministry of Culture, which controlled all state-subsidized theaters, accused Sapiro of not employing all the actors in the company, for stoppages, for choosing an "incorrect" repertoire that did not respond to the needs of children and teenagers. Perhaps the conflict could have been resolved, but no one tried. In the spring of 1992, the Ministry of Culture closed the theater and Sapiro left for Moscow.

Latvian Theater Today: Successes, Frustrations, Expectations

After some three years of chaos and frustration, a gradual improvement has become apparent in the state of Latvian theater. Theater is not intended as entertainment, but as an artistic activity that confirms the personal artistic tastes and interests of its creators. Theater seems to have become reconciled to the loss of its former role as spiritual leader and the only mouthpiece of truth. Although each director has his own set of principles and his own method of working, the main trend is becoming clear. Theater is beginning to feel more at ease with the diversity of aesthetic possibilities. It is acquainting itself with western experiences. Directors are experimenting freely, mixing techniques and trying to create new worlds of their own. On the other hand, theater is reestablishing its link to life. It is concerned more now with the inner processes of the individual, and even social conflicts and problems are discussed on the level of deep personal insight. At the same time, theater suffers from lack of funds and has to think about commercial success. However, only the National Theater is coping well with its financial problems. Their performances are sold out every night. How do they do it?

The Phenomenon of the National Theater

The theater building designed by the Latvian architect Augusts Reinbergs and built by the city of Riga at the beginning of the twentieth century is pompous and historic. It was in this building that Latvian independence was proclaimed on November 18, 1918. The auditorium's ceiling is decorated with gold and the chairs are upholstered in velvet. The very building inspires solemnity and respect for tradition. The large company consists of 50 actors who have become, or who are expected to become, legends of Latvian performing art. "The theater has based its work on realism, emphasizing human psychology and human actions validated by logic. At times one senses a tinge of naturalism. The most successful productions have revealed the scope of human nature within the context of history, tradition and the human experience."[2] says Lilija Dzene, the first lady of Latvian theater criticism. Still, this scenic realism is tinged with artificiality. The performers seem to underline every step, every gesture, every glance. They do not form an ensemble, but a group of soloists. Perhaps this collection of talented and fascinating personalities is one reason audiences love this theater. Another reason is that this theater understands the tastes of their audience and works hard to satisfy them. Their audience wants to be comforted and theater offers them a bit of illusion. They want to see what is publicly known and accepted and the theater gives this to them. Life does not find its double in the productions of the National Theater, but rather a slightly detached, slightly embellished reflection. A production of *The Shameless Old Men*, written by Anslavs Eglitis (who lived in exile in America) and directed by Mihails Kublinskis, may serve as an example. The play is about Janis Bertolds, an elderly man who discovers the pleasures of life after having retired, and is narrated with resignation and benevolence. It is a story about loneliness and overcoming that loneliness. The isolation of the actors on stage is used by the director to symbolize human loneliness and spiritual independence. *Shameless Old Men* is Kublinskis's attempt at leading his audience into a bright and vigorous world. Theatricality is evident not only in the actors' style of expression, but also in the colorful, illusory stage design by Ints Sedlenieks. For instance, each member of the Bertold family carries a piece of the car with which they go on a picnic. The Atlantic Ocean is represented by waving blue fabric and an apple tree grows luminous glass apples.

A very similar effect was achieved by Edmunds Freibergs in his production of *The Tailor's Days in Silmaci* by R. Blaumanis. It is probably the most beloved Latvian play. It would be difficult to find someone who had not seen it (it was written in 1904) several times. An entire museum is devoted to this play and its various performances. It is a "peoples' play", which Germans would call *Volksstück*, containing the peoples' vital humor, songs and dancing. The action takes place over a few days' time when the country people enjoy a short moment of rest before the summer solstice (St. John's Day). The rituals of the solstice form an integral part of the play. For the National Theater, this is a symbolic play. It has been running since 1921. In 1986, the production was transferred from the stage to natural surroundings, a move welcomed by thousands of spectators. It is quite understandable that this attitude towards the play has created certain stereotypes which are expected by the audience, but which at the same time stop the rich flow of creativity.

---

[2] Lilija Dzene, "The National Theater", Latvian Theater, N1, 1993, p. 42.

In his 1994 production, Freibergs managed to combine the seemingly incompatible. He paid homage to tradition (a country music ensemble plays throughout the performance and the song and dance is retained), but at the same time, he provides non-traditionally deep insight into the conscious and unconscious impulses of the characters. *The Tailor's Days in Silmaci* can be interpreted as a Chekhovian psychological study of human affairs.

Two more recent productions have contributed to the revival of psychological realism at the National Theater: Ibsen's *The Wild Duck*, and Lorca's *The House of Bernarda Alba*, directed by Olgerts Kroders. Both plays were staged in the 100-seat Actors' Hall (opened in 1976) and provide close-up looks at human existence. *The House of Bernarda Alba* opens with a procession of women dressed in black. Silently they draw around a small altar in the center of the room. Each brings a candle to place on the altar. Gradually, the symbolic meaning of the altar changes from religious to phallic. All the women are obsessed with sex. They are constantly peeping through vagina-like slits in the walls, hoping to glimpse some intimate moments in other peoples' lives, lives they are deprived of. Adela (played by Zan Jancevska) is the only one to break out. She is the winner, but she makes the losers suffer through her arrogance and cruelty. Kroders suggests via this subtle psychological study that the present socio-economic changes are not only desired, but also very painful.

Another attempt at analyzing the present day situation was made by Valdis Lurins in Lelde Stumbre's *The Dog*. Stumbre is a very prolific playwright and the only contemporary Latvian dramatist whose works are regularly staged by professional theaters. Lurins treats her psychological work as an Absurdist drama with elements of psychoanalysis. *The Dog* is designed by Ivar Noviks for a water tank with actors costumed in modern dress and waterproof boots. The world created by the director is real and unreal at the same time. Door bells ring unexpectedly, flashes of lightning and thunder and heavy showers reflect what is going on in peoples' lives. A woman in black takes off her dress and underneath she is wearing red underwear. Black and red symbolize the conscious and unconscious – states of being which Lurins explores. *The Dog* ends with a wood pile falling down. A picture of a spring landscape appears in the background as if promising peace and light after sin and suffering. In 1992, the audience interpreted the finale as a belief in the future of the community.

However, the few successful productions of the 1990s have not been able to solve the National Theater's problems. Opinions differ. Some think the National Theater should be kept as a museum of Latvian performing arts. Others think that it needs renewal. But will that not mean a loss of spectators? Meanwhile, the National Theater continues to be the most archaic and the most popular of Latvian theaters.

Diversity of Styles

Actually, the National Theater is the only theater whose aesthetic traditions constitute a specific artistic tendency. Other tendencies cannot be associated with particular theaters, but are connected with the work of certain directors. The New Riga Theater houses at least three different directors with differing production styles.

Mara Kimele belongs to the middle generation of Latvian directors and is the only woman director to have succeeded in advancing her own aesthetic program. She received an excellent professional education at the Theater Institute in Moscow where her artistic adviser was Anatoly Efros. He contributed greatly to Kimele's concept of theater. She believes that psychological action on stage is linked to biological roots. She rejects the authority of the text and looks upon theater as a means of metaphysical and spiritual breakthrough. At present, Kimele focuses on experiments with space and the relationship between the performer and the spectator. She is trying to discover whether or not the relationships between space, audience, and language can be revolutionized. In *Passion Play* (1993), *King Lear* (1994), and *The Book of Ruth* (1994) she broke with the proscenium stage. In *Passion Play*, by P. Nichols, the alter-egos of the partners in an adulterous marriage are given a chance to speak. Kimele treated this domestic play as a game reminiscent of ice hockey. The audience is seated behind a white rectangular barrier and watches the almost empty "arena" on which the actors portray the most intimate conscious and unconscious motivations of the characters. The presentation is almost naturalistic and closely resembles everyday life. However, the relationships between the partners are structured according to the rules of a risky game. They win and lose irrespective of their expectations and intellectual assumptions. They go at each other like fighters in a ring. Kimele's final admonition is that the human ego is a metaphysical microcosm full of inexplicable and unforseeable complexities.

Jan Kott interprets *King Lear* as a study in "philosophical cruelty." Kimele playfully substitutes "philosophical" with "children's". The action in her production takes place on a playground. The set and costumes are designed by Aija Zarina, a Latvian avant-garde painter. A piece of red satin with awkward drawings on it forms a backdrop against which the actors resemble bas-reliefs. A ladder, a rope, and a heap of pillows serve as props. There is no furniture. Lear's daughters wear short dresses like teenagers. Red and black for Regan and Goneril, bright green for Cordelia. The men are dressed in red and black shorts. Since *Lear* is viewed as children's play, several of the male roles (Edmund and Edgar, and the Fool) are played by women. The show opens with noise and chaos. All the actors rush to the playground laughing, screaming, and wreaking havoc. They show an amazing ability to jump, run, trip, and tumble. Their unpredictable movement lends itself to the abandonment of conventional patterns of speech. Many of the theatrical devices Kimele uses are taken from children's play. Regan and Goneril confirm their unanimous decision to thwart their father's demands by hopping over a jump-rope together. Cornwall writes on the wall "Lear is a fool." Regan kills Goneril by offering her a bottle of poisoned Coca-Cola. A thunderstorm effect is achieved by the actors throwing heaps of ping-pong balls like big hailstones. The ping-pong balls become Gloucester's eyes, crushed under the heels of Cornwall and Regan. Perhaps Kimele's playful vision of the world reduces the subtle complexity of Shakespeare's tragedy to a considerable extent. However, she has attempted to discover the play in terms of its modern equivalency. She sums up the social and political experience of the modern world, demonstrating how cruel it becomes without faithfulness, honesty, love, and humanity.

Kimele's reputation as an experimenter was confirmed with *The Book of Ruth*. The script is based on the texts of the Old Testament and it was produced for inclusion in an international theater festival in Finland, "The Bible '94." For Kimele, *The Book of Ruth* was to be an experiment in ritual. In it she worked with women only – all male roles were played by actresses – not to show postmodern disregard for *sex*, but in order to stress the most universal aspects of human existence. The ritualistic aspect of the production is plainly evident. It is performed in the center of a rectangular hall and the audience is seated in one row at right angles to the playing space. The actresses are dressed in plain blue, orange, and white gowns or slacks. Some of them carry big puppets. Their movements are simple and precise, The sounds recall primitive ceremony – screams, whispers, moans, incantation. The most basic episodes of human life are enacted: Harvest, by moving in a synchronized manner around the playing space, hissing; Marriage, by jingling bells and handing large bunches of grapes to the Bride: War, by the appearance of a woman clad in black violently rapping a clapper and screaming horribly. In the last moments of the play, the actresses kneel down in a circle, moaning: Child Birth. The piece is structured on the group's improvisations and responses rather than on any specific text. It is a ritual of life, a celebration of primordial existence. Kimele sees the piece as an infinite striving for harmony, a triumph of humanism.

* * *

There is a remarkable dialectic between Juris Rijnieks's ironic vision of new Latvian problematics and his universalist theater of poetic images. Rijnieks is 38 years old and at present is the only Latvian director to try to make socio-political comments on human affairs. His production of *The Seven Simpletons* (1994), a combined adaptation of Rainis's mock-epic and the nineteenth century writer Jekabs Zvaigznite's stories about simpletons, received an enthusiastic reception. It deals with different hot topics of discussion: recent political events, the structure of authority, the building of a national state, the heritage of the socialist system, human interaction, and multiculturalism. Rijnieks sees the ideological-political chaos as ridiculous and alien to the individual. At the same time, he sees that politics are vitalizing the country. In *The Seven Simpletons*, Rijnieks worked with young actors from the Daugavpils Theater company and tried to find a non-stereotypical way of combining politics and art. Odums Vucans, played by Andris Makovskis, is a mock version of a cultural hero. He is an unsophisticated child of nature who sets out to learn the wisdom of the world. The world turns out to be a world of simpletons. They build a town hall without any windows and then try to bring light into it with their hats and sacks. They undress in order to present their national costumes to a mighty sovereign who has come to visit the small land on the shores of the Daugava. Though the problems of contemporary Latvia may not be immediately apparent, the actors succeed in saying something true and honest about their native milieu and the absurdity of the present-day situation in Latvia. The dominant principle of this production is eclecticism. Rijnieks combines elements of epic theater with *Volksstücke*, clownery, and absurdism. Eight actors dressed in black slacks, white shirts, and ties – simpleton "uniforms" – tell stories, enact intellectual jokes, sing, and dance, trapping the audience in a blend of existential and historical realities. The tone of the production is bold, virile, good-natured, and ironic. And slightly sad.

The other trend Rijnieks has been following is the theater of poetic images, of sophisticated scenic metaphor. Little wonder that he is obsessed with Harold Pinter. In *The Caretaker* (1987), *The Dumb Waiter* (1993), and *Betrayal* (1994), the irrationality of experience was transferred to the stage. These productions were fusions of naturalism and surrealism, of expressionistic movements and kitschy music. Parallel action helped create an illusion of a strange, dreamlike world which proved to be much larger and more mysterious than that inhabited by the characters. In each case, Rijnieks tried to evoke what was behind the text.

In Rijnieks's more recent production of F. Wedekind's *Spring's Awakening* (1995), he continues his search for a sensuous, theatrical vision of the world. The tragic, eerie tone of the play is somewhat mitigated by Rijniek's calm, placid, and meditative approach. He replaces the theme of the need for a repressive society to recognize the stirring of puberty in its children with a poetic study of human loneliness. *Spring's Awakening* opens with the actors standing in a line on the edge of the stage in bluish darkness as the lonely voice of Rudolfs Plepis recites words, the meaning of which is unimportant. What really matters is the tone of his voice. Bitter and tragic, it suggests the total emptiness of the world. Then the lights come up and the space comes to life. The location is indicated by an arch, which is used as a bridge, and a bare tree with bright colored kerchiefs for leaves. Schoolboys and schoolgirls are singing, dancing, and laughing under light that seems to be shining through stained glass windows. Rijnieks shows this world touched by deliberate artificiality. The scenes follow one another like shots of modernist pictures, each expressive mise-en-scene or pose lingers on. The central characters' actions are mimed by their doubles. Sexual intercourse between Melchior and Wendla takes place on a flower-entwined swing, and Wendla and Moritz – both the victims of the puritan repressiveness of the grown-ups – climb the stairs and sit on the bridge. They have moved to some other reality and look down on the playing space where those who are alive feel so lonely. *Spring's Awakening* is not a condemnation of hypocrisy and puritanism that leads to institutionalized barbarity, but rather a poetic reconciliation with the fact of human loneliness.

* * *

30-year-old Alvis Hermanis belongs to the younger generation of Latvian directors and is quite often called a postmodern director. Trained as an actor at Mara Kimele's studio, he often plays the leading parts in his own productions. He spent a couple of years in America. He attempts to break radically with theatrical conventions endorsed by his contemporaries. The underlying conviction in all of Hermanis's productions is that conventional signs and images do not fully express reality. He plays with different objects, creating assortments of images that belong to different epochs and styles. In *Secret Pictures*, Hermanis seems to be inspired by a novel by Marguerite Duras as well as by the work of Robert Wilson. He isolates meaningful speeches instead of integrating them. The audience can watch slides of paintings by Andrew Wyeth, or video clips of ocean waves. They can listen to the sound of waves on tape or turn to the young actor sitting in a glass cage reciting a text by Duras into a microphone. Each component is seen as a piece of a collage and the text is detached from the image and the sound. In *The Marquise de Sade*, by Y. Mishima, Hermanis solemnly and ceremoniously demonstrates how six women attempt to reach sexual satisfaction by remembering de Sade and his horrible experiments. The set, designed by Hermanis himself, is an empty white rectangular playing space. The lights remain on-white and at full strength. Spectators sit at one end of the hall. The actresses face the audience wearing masks of eighteenth century French noblewomen. Their faces are painted white to conceal their natural color. They wear tall headdresses and rococo costumes designed by Vecella Varslavane. The actresses arrange themselves in symmetrical groups, their movements are rhythmical, slow, and purposefully graceful. They chant their lines – the meaning is not important, but the melody is: words are used merely for their musical value. Hermanis's theater feeds on archetypes and images of the past. In *The Madame de Sade*, the image of Christ goes together with de Sade and Mishima. The actress who plays Charlotte and who simultaneously embodies the spirit of de Sade, appears half naked in the second act in a wreath of thorns. She becomes Christ bleeding from his wounds and is reminiscent of de Sade, crucified by the sexually obsessed women. Hermanis views his production as a meeting of cultures, trying to fuse French and Japanese styles of movement, music, and costume. His theater is a hybrid world in which all forms coexist effortlessly.

Hermanis's dramatization of *The Portrait of Dorian Gray* (1994) was staged as a chain of separate scenes, including mime, skits, and dances set to music by Prokofiev. Both Dorian Gray and Lord Henry were played by women, and Dorian's descent into dissipation and evil was portrayed on a video screen: the beautiful face of Elita Klavina's Dorian becoming more and more cynical, worn out, and perverted. Hermanis continued his artistic quest in his production of *In The Burning Darkness* (1995) by A. Buero-Vallejo. This play, which is rooted in political reality, was treated by Hermanis as a study in the universal aspects of human relationships. The story deals with the supposedly harmonious existence of blind students. Blindness has been a commonly used metaphor, but for Hermanis is still provoking. He does not encourage the actors to enact their blindness symbolically. Instead they depict blindness naturalistically: odd movements, hypersensitive reactions to noises, fixed gazes. The central theme of the production, revealed through the conflict between the characters of Ignasio and Carlos, is the uncovering of human complexities, the search for self-definition and the absolute freedom that can only be achieved in death. The actors are not limited to conventional modes of expression. An external situation, sign, or word corresponds to an internal state of emotion. Therefore, the performance is based on the group's improvisations and responses, and the message of the play depends very much on who takes the upper hand – Ignasio or Carlos. The unpredictability of the psychological pattern within the production is fascinating. The unpredictability of Hermanis's projects is likewise fascinating. In the fall of 1995, he staged the opera *The Fire and the Night*, with a libretto adapted from a work by Rainis and music composed by Janis Medins. Most recently, he has begun working on Chekhov's *The Seagull*.

* * *

Film director Peteris Krilovs's productions at the Daugavpils Theater have prompted critics to view him as an important theater figure as well. During the Soviet regime, Krilovs made several films of considerable artistic value. *Perestroika* put an end to the Latvian film industry, but

Krilovs's desire to experiment fortunately coincided with the needs of the newly established Daugavpils Theater. He was invited to teach at the young actors' studio. His training methods encouraged actors to freely express their psychological and physical motivations while controlling them at the same time. In the terms of Grotowski, he helped them construct their own "psychoanalytic language." The stage adaptation of William Faulkner's *The Sound and the Fury* (1991) was the first production in which Krilovs demonstrated the results of his training methods. The actors in the production all play several roles, but do not use make-up, props, or costumes to effect the transformations from one role to another. They are able to create a wide range of characters using facial expressions, physical comportment, and voices alone. Krilovs does not reject the script altogether, but uses it as a structure for a new piece. That may be one reason why he prefers to work directly from non-dramatic texts. Another reason is his experience as a film director. His productions consist of series of cinematographic "shots" that have a deeper unity and appeal more strongly to the emotional and cognitive faculties of the audience. In *The Sound and the Fury*, Krilovs "has achieved the effect of the continuity of life, the stage is invaded by a series of simultaneous actions. The actors' performances are 'hot tempered' – swift, energetic, explosive, and extremely concrete, physically and psychologically. The director has stimulated them to penetrate into madness. The atmosphere is created through contrasts: noise, intensity, dynamics, and bright light are alternated with dark, meditative scenes. Several episodes might seem superfluous as they are not integral to the action, but they are necessary in order to create the impression of the complexity and mystery of the world."[3]

Krilovs has staged works by Goethe, E. T. A. Hoffmann, and Heinrich von Kleist, but he established his reputation as an experimenter with his production of *The Possessed*, by Dostoyevsky (1993). *The Possessed* is an apocalyptic novel, an exposé of unbridled, unprincipled radicalism. Krilovs was attracted to the novel because it expresses the contradictions of human life, the transformation of ideals into tyrannical ideology. Morality clashes with daily life, established values disintegrate. This world is the absurd, inexplicable world of post-socialism. Krilovs staged *The Possessed* on a single set which does away with time sequence and linear continuity in favor of simultaneity and a total symbolic image. The set is a circular railway. A small wagon carries the characters around and around the circle and no one can get off. As the social and political realities of post-socialist Latvia inspired Krilovs's intellectual concept of

---

[3] Silvija Radzobe, "The First Graduates of the Daugavpils Theater," *Teatra Vestnesis*, n. 6, 1992, p. 38.

the play, the work of Marc Chagall inspired his visual concept of the production. Natural proportions are distorted. Clownery, grotesquery, and tomfoolery replace despair, violence, and suffering. Actors' physical actions correspond to their inner emotions. They use grotesquely exaggerated movements, piercing voices, shouts, cries, and puppets. The unifying element is rhythm. Krilovs insists that Dostoyevsky is carnavalesque and shocking, that excruciating human existence can be laughed at. Stavrogin's story is not the story of the fall of a tragic hero, but the fall of an insignificant man who pretends to be a hero. The character of Peter Verkhovensky who represents the mysterious, metaphysical evil in the world has turned into a slight, fidgety, cheerful jester. The universe is incomprehensible and indifferent, and man is alone and alienated.

* * *

In the nineties, several theater centers have developed in Latvia. The National Theater (founded in 1919) and the Daile Theater (founded in 1920) which have firmly established traditions and are well known by audiences can be considered the formal centers, but the most interesting projects have taken place at the New Riga Theater (founded in 1992) and at the Daugavpils Theater (founded in 1988). These theaters have become informal centers for the performing arts and their audiences are made up of young people and intellectuals.

1996

LITHUANIAN THEATER

FOREWORD

Eimuntas Nekrosius

After the political changes in Lithuania, problems related to the creative arts did not disappear. They torment me now just as they did before. I have always thought that true art is not born independently of political, economic, or social conditions. Take for instance Shostakovich's music during the blockade of Leningrad. What will change in the actor's profession if a computer is installed in the rehearsal studio? Will actors act better? Now, many say that the symbols and metaphors of the theater in former times were a way of deceiving the authorities. But metaphor is not guerrilla warfare. I did not deceive anybody when working in the theater. I was sincere. And now I am doing the same things; I like metaphors on the stage.

Perhaps many artists are disconcerted by the loss of their privileged position. They represented an exceptional race under the socialist system. Psychologically it is difficult to give up the importance one had attributed to oneself. Young actors think they are valuable after only four years of study: after all, theater is the lowest art form, requiring the least investment of intellect, talent, and labor. I see a great imbalance between what people who work in theater give and what they receive in exchange: popularity, recognition, success. A painful paradox. Sometimes I feel ashamed. After speaking to serious musicians, physicists, or doctors, I feel like an absolute zero. When the public stopped going to the theater, it punished the theater for its allegedly exceptional importance. People had surpassed the theater in experience and knowledge.

At present, theater tends more and more towards entertainment. And maybe theater really is only a way of passing time? Now everyone is openly enticing audiences into theaters. I also want to be liked. I try to stop myself. It is awful when one attempts to please others, to win them over at any cost. Maybe this is the beginning of the artist's downfall?

We tour a great deal. However, should tours be a measure of success for theater? We've been to many places. What did we leave there? I don't believe that the theater can cut a fatal mark – like a knife in a table – in the memory of another nation. On the other hand, a trip creates the illusion of drawing nearer to our dream. As in Chekhov's play, "to Moscow, to Moscow!" One must have a dream.

NEW SEASONS OF HOPE AND CRISIS

Ramune Marcinkeviciute

The Audience Preferred Life

Theaters were deserted during the first seasons of freedom. Spectators went out into the streets and squares. People got involved in the affective and adventurous process of creating history. Theaters were shocked at the loss of audiences, because over the last ten years, theaters had felt a special love and attention from their public. People had liked going to the theater. People waited in long lines at the box office in order to get tickets for the best shows. This was due to the fact that the quality of the theater was good but was also a result of living in a society where entertainment options were limited. In Soviet Lithuania, theater and literature provided an escape from everyday life. A false and deceitful reality seemed more artificial than a life that was invented on the stage. Actors' performances were more natural than lives of ordinary citizens who were afraid to be frank and who were weighed down by daily routine. There is a well known Lithuanian saying that real life during the Soviet era began at night in "kitchen talks." Theater in Lithuania was like a symbolic "kitchen night." A special symbolic and metaphoric language was invented. One felt as though the audience and actors were united by the same thoughts and ideas. This "artificial reality" was brought to a halt by historical events. Theaters seemed to empty overnight. It seemed as if audiences, preferring life now to the stage, would never return. The new language of politics was so attractive and strong that its current swept away the language of the stage.

The Period of Repaying Debts

"Today we trust artists!" said the former Minister of Culture of the Soviet Government prior to the Declaration of Independence. We were now allowed to produce the plays we pleased. In 1989 this sounded like a triumph, but after a few seasons, it became a problem. It became clear that if you wanted your audience to return, you not only had to decide what to stage, but how to do it.

First of all, theaters began repaying debts – concentrating on some of the events of the twentieth century that had, until now, been ignored. They began by recognizing formerly banned works by emigrants such as Antanas Skema, Algirdas Landsbergis, and Kostas Ostrauskas. In 1989, the director Jonas Vaitkus produced Antanas Skemas's play *The Awakening* at the Lithuanian State Academic Drama Theater. Skemas's play dealt with the beginning of the Bolshevist occupation in Lithuania and it aroused a great deal of public interest.

While theaters still had to meet political requirements, they refused to compete with politicians or to stage overtly political plays. An interesting result of this situation was the creation of the political puppet theater, Sepa, founded by Gintaras Varnas and nine of his colleagues who, at the time, were studying directing at the Academy of Music. Tickets were free and the house was always packed. Audiences were able to see political personalities such as Gorbachov and Landsbergis on stage. Some politicians became the object of mockery at this theater and people were able to laugh at situations they had to face in real life.

The theater has also taken an interest in formerly neglected classic works by the absurdists Beckett, Ionesco, and Pinter. In Soviet Lithuania, a play by Beckett had been staged only once, and then quite by chance. In 1982, a young actor/director, Kestutis Zilinskas, produced *Waiting For Godot* at the Klaipeda Drama Theater. When the political changes began, Zilinskas left the state-run theater and founded his own private theater, a fifty-seat house which only functions sporadically. Zilinskas also set up a cafe next door, saying, "I need a business to support the theater." The theater director/cafe owner did not forget Beckett and went on to produce *Endgame*. Another well-known actor, Valentinas Masalskis, also left the state theater and founded the Leeway Art Center in Kaunas where he staged *Krapp's Last Tape* and *Waiting For Godot*. Masalskis says that absurdist drama goes against the conventional mechanism of the theater. Lithuanian artists needed the Theater of the Absurd in their attempt to overturn their situation and find their place in the former communist society.

The third feature of recent seasons is the death of Lithuanian drama. Since gaining independence, not a single new Lithuanian play worthy of notice has been staged. The years under the Soviet regime made us mythologize the past, look forward to the future, and hate the present. This tendency is reflected in Lithuanian drama. A strong tradition of historical drama exists, exemplified by the work of Juozas Grusas and Justinas Marcinkevicius. Writers were very much against "vulgar reality", and preferred to deal with themes of inner, spiritual discovery. Most Lithuanian playwrights have been well known writers, but have had no direct link to the theater. The lack of native plays is the most crucial problem facing Lithuanian theater today. Contemporary playwrights are not able to transform contemporary life into art.

Are Lithuanians Conservative?

Lithuanian theater is over 425 years old. The first theater performance in Lithuania took place on October 18th, 1570, in Vilnius. It was a performance of *Hercules* by the Italian S. Tucci. Professional theater in Lithuania was formed much later, at a time when directing was undergoing reforms in most other countries. This historical coincidence determined the future course of Lithuanian theater: its emphasis on serious, artistic direction. This explains why literal forms of theater in Lithuania are considered academic and traditional, and why artistic innovation is most often found in the area of directing. Certain criteria of evaluation were established under the Soviet regime. Artists had to invent new ways of telling the truth. This is why a theatrical language consisting of various artistic symbols evolved. At that time, the theatrical metaphor of director Eimuntas Nekrosius became very popular. In speaking about his method, he said that he was looking for "space behind words." The "space behind words" is still very important today.

During the recent years of political change, none of the state theaters have been forced to close. Of these state theaters, the Drama Theater in Kaunas is the oldest. Kaunas, the second largest city in Lithuania, was the temporary capital of the Independent State of Lithuania between the wars. The first premiere of a professional production (Zuderman's *St. John's Eve*) took place there on January 19, 1920. The Drama Theater was the first to form the traditions that would shape Lithuanian theater. The Drama Theater also took an interest in foreign artistic achievements. The famous Russian artist and innovator Mikhail Chekhov worked for some years with a company of actors in Kaunas. Two directors contributed significantly to the Drama Theater during the Soviet era. From 1968 to 1971, the theater was under the direction of Jonas Jurasas, who was famous for his nonconformism. He was forced to emigrate because of his political convictions and his name was not mentioned in official histories of Lithuanian theater for almost 20 years, although he continued working in The United States, Canada, West Germany, and Japan. When the changes took place, Jurasas returned to Kaunas to help the company he had known since his youth create a modern, model theater. He was welcomed at the Drama Theater and staged three previously underrated plays there: a successful environmental production of *The Lithuanian Piano*, and versions of Harold Pinter's *Mountain Language* and Ariel Dorfman's *Death and the Maiden*, which were not so warmly received. Jurasas could not share the experience he had gained abroad because of the company's old, bad habits. At that time, some incompetent actors were fired, but they took the case to court, won, and were allowed to return to the theater. This incident, along with the trying political and economic conditions in the country in general, discouraged

Jurasas who had become accustomed to the western way of life, and he left Lithuania again.

Jonas Vaitkus, the director of the Kaunas Drama Theater from 1970 to 1980, is a unique and interesting personality in the history of Lithuanian theater. He is a master of the grotesque and of "total" theater. His favorite theme is the conflict between the individual and society. During his time at the Drama Theater, he staged versions of Gorky's *The Last Ones*, Ibsen's *The Master Builder*, Jarry's *Ubu Roi*, and Camus's *Caligula*. These productions moved the audiences and taunted the officials who were responsible for the theater. When the political changes began, Vaitkus moved to Vilnius and became the director of the State Academic Drama Theater.

The current director of the Drama Theater at Kaunas is Gytis Padegimas. He is of the middle generation and his views are rather idealistic. During the Soviet era, he staged versions of Strindberg's *The Creditors* and Thornton Wilder's *Our Town*, which made him famous. Now, he has made the Drama Theater very successful and frequently invites guest directors from countries like England, Norway, and Japan to work with the Kaunas company.

The Drama Theater of Klaipeda was established in 1935. Klaipeda is a port city situated on the Baltic Sea. The theater survived both the German occupation and the Soviet era. Povilas Gaidys has been the director of the theater since 1963. He is the only director of this theater who has enjoyed staging comedy and who does it well. There is a general feeling in Lithuania that comedy as a genre is not representative of the country. Lithuanians are not merry by nature. The deformed fate of the nation had an impact on our ability to laugh: it became deformed as well. On stage, laughter was transformed into grotesque and irony. In Gaidys's staging of Soviet comedies such as Mayakovsky's *The Bathhouse*, Kocergo's *The Masters of Time*, and Kapkov's *The Elephant*, the traditional Gogolian question, "What are you laughing at?" was always addressed to our neighbor, never to us. Young actors came to the theater at the time of the political changes and they made audiences laugh again. They did not produce traditional comedies, but saw the humorous side of themselves and of the world, and were not afraid to laugh at it. Polls taken in 1995 showed that many spectators would like to see more comedies on stage. The Lithuanian theater will have to take this into consideration in the future.

The Drama Theater of Panevezys was established in 1940. By the 1960s, it had become a legend in the former Soviet Union and was like a forbidden fruit for Lithuanians. The director Juozas Miltinis, who had studied at the Charles Dullin studio in Paris, turned this provincial theater into an oasis of western atmosphere in the middle of Soviet Lithuania. He trained a new company of actors at his own studio.

The company was like a closed sect. They were interested in the aesthetics of Western European theater rather than the obligatory social realism. They staged plays by Ibsen, Strindberg, Wolfgang Borchert, Arthur Miller, and Dürrenmatt. Miltinis made audiences understand intellectual drama. Today, the theater is named after him and the current director, Saulius Varnas, follows the traditions Miltinis began in his own productions of Kafka's *The Trial* and Strindberg's *Dream Play*.

The State Theater of Vilnius opened in 1940. It later became the State Academic Drama Theater of Lithuania and today it has been designated the National Theater. The State Academic Theater's acting company with its hierarchical structure, is the largest in Lithuania, and being accepted into it establishes an actor's career. Despite political obligations and compromises, the State Academic Theater has continued to play a positive role, producing many Lithuanian plays. In 1989, Jonas Vaitkus became the head of the theater and attempted to reform the "spoiled" acting company. The experiment ended in conflict. In 1995, he handed partial leadership over to Rimas Tuminas, a member of the middle generation who had studied directing in Moscow and who had been working at the State Academic Theater since 1970. Tuminas had put together a small troupe of actors and taken up residence on the State Theater's small, second stage. Both companies now exist side by side at the same theater. In 1990, the Town Board of Vilnius acknowledged Tuminas's company as the Small Theater of Vilnius. Tuminas's productions of Chekhov's *The Cherry Orchard*, Brecht's *Galileo*, and *Smile Upon Us, Lord*, based on the work by the Jewish writer G. Kanovicius, have recently made the Small Theater a favorite.

The Russian Drama Theater was established in Vilnius in 1946. Such a theater was obligatory in all the former republics of the Soviet Union. The company consisted of Russian actors. Gradually, this theater became the most popular. Its repertoire was interesting and the acting was unusual. Directors, such as Roman Viktiuk, who were misunderstood in Moscow at the time, found shelter here. Now the situation has changed. Today, the actors of the Russian Drama Theater are trying to find their place in Lithuanian society. They do not want to represent the theater of the national minority. They are trying to gain popularity by staging plays about current, immediate issues. Linas Zaikauskas, the theater's director, supports experimental theater, but only a handful of specialists are interested in the plays he has staged: *Medea*, by Euripides; *On the Edge of the World*, based on the play *Wielopole, Weilopole* by Tadeusz Kantor; and *The Time When We Knew Nothing About Each Other*, by Peter Handke.

The situation at the Russian Theater is similar to that at most theaters: the companies do not know how to communicate with the audience. Directors on staff devote themselves to experimental work, while

guest directors stage popular plays which interest audiences. A growing number of artists prefer to create elitist theater which is often self-
indulgent and does not satisfy the needs of the public.

Puppet Theaters have been operating in Vilnius and Kaunas
since 1958. They are far more stable institutions than theaters which were
established in independent Lithuania at the time of the economic crisis.
Parents want their children to go to the theater. Private sponsors are willing to help. The Funny People Theater, one of the first non-government
theaters, is popular nation-wide. The young actors trust the imagination
of a young audience. They perform improvised versions of popular
stories which are relevant to the lives of contemporary children. The
Funny People Theater also stages cabarets for adults. Julius Dautartas
founded the Art Theater in Panevezys where he produces plays based on
international children's classics. The state theaters also stage special performances for children.

The State Youth Theater opened in Vilnius in 1965. It became the
leading theater in the country in 1980. In 1975, Dalia Tamuleviciute,
a well known teacher and long-time director of the theater, invited ten of
her students to join the company there. Among them was Eimuntas
Nekrosius, who, at her suggestion, had also studied at the Institute of
Theater Arts in Moscow. His productions of *The Square* (1980), *Pirosmani,
Pirosmani* (1981), *A Day Over a Hundred Years* (1983), and *Uncle Vanya*
(1986), made him famous throughout Lithuania and abroad. Arthur
Miller, on a trip to Lithuania in 1985, saw Nekrosius's work and said,
"Nekrosius must be a genius."

The life of the State Youth Theater was disrupted by the political changes in 1989. Well-known actors felt depressed by a perceived
betrayal by their audience. In this oppressive mood, not a single new
production was mounted for 15 months. Ruta Wiman, a well-known
theater critic, became director of the theater and Bernard Sahlins, an
organizer of the International Theater Festival of Chicago, became a
consultant to the company. He proposed the idea of a moratorium.
On November 21, 1990, the Youth Theater closed for 100 days in order to
conduct an experiment. Sahlins and Wiman selected six new plays
and six directors. They drew up a rehearsal schedule and obtained additional funding from the Ministry of Culture. At the end of the hundred
day period, five new plays had been produced. The most important
was Nekrosius's *The Nose*, based on Gogol's short story – his first
production in five years. Sahlins was shocked by the state of theater
management in Lithuania. He could not understand what people were
doing or what their responsibilities were. He could not understand
why Lithuanian actors were incapable of satisfying the needs of their
public. He also spoke about the theater's arrogance. He noticed that
actors were afraid of the audience. Gradually, the company at the famous

theater became apathetic, and the combined American/Lithuanian forces could not overcome this despondency. Wiman, Nekrosius and others eventually left the theater and today it exists on the periphery of the theater scene.

Empty houses and a difficult economic situation demand new reforms. Everyone talked about it but no one had the courage to leave the security of the state theaters. Even young directors and actors look for openings with existing companies, refusing to create their own independent theatrical territory. They prefer to work on the small stages of established theaters. Most actors agree with Tumin's belief that theater should be like a home with enough room for everyone. Are Lithuanian actors a patriarchal community? They want a theater/home ruled by a caring, artistic director/father.

A Well-Known Actor is Shining Shoes at the Door of the Theater

Jonas Vaitkus attempted to reform the Lithuanian State Academic Drama Theater by firing several actors, including famous older actors. In protest, the dismissed actors organized a farewell party to which an audience was invited. A popular actor disguised himself as a shoe-shiner and met the audience at the door of the theater. The theater community split into two groups: those who supported Vaitkus, and those who did not. Convinced that it was new, young people who would be able to re-energize theater, he invited his own students to work with him. The young actors experimented successfully on the small stage. Vaitkus himself, faced with organizational problems, was not very productive artistically. During a three-year period, he produced Mishima's *Madame de Sade* and Bergman's *Persona* on the small stage, but nothing on the main stage. Instead, it was rented out to different organizations for various events that had nothing to do with theater. In 1995, the Ministry of Culture canceled their contract with Vaitkus. Before leaving the theater, however, he staged the most avant-garde production in recent seasons, Strindberg's *Dream Play*, which was warmly received by the young intellectual audience.

A group of actors who had been fired by Vaitkus established the Vaidilos Ainiai Chamber Theater in the center of Vilnius. It is a commercial theater aimed at a wealthy audience. It produces plays such as Molière's *The Miser*, Anouilh's *Ornifle*, Luce's *The Beauty of Amherst*, and C. Manie's *Blez*. The director Adolfas Vecerskis is proud of the theater's independence and the fact that it receives no financial support from the state. Every Lithuanian theater is looking for private sponsors at the moment, but they are not easy to find as tax laws do not favor those who support cultural programs. Vecerskis views theater as a means of interacting with people, but not as a separate kind of art. In 1995, the Vaidilos Ainiai Theater and the Metropolitan Playhouse from New York began the "Theater Without Walls" project through which they intend to stage joint productions.

The Effect of Falling Walls

The lifting of the Iron Curtain disrupted theater life in Lithuania. But breaking through the walls of uncertainty and reticence produced positive changes. For almost 50 years, theaters had been working in total isolation, suffering from a constant blockade of information. In 1984, a Lithuanian troupe was allowed to take part in an international theater festival for the first time: Eimuntas Nekrosius's play *Pirosmani, Pirosmani* was performed by the State Youth Theater at the International Theater Festival in Belgrade (BITEF). This was the first attempt at pulling down "ideological walls." In 1988, after their first tour in the United States, Nekrosius was asked about American audiences and their reaction to this plays. He answered that they understood his ideas because, "all people have their hearts on the left side of their body." This metaphor was very apt. Long years of isolation had made us long for information while at the same time feeling inferior to the rest of the world. The Lithuanian theater was afraid of facing the free, but unknown world and of embracing it.

After the initial passions brought on by freedom had calmed down, contacts with foreign theaters began to stabilize. The changes made us approach reality from new angles. We began to tolerate differences in others and stopped fearing differences in ourselves. We became capable of making comparisons, and are now willing to criticize and be criticized. Some young actors have made interesting observations in this regard. In 1990, a group of students from the Music Academy went to the Julliard School on a three-week-exchange program. On returning, Daiva Burokaite remarked, "American actors are more technical – they do not depend on their inner emotional state. They are very pedantic and do not pay attention to their surroundings. Lithuanians, on the other hand, are used to being content with very little. That is why it is necessary for us to improvise." The American student Robert Sella commented, "In America, a table on the stage is always a table, but on a Lithuanian stage it can become a symbol. I was overcome by a strange feeling in Lithuania – I had to fly instead of standing." Another American, Michael Hyden, said that it would be difficult for Americans to act in Lithuania.

In 1993, at the suggestion of Ruta Wiman, the first international theater festival took place in Lithuania: LIFE. The second LIFE festival was organized in 1995 and its next editions are being organized now. Lithuanians are already fond of LIFE. Thousands of people admire it, speaking about it on television and everywhere else while it is going on. Theaters from Hungary, Japan, The United States, and Russia took part in the first festival. Lithuanians were able to see Bergman's *Madame de Sade* by Mishima (performed by the Swedish Royal Drama Theater) and *The Street of Crocodiles* (based on Bruno Schulz, Théâtre de Complicité). Audiences were astonished by the pyrotechnic effects displayed by the Xarxa Theater from Spain. In 1995, LIFE organizers wanted a great variety of companies to participate in the festival. One could see the adventurous French play *The Mummy's Funeral* by Turbo Cacahuute, as well as the modern *Bonjour, Madame…*, produced by Belgium's Modern Ballet Theater. LIFE is also very interested in Nekrosius's work and has produced some of his productions.

In Search of Theater

The former leaders among Lithuanian directors, Jonas Vaitkus, Eimuntas Nekrosius, and Rimas Tuminas, have maintained their status in the new Lithuanian theater. In the 1994/95 season, their shows became real cultural events and proved the ongoing vitality of the theater arts. Rimas Tuminas directed *Smile Upon Us, Lord* at the Small Theater, based on Grigorijus Kanovicius's novel about Jews in Lithuania. In this show, the nation's fate and character are considered and an attempt is made at understanding universal problems. The Jews travel and look for the Promised Land. Their journey is the starting point of the play. We can regard their journey as our journey into the land of hope. It is similar to our search for a nicer, more truthful world. Tuminas is known for intimate, psychological theater, in which the acting is the most important element and the viewer must pay attention to the actors' every sigh and glance. Audiences like the performance. The Small Theater is always packed. Here, a person is understood: his dramas and tragedies are not ignored.

Vaitkus's production of Strindberg's *Dream Play* at the Lithuanian State Academic Drama Theater is quite different. It is a severe performance. The director demonstrates a striking ability to combine various means of expression, including opera and video. A continual flow of sights and sounds, and their sudden changes create a dream-like impression. The play's atmosphere is further enhanced by a moving crowd of people, roaring, singing, shouting. We can find neither love nor sympathy here. The show is an open conversation about peoples' foolishness, weaknesses, and blindness.

Nekrosius's production of Chekhov's *Three Sisters* (produced by LIFE) is a modern interpretation of a classic play. Nekrosius knows how to stage a well-known play as if it had been written yesterday and is being performed for the first time. He also puts his own artistic insight into the text, filling Chekhov's pauses with theatrical substance. *Three Sisters* is the third play by Chekhov that Nekrosius has directed (following *Ivanov* and *Uncle Vanya*). His devotion to the playwright is not static. One can see the changes in Chekhov's theater. It becomes more dynamic and tragic. In *Three Sisters,* nothing is expected of "those who are going to live in one or two hundred years" (*Uncle Vanya*), because it is *we* who are going to live then. The image of Moscow in *Three Sisters,* which has traditionally been understood to represent the anticipation of a wonderful future, is interpreted here as an irrational and vanishing mirage. The sisters try to keep cigarette smoke under glasses on the palms of their hands. They try to keep it from clearing away, but it is too temporary. All our life is too temporary. One can feel the rapid flow of time and see the future turn into the past. Every instant is both temporary and eternal. Every moment may become our last – like Tuzenbach's last moment, seated at the big table, eating slowly before going to fight his duel and meet his death. Nekrosius says, "Sometimes it seems as if there will be no tomorrow. But life keeps moving forward, even if at varying speeds."

These three directors prefer plays that have no direct link to everyday life, but they approach their material in different ways.

Some members of the new generation of directors should also be mentioned here: Gintaras Varnas, Jokubas Turas, Ignas Jonynas, and Oskaras Korsunovas, all of whom finished their studies in independent Lithuania and now produce plays by Camus, Gogol, Cocteau, and Strindberg. The undisputed leader of this group is Oskaras Korsunovas, a former student of Vaitkus, who became famous for his trilogy, *There To Be Here, The Old Woman,* and *Hello, Sonya New Year,* based on OBER (OBER is a union for the creation of realistic art, centered on the work of Russian avant-garde artists of the thirties: Zablocky, V. Vedensky, and Kharms). Korsunovas has founded his own theater, which has already created its own very popular theatrical language – very precise and ironic. He says, "We simply want to be straightforward. We want to rid ourselves of all unnecessary things: actors' narcissism, meaningless sets that merely take up space, costumes that stifle movement, music that is meant to save bad acting and direction, text that encourages actors not to think but merely to babble, or that serves only to reveal the plot. We try to create intense action that destroys the sense of time passing. We try to show paradoxes, to shock, to amaze, to impress the audience into thinking about that which they are witnessing."

* * *

Theater plays an important role in the development of the state. Lithuania's theatrical experience is very valuable. Historical changes, while causing dissatisfaction among some actors, have created new conditions under which theatrical life has become more intense and more diverse. In 1994 and 1995, 62 new productions were mounted, while during the Soviet era, only half that number were staged each year. Today, both actors and directors are trying to define their new roles in life. This process proves the creative vitality of the Lithuanian theater. Life in the theater goes on.

1995

1. Alternativa 2000 Theater, Albania, *Nightmare Pains* (*Exodus*) by Kudret Velca and Elona Velca, directed by Elona Velca. Photo: Alternativa 2000 Theater.

2. Alternativa 2000 Theater, Albania, *Nightmare Pains* (*Exodus*) by Kudret Velca and Elona Velca, directed by Elona Velca. Photo: Alternativa 2000 Theater.

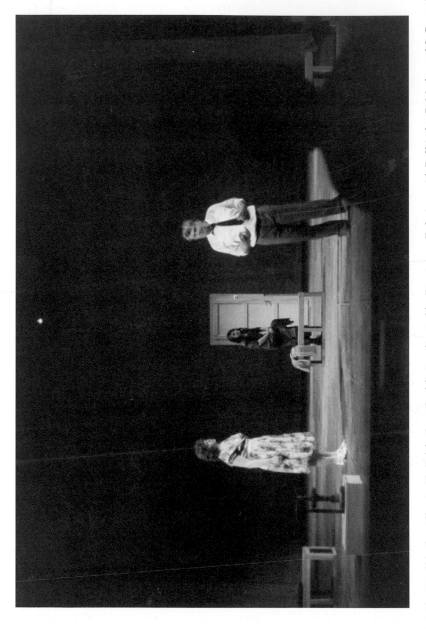

3. Midjeni Theater, Shkoder, Albania, *No Exit* by Jean-Paul Sartre, directed by Dominique Dolmieu, with B. Shiroka, R. Marku and S. Garrusi. Photo: Midjeni Theater.

4. Bulgarian Army Theater, *Waiting for Godot* by Samuel Becket, directed by Leon Daniel, with I. Surchadjiev and I. Hristov. Photo: Bulgarian Army Theater.

5. Theater of Satire, Bulgaria, *Leonce and Lena* by Büchner, directed by Galin Stoev. Photo: Sv. Slavov.

6. The Bulgarian National Theater, Sofia, *Lorenzaccio* by Alfred de Musset, directed by Margarita Mladenova, with M. Kavardjikova and St. Danailov. Photo: The Bulgarian National Theater.

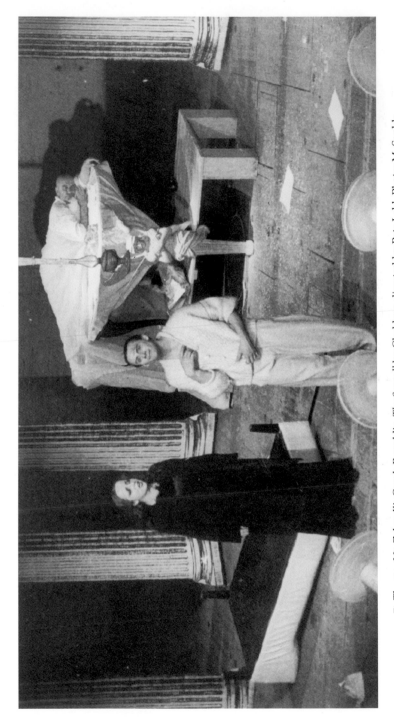

7. Theater Na Zabradli, Czech Republic, *The Seagull* by Chekhov, directed by Petr Lebl. Photo: M. Spelda.

8. Theater Labyrinth, Czech Republic, *Dada Opera* by K. Kriz, V. Gallerova and J. Gerha, directed by Karel Kriz. Photo: Theater Labyrinth.

9. Theater Comedy, Czech Republic, *Hamlet* by Shakespeare, directed by Jan Nebesky. Photo: Theater Comedy.

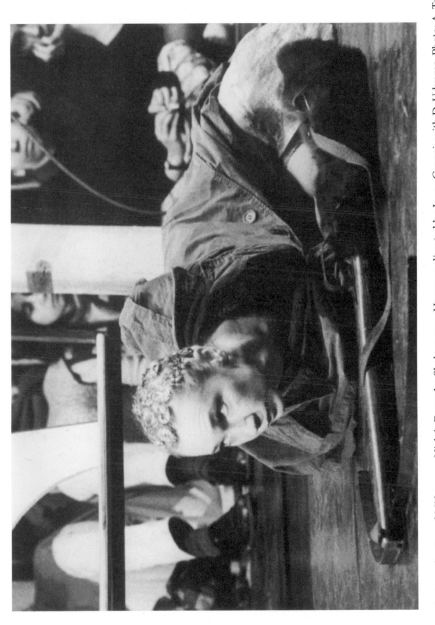

10. Independent production of *Midsummer Night's Dream* by Shakespeare, Hungary, directed by Janos Csanyi, with D. Udvaros. Photo: A. Tamassy.

11. Asroth Utca Theater, Hungary, *Leonce and Lena* by Büchner, directed by Eniko Eszenyi, with V. Papp and A. Kaszas. Photo: I. Bela.

12. Muvesz Theater, Hungary, *Uncle's Dream*, directed by Vassiliev. Photo: K. Peter.

13. The New Riga Theater, Latvia, *The Portrait of Dorian Gray* by Oscar Wilde, directed by Alvis Hermanis. Photo: J. Deinats.

14. The Latvian National Theater, Riga, *The Tailor's Days in Silmaci,* directed by Edmunds Freibergs. Photo: A. Vitins.

15. The Daugavpils Theater, Latvia, *The Sound and the Fury* based on William Faulkner, directed by Peteris Krilovs. Photo: The Daugavpils Theater.

16. Lithuanian International Theater Festival, Vilnius, *Three Sisters* by Chekhov, directed by Eimuntas Nekrosius, with D. Micheleviciute, A. Bendoriute and V. Kuodyte. Photo: A. Zavadskis.

17. Lithuanian State Academic Drama Theater, *The Old Woman* by Danil Kharms, directed by Oskaras Korsunovas. Photo: Lithuanian State Academic Drama Theater.

18. Lithuanian State Academic Drama Theater, *There To Be Here* by Danil Kharms, directed by Oskaras Korsunovas. Photo: Lithuanian State Academic Drama Theater.

19. Eugène Ionesco Theater, Chisinau, Moldova, *The Bald Prima Donna* by E. Ionesco, with N. Kozaru and B. Kremen. Photo: S. Cartashev.

20. Gugutza Puppet Theater, Moldova, *Hirzobul*, directed by Victor Stefanine. Photo: Gugutza Puppet Theater.

21. Karman Theater, Moldova, *One Hundred Years of Solitude*, by G. G. Marquez. Photo: Karman Theater.

22. Grupa Chwilowa Theater Company, Poland, *A Stop in the Desert* with A. Zaitsev. Photo: Grupa Chwilowa Theater Company.

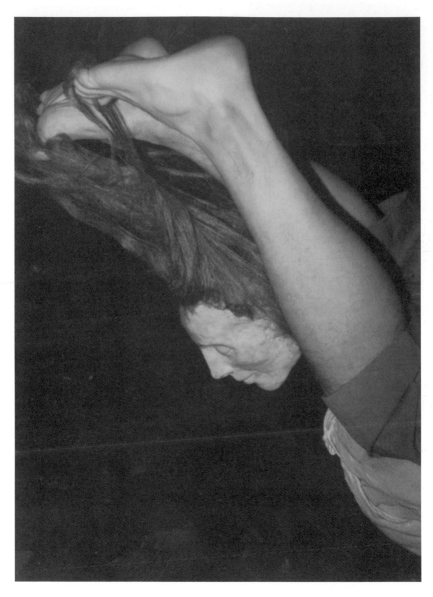

23. Academia Theater Company, Poland, *A Meek Girl*, based on Dostoyevsky. Photo: Academia Theater Company.

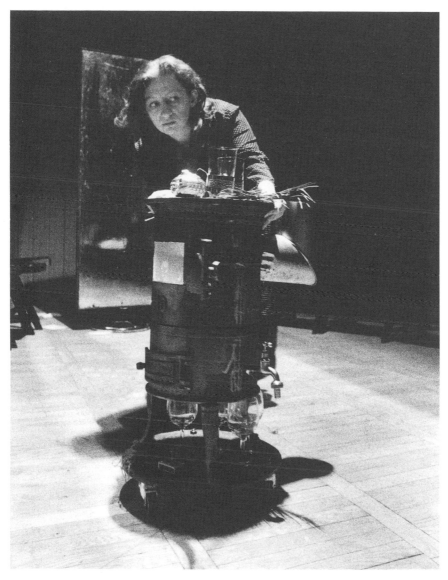

24. Grupa Chwilowa and Z Lublina, Poland, *A Home by the Sea,* with E. Bojanowska. Photo: I. Burdzanowska.

25. The Romanian National Theater, Bucharest, *The Ancient Trilogy* (*Medea, Electra* and *The Trojan Women*), directed by Andrei Sherban. Photo: S. Hudson.

26. Lucia Sturza Bulandra Theater, Romania, *The Winter's Tale* by Shakespeare directed by Alexandru Darie, with D. Astilean and S. Cellea. Photo: S. Lupsea.

27. Puppet Theater of Arad, Romania, *Trufaldino*, directed by Ion Minzatu. Photo: Puppet Theater of Arad.

28. The Young Spectator's Theater, Perm, Russia, *Candide* by Voltaire. Photo: A. Zerin.

29. Saint Petersburg's Puppet Theater, Russia, *Hantor's Secret* by L. Sevbeau, with A. Mitrohin. Photo: P. Markin.

30. The Russian Army Theater, *The Oresteia* by Aeschylus, with E. Mironov. Photo: O. Chumachenko.

31. The Slovak National Theater, Bratislava, *Karate Billy is Coming Home* by Klaus Pohl, directed by Vladimir Strmisko with J. Kroner, E. Horrath and M. Labuda. Photo: M. Olha.

32. The Slovak National Uprising Theater, Martin, *Decease of Palo Rocko*, written and directed by Matus Olha with F. Virostko and J. Olhova. Photo: M. Olha.

33. Stoka Theater, Bratislava, Slovakia, *Komora*, directed by Blaho Uhlar. Photo: Stoka Theater.

34. Suzirya Theater, Kiev, Ukraine, *Radiation of Fatherhood* by Karol Wojtyła (Pope John Paul II), with L. Kadyrova and S. Djugurdya. Photo: O. Lypsky.

35. I. Franko Theater, Kiev, Ukraine, *Tevie-Tevel* by Grigori Gorin, based on Sholom Aleichem, with B. Stupka. Photo: V. Marushchenko.

36. Zankovetska Academy Theater, Lvov, Ukraine, *Marusya Churay* by L. Kostenko. Photo: Zankovetska Academy Theater.

MOLDOVAN THEATER

FOREWORD

Mihai Chimpoi

Usually the theater is compared to a mirror. The analogy comes from Shakespeare, the uncrowned king of the theater, but the roots of this metaphor go further back. Actually, the theater is a system of parallel, dynamic, revolving mirrors in which both a nation's history and identity are reflected. Life is a theater also, and we are all actors on this great stage, and the director is he who created us – the demiurge.

The world as a theater is also a distinct theme of Romanian (and Moldovan) literature, used by writers such as Cantemir, Alexandri, Creanga, Eminescu, Carajiale, and later on by Ioneso, who carried this theme to its ontological extremes. Therefore, the theater remains for us the perpetual paradigm of that *theatrum mundi* which is given to us as a *fatum*, a Sword of Damocles.

Contemporary theater in Moldova has a distinct role in the process of democratization, in the promotion of cultural values, and in the opening up of the nation to the rest of the world.

AT THE CROSSROADS:
MOLDOVAN THEATER IN
THE YEARS OF LIBERALIZATION

Leonid Chemortan

A Glimpse at the Pre-*Perestroika* Years

In order to better understand the evolution of theater life in Moldova after the fall of totalitarianism and in order to clarify from where and to where it is going, one must take a glimpse at our stage during the years prior to *perestroika*.

Naturally, professional theaters operated in Moldova during the period of the Soviet regime. There were five drama theaters and one puppet theater, all of them, of course, state-owned. There were famous actors, directors, designers, critics, and productions which provoked real public interest. Our theaters mounted classic national and international plays, and modern drama was staged widely. Theater workers won government awards, official honorary titles, state prizes, etc. But in taking a more critical look at the situation at that time, one's evaluation of it changes radically. One has only to remember the repression of ideology in all creative work. Restrictions and taboos were imposed not only on ideology, but on purely artistic matters: art forms, scenic decisions, and methods. The canonization of stage principles, usually disguised under the name of Stanislavsky (though they often had nothing in common with his well known system), limited the variety of directorial, design, and acting decisions. The postulates of "socialist realism" stimulated antagonistic, simplified conflicts between characters, actions, and ideas, and the kind of happy ending where "ours" (i.e. the "good" ones) won over the "bad" ones (i.e. "not ours"). A step outside the boundaries prescribed "from above" could cause great troubles.

It is impossible to ignore the unnatural isolation of the Soviet republics' theaters from western culture, which was denounced as bourgeois, harmful, and destructive. As a matter of fact, after Stalin's death, major European theater companies (especially those of a classical and realistic bent) began to visit Moscow and sometimes Leningrad. But as a rule they did not go to the peripheral Soviet republics and the wall separating Moldova from the western world was especially strongly felt. Of course, our cultural connections were encouraged too, but mainly with the rest of the Soviet republics and rarely with countries from the Soviet block. This was realized in the following way: artists and cultural workers regularly went to Moscow on "report performances" and ten day festivals of literature and the arts. As for direct contacts between the Soviet republics or connections with other countries and even socialist ones, the Kremlin viewed such relations warily, as though they would weaken Moscow's power.

Of course, the strength of the ideological regime and the intensity of castigation was dependent mainly on the local authorities, but Moldova was unlucky even in that. Some of the most confining ideological restrictions existed here. Political powers were always on the alert, especially for any contacts between Moldova and Romania, although we have much in common with the Romanians: not only language, history, and folklore, but classical literature, which even the Stalinist regime had to admit. But who and what were classics was very carefully decided. And after Krushchov's short "thaw", Romanian books, newspapers, and magazines were banned from Moldova. Romanian directors, actors, designers, critics, and authors could not be invited to visit. Romanian theater companies could perform in Moscow, Leningrad, Kiev, Siberia, and anywhere else in the Soviet Union, but not in Moldova – never mind that they entered and left the USSR through Moldova … . The ideological censors were very careful to make sure not only that modern Romanian plays were not being produced, but that plays in Romanian translation by Shakespeare, Molière, and Gogol, among others, were removed from theater repertoires.

A characteristic feature of Soviet conservatism and cultural policy was their innate fear of the creative work of the younger generation. This caused a certain generation imbalance in the Moldovan theater, especially in the area of directing. For 20 years (since the late 1960s), the Ministry of Culture, which controls the theaters, accepted no students into directing programs. Moreover, directors who were already working were systematically disgraced and prosecuted so that leading directors such as Ion Ungurianu, Valeriu Cupchia, Ion Sandri Shkuria, and Ilie Todorov were forced to either leave the country or work just as actors. The shortage of directors (at the Luchaferul Theater for example, there were no directors for three years), and the lack of young, modern-thinking directors, designers, and actors caused much damage to the Moldovan theater.

But the Moldovan stage knew better times. During the years of the post-Stalinist "thaw" in Moldova, three new theaters were started: the V. Alexandri Theater in Belts (1957); the Luchaferul Kishinev Youth Theater, formed by the graduates of the Moldovan studio of the B. Shchukin Theater School in Moscow (1960); and the Kishinev Poetry Theater (1975). Different artistic styles and trends made theater life during those years colorful, a fact noticed not only by local critics, but by critics in Moscow, Leningrad, Latvia, Estonia, Georgia, and Ukraine where Moldovan theater companies made guest appearances.

Nevertheless, due to the ideological pressure and unifying canons of socialist realism, the lack of young professionals, and the fact that all theaters spent a significant part of every year providing the peasant public with a special lighter repertoire, the stylistic individuality of the different companies gradually vanished. As a result one general, uniform, so-called "natural" style was established in all Moldovan theaters. This style was characterized by artificial, elevated poetry and was geared toward the mass unpretentious public.

In the late 1970s, it became apparent that these problems were not just related to the inner conflicts and crises within the companies, but stemmed from an overall depression in Moldovan drama, and in the area of directing. This crisis was especially serious and prolonged because it had its roots in the general social crisis of the time and in the whole spiritual culture.

More and more directors and actors began to understand that not only theater but social life in general needed fundamental changes. That is why Gorbachov's *perestroika* received the unanimous support of the intelligentsia. Around 1990, the foundations of totalitarianism were destroyed, the ideological barriers that had paralyzed cultural and artistic development for many long years fell down. Thus it can be said that the renovation of the Moldovan theater began not in 1991 when the Soviet Union collapsed and Moldova announced its independence, but much earlier – in the late 1980s, under *perestroika*. Some of the first to involve themselves with radically changing social life were Moldovan writers, while the theater movement was headed by the Union of Theater Actors (UNITEM). In fact, at that time even the Ministry of Culture was well aware of the urgent need for radical change in the sphere of theater arts.

Healing the Wounds: What Happened After *Perestroika*?

Obviously, the first thing to do was to solve the problem of the lack of young theater professionals. In 1988 and 1989, two groups were sent to the B. Shchukin Theater School in Moscow and to the school of the Moscow Art Theater. Another group of future actors was sent to Georgia. At the same time, the Kishinev Art Institute increased enrollment at the actors' studio of the theater faculty and formed puppetry groups for the first time. In 1991 they began to educate professional drama critics, repertory directors, and managers. Some of the young actors who had revealed directing abilities were sent on two-year training programs with famous theater masters in Moscow, Leningrad, and after the fall of Ceaucescu, in Bucharest. In 1990, a class for theater directors's training was formed at the Theater Faculty of the Moldova Institute of Fine Arts.

But the stormy joy inspired by that creative freedom which unified all the creative powers of the people worked in some negative directions at the same time. Peoples' analytic intellectual activity had become a bit dull. Obviously, it is not accidental that for the last ten years, not one deserving play, novel, poem, film script, etc. has been written in Moldova. It became fashionable to nihilistically reject nearly all the old values. For example, the oldest Moldovan theater, the Academic Theater, was closed. Some suggested that in its place an entirely new company of actors from Romania should be formed because they knew the literature and language better, and for three years, new productions should be staged only by foreign directors. No good resulted from all this, of course. A strong, albeit somewhat conservative company, which had existed for years, was broken up and the M. Eminescu National Theater, newly founded in its place, has not even gotten on its feet yet.

However, this negative side to the general excitement of social and political change, this desire to remake everything could pass in time. At the height of the liberal reforms, the Moldovan intelligentsia hungrily acquainted themselves with western social ideas, philosophy, literature, drama, and painting. Romanian drama and indeed Romanian culture in its entirety was especially popular – art, literature, social trends, and historical studies about Bessarabia – all that was unknown in Moldova for such a long time.

The increased interest in western theater led Moldovan actors, directors, and critics to participate in international festivals and competitions and to perform and tour privately abroad in order to see different productions of classical and modern plays and gain knowledge of spiritual life in other countries. All the new and unfamiliar things were accepted enthusiastically without criticism. Some time had to pass, one had to see many productions by different companies with different styles and ways of performing in order to analyze and compare. Only then could one arrive at the understanding that all that glitters is not gold … .

Gradually, the comprehension set in that there was no need to reject everything at home and that we should give ourselves more credit for our own achievements. The awards received by Moldovan theater companies at international competitions and the positive response of foreign critics helped us to regain self confidence and become aware once again of our own creative powers. It became clear that the Moldovan theater was able to reach western audiences and participate in contemporary European culture.

Discontent arose within the old theater companies. Many actors and directors, especially young ones, changed theaters, turned to TV, or formed new companies. New theaters sprang up one after another. In the late 1980s and early 1990s, eleven new professional theaters appeared, along with numerous amateur groups, experimental studios, and drama circles. And of course, as theater and society as a whole were seeking new ways and principles, each group laid out its own aesthetic program. The theatrical landscape in Moldova became quite diverse, even picturesque. Different schools, trends, and styles now exist side by side: the Kishinev Municipal Theater, the Ion Kryange (a company formed mainly by actors from the former Academic Theater) which primarily produces plays based on folk themes, the Luchaferul Theater in Kishinev, the Vasile Alexandri Theater in Belts, and the B. P. Hashdeu Theater in Kagul all follow the realistic tradition; and the young troupe at the Eugene Ionesco Theater of the Absurd tends toward more modern styles.

Enter New Drama

One of the most characteristic features of the modern theater in Moldova is the wide scope of the repertoire and new methods of choosing plays. This is due mainly to a general desire to stage European (especially Romanian) plays and plays dealing with national history and real life social and political problems. Now the names of Aristophanes, Shakespeare, Molière, Goldoni, Gozzi, and many other playwrights can be read on theater posters. Works by V. Alexandri, I. L. Carajiale, B. P. Hashdeu, and others that are viewed by Romanians and Moldovans alike as national classics are staged with great popularity. So are plays by modern Romanian authors like V. I. Popa, M. Sebastian, and V. Eftimin. And of course, plays by Moldovan dramatists like Ion Drutse, Aureliu Busuiok, and Petru Kerare are not forgotten.

　　　Now, instead of needing to speak allegorically, to use Aesopian language in revealing social problems, it seems that everything can be said quite openly. Nevertheless, the modern Moldovan theater is much given to the use of parable and metaphor. They inspire, excite and deeply touch the imagination with their unique freshness. Imagery and metaphor are even considered to be the most characteristic ways of thinking in this new epoch. As a matter of fact, folk productions representing concrete folk characters have already lost their appeal. Critics explain this not only by changes in cultural acceptance, but mainly by changes in social conditions. At the time when slogans of internationalism disguised a policy of de-nationalization of the different peoples in the Soviet Union, and the term "community of Soviet peoples" meant no more than Russification and the assimilation of all non-Russian peoples into the Soviet empire, national folk traditions held a special place in the hearts of the public. Then, national folk values and spiritual tradition were a kind of defense against and even in opposition to the official policy of assimilation. Today there are no limits placed on the demonstration and acceptance of national cultural values, thus there is no need for that kind of resistance.

During the first years of liberalization, when the general enthusiasm for western and Romanian drama arose, it seemed that Moldovan plays would be staged with difficulty. However, this soon began to change. The spectator became more discerning, voicing a preference for certain dramatists, theaters, styles, etc. Although in general an interest in national historical themes remained, audiences became more critical of the political exaggeration and didactic style from which some historic, heroic plays suffered. Time showed that interest in modern Moldovan playwrights had not merely been preserved, but had grown. This was not a result of local patriotism. Such productions gave the spectator the opportunity to see his own problems, his own difficult confused life, and everything that happened around him. And even if some of the new Moldovan plays cannot be compared to the works of the outstanding European dramatists, they do reveal their authors' openness to the new.

One of the features of modern Moldovan plays that appeals most to audiences is that they are very topical. Another important characteristic is their fragmentedness. It is not accidental that over the last few years almost all the theaters, even puppet theaters, have staged revue productions in which the topical problems are revealed through irony or satire, connected, of course, to politics. The texts for these productions (*We*, at the Luchaferul Theater; *Country, Wait!* and *Where Are We Going, Gentlemen?* at the Satiricus Theater; *Hodoronk-tronk*, at the A. Mateevitch Theater; *Half Past Six*, at the E. Ionesco Theater) read more like scripts, giving the actors a greater opportunity for improvisation. Within the revue format exists another type of production, the pop-show (*Shock, Shop, Show*, at the A. Mateevitch Theater; *Pecale's Adventure*, at the Kagul Theater; *Show*, at the Jinta Latine Theater).

Unfortunately, formerly famous playwrights practically disappeared from view over the last few years, some because they had actively involved themselves in politics and others because they could not respond to the new needs of the times. New playwrights took their places. Valeriu Butnaru is one of the most interesting young playwrights. His play *In Venice, Everything Was Different*, a witty satire that uses elements of absurdity to expose the vices of the communist regime, and his philosophical drama *Joseph and His Concubine* were both staged at the E. Ionesco Theater and won public recognition. Nicolae Eminescu's witty comedy, *The Smoking Room*, and Seraphim Saka and Valeriu Matei's historical drama, *Prologue*, were two popular productions at the M. Eminescu National Theater. Georgie Urski's play concerning different aspects of contemporary Moldovan peasant life, *Let's Live and See*, has enjoyed many performances during the last few years on the stage of the Luchaferul Theater.

In recent years, many classical Moldovan poems and works of prose by V. Alexandri, K. Negrutsi, I. Kryange, M. Eminescu,

B. P. Hashdeu, and I. L. Carajiale have been adapted for the stage as have works of classic world literature by Chekhov, O' Henry, Hans Christian Andersen, the Brothers Grimm, Karel Chapek, and even Choderlos de Laclos (*Dangerous Liaisons*).

Moldovan Theater: A Noah's Ark of Directing Styles

The variety of theater life in Moldova is apparent not only in the repertoire, but in an increase in interpretational styles, acting methods, and the importance of the role of design. The orientation to so-called conceptual productions has been preserved and has become even more pronounced. In this kind of productions directors not only cut out certain lines, but even entire acts and plot lines in order to adapt the text to their own interpretation. A penchant for non-verbal theater has also become more apparent in recent years. This is expressed by abridging the text, giving it a secondary role, or eliminating it altogether. For example, in the Eminescu Theater's production of Peter Shaffer's *Amadeus*, director Sandu Vasilacu preserved only a few lines of text, staging in fact a sort of ballet-pantomime. Supporters of this kind of theater think that taking the accent off of the text and placing it on the visual aspects of the production enriches the drama. But it must be said that this kind of radical editing of the text can lead to serious losses of artistic values and meaning, generalized productions, and/or the loss of many of the play's ideas. Undoubtedly, if the director is very talented and on a very high level of dramatic understanding, productions of great interest and importance are born. But when the director's desire to shape the play through his own eyes becomes merely a fad, and when mediocre directors who are unable to deeply comprehend the text follow this trend, it is a real disaster.

When a play is well known to the audience, especially classical texts which they almost know by heart, the success of the production depends heavily on things such as the novelty of the "reading" – to what extent the different interpretations respond to contemporary feelings and thoughts. When a spectator has to watch artificial and lifeless inventions and boring, exhausting, and emotionless puzzles that do not touch the soul – then it is just bad staging. As Pirandello said, "Art – it is life, not rationality."

There are many theoreticians of modern drama who claim that the European theater has already overthrown the dictatorship of the director. In a recent interview, Giorgio Strehler spoke quite definitely against Artaud's principle of rejecting the role of the text.

The discussion over the dominant role of the director and the theater's attitude toward the script is particularly relevant in the present day development of the Moldovan theater. The problem is that theater life in our country today is like a compressed version of the last 70 or 80 years of West European history. We simply were not familiar with actual European theater history before. Now that it has become accessible in all its richness, each director, designer, and actor has begun to chose what seems to them most interesting and useful. Thus, Moldovan theater is like Noah's Ark, containing side by side various styles, trends and methods. Of course, sometimes something that seems new, fresh, and avant-garde to us is already passe in the west. There has even been a discussion on this theme: Need we repeat every stage passed through by the western theater? Most participants in the debate felt there was nothing wrong in repeating western development, even in a very short time. Repetition would enrich our theater with a deeper understanding of theatrical nature and would expand our repertoire of methods of dramatic expression. This fashion of course will pass, but the influences will stay, and Moldovan theater as a whole will gain from it.

Young, New Theaters Steal the Show

The transformation in Moldovan theater coincided with changes in generations. Only one director is left of the directors who began to work in the 1960s and 1970s, Anatol Punzaro, who works at the V. Alexandri Theater in Belts. Currently active directors and actors began working for the most part in the 1980s and 1990s. Of course, the leading figures in the theater have changed also.

The most popular and critically highly acclaimed theater at home and abroad is the E. Ionesco Theater. Its troupe, led by the young actor/director Petru Vutkereu, is composed mainly of actors who graduated from the B. Shchukin Theater School in Moscow in 1985 and 1992, and graduates of other theater schools in Moscow, Tbilisi, and Kishinev. Leaning toward modern styles of theater, the troupe made its debut with a production of Beckett's *Waiting for Godot*, a mock tragedy, which under the direction of Vutkereu and Mihai Fusu was quite appropriate to our reality. The interesting, new interpretation of the text, the abundance of visual metaphor and witty improvisation, the original combination of the grotesque and an overwhelming sadness, the expressiveness of the scenes and details, all carried the production to great success. At the International theater festival in Tallinn, it won Best Production Award, and in 1992, it won awards for Best Production and Best Actor at the Festival of Experimental Theaters in Cairo. The credo of this theater, named after the creator of the theater of the absurd and which began its life with a Beckett play, was well expressed in productions like Ionesco's *The Bald Prima Donna*, which won a prize at the Carajiale Festival in

Bucharest in 1991, and *Exit The King*, which won prizes at the festivals in Cairo, Brashov, Sibiu, and Kishinev. In 1993, the theater toured France for a month with *Exit The King*, *The Bald Prima Donna*, and *Waiting For Godot*. At the same time, they became the organizers of the International Theater Festival in Kishinev. The first edition of the festival took place in May, 1994, with groups participating from Moscow, Stockholm, Bucharest, Tirana, Kaunas, Kishinev, and Belts (among others). Gradually, the theater is expanding its repertoire and techniques. They perform *The Time of Your Life* by William Saroyan, Chekhov's *The Seagull*, the classic Romanian comedy *Lady in the Country* by V. Alexandri, *Joseph and His Concubine* by the modern Moldovan writer Valeriu Butnaru, and *Half Past Six*, a revue production. This company's charming and playful work already shows great creative power, philosophical depth, and subtle psychological understanding. They have gathered together a bright constellation of actors: Alla Menshikova, Petru Vutkereu, Michaela Strambyanu, Andrei Sokirke, Igor Kistol and others.

One of the most interesting Moldovan theaters is the Pocket Theater, led by the young actor/director Sandu Vasilake. Their ceaseless experimentation has given life to many original productions such as *Dangerous Liaisons*, based on the novel by Choderlos de Laclos and directed by Sandu Vasilake. Vasilake's production of *One Hundred Years of Solitude*, based on the novel by Gabriel García Márquez recreates Márquez's atmosphere of "magic reality", expresses the tense contradictions between mystic feeling and the ironic concept of fate, and reveals in a unique way the existential extremes and the lonliness of love and hate. Critics highly praised Vasilake's production of *Nameless Star*, a musical based on the Romanian playwright Mihail Sebastian's comedy of the same name, with music by the American composer David Bishop. The Pocket Theater has toured successfully in Romania, Ukraine, and Russia.

Outstanding work is staged at the V. Alexandri Theater in Belts. The original company of skilled actors (Mihai Volontir, Emilia Lupan, Calin Maneatsa) was enlarged recently with the addition of talented young actors. The young directors Ion Chibotaru, Dimitriu Grichuk, and Niki Ursu work together there with the experienced director Anatol Panzaru. Ion Puiu's design work is characterized by original poetic and philosophic metaphor. The desire to throw away old rules but to retain realistic traditions led the group to a blend of old and new forms, demonstrated in productions such as *Miss Julie* by Strindberg, directed by Ion Chibutaru and *Lysistrata* by Aristophanes, directed by Ion Sandri Shkuria.

The Kishinev municipal theater, Satiricus, is very popular especially with younger audiences. Founded in 1991, it is led by the director Sandu Grecu. This company's productions combine dramatic improvisation with music, dance, and mime. They prefer comedies with grotesque elements, satire, and irony. They avoid deep philosophical ideas and subtle psychology. They present comedies by Molière, Carajiale, Dürrenmatt, Alexandri, Bulgakov, and contemporary plays. In 1995, the Satiricus successfully toured the United States.

Changes have also affected the puppet theaters. The oldest, the Likuritch, was home to two companies, a Romanian one and a Russian-speaking one. In 1992 two new puppet collectives were formed, the Gugutse Theater in Kishinev, and the Gadilich Theater in Belts. The new companies are comprised mainly of graduates of the puppetry studio of the theater department at the Moldovan Institute of the Arts. These companies stage world and national dramatic works, but each has its own individuality. The Likuritch, led by Titus Bogdan Zhukov, tends to use classical puppets and marionettes, sometimes with live actors who even use pantomime. The Gugutse Theater, led by Victor Stefaniuk, tends to use primarily old traditional folk puppets and shadow puppets. At the Gadilich Theater, productions are staged by different directors and one could say that this company has not yet found its own identity. Moldovan puppeteers have toured Bulgaria, Georgia, Russia, Romania, Ukraine, and France. In November, 1995, on the 50th anniversary of the Likuritch Theater an international gala performance of puppet theaters took place. Groups from Bulgaria, Romania, Germany, Russia, Ukraine, and, of course, Moldova took part.

Definite achievements have already been made in the transformation of the Moldovan theater. Nevertheless, in order to completely overcome the old canons and integrate fully into the rest of European theater much remains to be done. It is easy to see that the young companies arrive at modern forms more easily and are not afraid to experiment and invent new theatrical languages.

Difficult Times for Older Theaters

The situation in which the old theaters find themselves is very complicated. The Luchaferul Theater was famous for its fresh and original ideas in the 1960s and 1970s. For that reason, it fell into disgrace with the Soviet leaders who saw in its productions a supporter of modernism and nationalism. In the late 1970s the Luchaferul was deprived of its directors and fell into a deep crisis. Although the artistic directors have changed many times in recent years, the theater could not find its way out of its stagnation. Now the company is led by the young director Mihai Fusu from the E. Ionesco Theater and maybe he will lead the theater out of its crisis.

The situation of the oldest Moldovan theater, the M. Eminescu Theater, is even more complicated. Reorganization of the company and reconstruction of the building caused the disbanding of the company. A small group from the theater remained together using another space and staging some productions, but nothing of note. In 1994, the renovation of the building was completed and it suddenly became evident that there was no one left to work in this splendid building.

The Ministry of Culture had wanted the Pocket Theater to join the company of the National Theater but that did not in fact happen. The problem of the National Theater has remained unsolved. Most of the famous actors did not return to the company. Many of the productions staged by the remaining group were unsuccessful and closed quickly. Here as at the Luchaferul, the problems can be attributed in large part to the lack of modern-minded directors.

In Summary

In Moldova today, whereas there are enough good actors, skilled professionals, and interesting young artists working, the theater is developing slowly due to the lack of directors. Recently, the condition of theater as a whole has worsened as a result of the general social and economic crisis in Moldova Deprived of financial support not only from the state and municipalities but also from private sponsors, many of whom are on the edge of bankruptcy themselves, many theaters' very existence is threatened.

Another serious problem is the audience. During the first years of liberalization when real life was eventful, passionate, and emotional, people often preferred their own life to the theater. Theaters, concert halls and galleries were practically empty. Now that the social and political situation in the country has stabilized, the public's interest in theater has reemerged. But even if young people, especially students, are ready to accept new forms of theater and new ideas, the public at large prefers productions with a clear plot and clear conflicts, without complicated metaphors – to put it bluntly, comedies and melodramas. Under these conditions, the theater has to resist the temptation to satisfy the masses. It must oppose commercialization. But the fight to keep audiences is a matter of life and death for some theaters.

Critics have also played a role in complicating the situation. Some have taken a one-sided position, insisting on new forms of staging and nihilistically rejecting all the acheivements of the past, or, reversely, accusing Art of snobbism and defending all the old stereotypes.

Contemporary Moldovan theater is passing through a very difficult time of inner transformation. Directors, designers, and actors are all searching for new ways, learning from others, experimenting, trying to overcome stereotypes.

On an Optimistic Note

Actually, large possibilities exist for developing an elite theater and for staging productions oriented to the general public. And, of course, innovation and experimentation do not equal elimination of traditions. On the contrary, they encourage development of traditions – all the valuable experience of the Romanian and Moldovan theater. As Peter Brook says, "the theater lives its own life [...] but it changes in accordance with reality." Theater, he underlines, "has to reflect the moving, contradictory society of our century through its own structure."

1996

POLISH THEATER

FOREWORD

Zofia Kalinska

My few reflections on Polish theater of the last years will be very personal. Being an actress and director, I have no right to speak from the position of a critic. I don't feel an intellectual either.

What is the main aim and function of theater from my point of view? I think, I am also able to be an ordinary spectator and as a spectator I expect, I need, to be deeply moved and touched by the theater. I long for catharsis. Of course, I haven't seen every performance, every theater or every company in Poland. I can try only to remind myself of the strongest moments I've experienced as a spectator in Poland over the few last years being at the same time a spoiled and merciless actor/critic.

So what I remember is: Kantor, Kantor, and once more Kantor, with his Cricot 2. Watching his absolutely cathartic performances was for me like drinking from the source of real art. So simple and powerful, so incredibly human, his theater was able to move audiences all over the world. His charisma was immense. Of course, I had a dual relationship with Cricot 2 – that of an actor and spectator. I cannot compare this experience with anything else.

On the other hand, Lupa's psychodramatic theater was thrilling for me too. I worked with both these titans of Polish theater as an actress. Their incredible power is quite differently manifested in their method of working with actors. Kantor inspired actors with his furious energy – energy sometimes close to the rage, whereas Lupa's charisma consisted of patience and love. Kantor loved his actors too, but his love was also full of jealousy and he used to consider actors his property in some sense.

What is my "Cassandric" vision of the future of Polish theater? I see it in the newborn actors who are always the heart of the theater ... I must say that the Polish theater schools are not so interested in using the methods of such innovative teachers as Grotowski. You probably can't be a prophet in your own country. I am very much interested in teaching also and I used to lead a lot of workshops in Europe and Australia. I found that encouraging actors to be creative and proving that acting is a real creative process, is the way for "new age" for the Polish theater.

We have a lot of new, interesting directors with great visions, but very often they don't know how to work with actors. They should not exclude actors from the creative process during rehearsals. Actors make theater credible and human. The actor is the medium through which the audience achieves catharsis.

CONTEMPORARY POLISH THEATER: A HAMLETESQUE "BODY OF TIME"

Tomasz Kitlinski

Hamlet and the Polish Cause?

It is none other than Hamlet which has marked political changes in Poland. In 1956, the Cracow's production, with its set designed by the avant-guard Tadeusz Kantor, bid farewell to Stalinism. Another staging of *Hamlet* portrayed the Prince of Denmark as a Jew. It was mounted in 1968 by the experimenter Jerzy Grotowski when the rise of anti-Semitism within the Communist Party culminated in purges and expulsions. In 1989, the cult-film director Andrzei Wajda directed his fourth *Hamlet* – a Polish *Hamlet* which could at last dispense with anti-Communist innuendoes as the Iron Curtain had been lifted up.

Wajda's *Hamlet IV* was set backstage of Cracow's Stary Theater. Hardly had the audience been admitted to the privacy of a dressing-room when the reflection of a seated figure dressed in black appeared in the mirror. What the audience saw were sublime features, cropped hair, and ultimately a Mona-Lisa-like smile. Hamlet's first words confirmed perfect androgyny. It was only after time that the actress Teresa Budzisz-Krzyzanowska could be recognized. She made a Prince of Denmark who rehearsed the part no more for History than for a personal story. With script in hand, s/he played Wajda's play within a play discreetly revealing the monologues spoken "trippingly on the tongue". Free "in a nutshell", in front of a mirror, on and off stage, a Polish Hamlet in all higher human singularity.

Painters Make Theater Champions

Wajda filmed Tadeusz Kantor's *The Dead Class* after agonizing hours spent talking Kantor into it. Both artists had something in common: a painter's background which spurred their ambition to mix literature, music, and visual arts into theater. This can be traced back to Wyspianski's vision early in the century of creating a total piece of mixed-media theater, while designing a production of *Hamlet* in Cracow's Royal castle.

Kantor seemed to have been fascinated both with the open theatrical form of Polish Romanticism whose model was Shakespeare and with his and Wyspianski's homeland, Galicia. Part of the

Austro-Hungarian Empire, Galicia contained his tiny town of Wielopole. After years of experimentation, he in a way returned to his home on stage, resurrecting his experience of a mixed milieu in a Proustian way through classroom benches, echoes of a roll-call or near-magic country games, and the sensuality of a tango.

    Today Is My Birthday was Kantor's last production. As ever, his Cricot 2 ensemble achieved a painterly quality of contrasts reminiscent of the film *The Cabinet of Dr. Caligary*. To Kantor's junior colleagues, Jerzy Grzegorzewski, Krystian Lupa, and Leszek Madzik, visuality was as dear as it was to Kantor. They devised silent plays about life and death – ascetic spectacles dealing with archetypal images and themes, which left audiences breathless, especially when they were staged in a salt mine. Madzik only recently approached Sophocles's *Antigone* and *Cassandra* by Christa Wolf. Actress Anna Chodakowska made a considerable contribution to the staging of the latter through her insightful research.

Kantor's Disciples

While the Janisci twins who had epitomized the Master's uncanniness, turned to Beckett, an ensemble led by Andzej Welminski (yet another painter!) staged a witty adaptation of Kafka's *America*. Although Zofia Kalinska acted in it, she simultaneously took a different, single route. Most telling about her background: having graduated from Cracow's Theater School where she made her debut in a Chekhov play with legendary Jerzy Grotowski, Kalinska joined both a repertory company and the Cricot 2 troupe. Under Kantor her parts included the eponymous Water Hero of Witkiewicz/Kantor and the Lunatic Streetwalker in *The Dead Class*. The latter production was her last with Kantor. She went on to found an all-female company and mounted Genet's *The Maids*. She devised *Nominatae Filiae* for the Magdalena Festival in Cardiff and the Odin Theater. The audience was presented with Salome, Medea, Cassandra, Mrs. Havisham, and the Little Mermaid who, in exquisite costumes designed by Zofia de Ines, screamed or whispered their transgressive tales of love. In *The Sale of the Demonic Women*, produced at the Nottingham Meeting Ground and presented at Cracow's Witkiewicz Festival, even more Art Nouveau color, posing, and music were combined with Kalinska's method of putting actresses into trance. Alongside *Plaisirs d'Amour* with which a Polish cast won Fringe First in Edinburgh and with which a British cast toured England, Kalinska directed a Scottish play, *Mooncalf*, based on *The Tempest*. Whereas Kantor revealed what he called the "reality of the lowest rank", his disciple Kalinska celebrated the opposite: our ecstasies of love.

Mainstream Actors with Alternative Techniques and Off-Classics

Tadeusz Lominski, not unlike Laurence Olivier learning from "the angry young men", drew on Grotowski's exercises and sought inspiration from the absurdist poet and playwright Tadeusz Rozewicz. His one-person shows, based on *Krapp's Last Tape* by Beckett and Bernhard's *Theater-Maker*, were unsurpassed in technique and intelligence. He died in 1992 at the dress rehearsal of his title part in *King Lear*.

Wajda's film star Andrzej Seweryn acted in Peter Brook's *Mahabharata* and played the part of Don Juan at the Comédie Française. Time and again, he gave workshops to young actors in which he demonstrated unconventional voice and movement training.

In turn, the members of an off-troupe, Gardzienice, were invited to train the actors of the Royal Shakespeare Company. Gardzienice had developed a unique vocal system during their expeditions to study the oral culture of the borderlands of Poland, Belarus, and Ukraine. Following their show, which was immersed in traditional Russian culture, Gardzienice premiered *Carmina Burana* in 1991. Later, Gardzienice invited *Hamlets* from Europe and Asia to their village near Lublin.

Fringe Hits

Poland produces much experimental theater and this has often been proven at the Edinburgh Festival. One of the most famous experimental theater groups is Akademia Ruchu, which at its creation in the mid 1970s, was all too easily classified as an alternative company, along with a hundred other troupes at the time, including the Theater of the Eighth Day.

Another company which went beyond the alternative was Grupa Chwilowa, which used sets and props ingeniously. Whereas *A Miraculous Story* was based on a romantic short story about a painter who sold his shadow to the devil, their next show presented the biography of a celebrated Russian film actor who played himself. The latest *House by the Sea* used Ritsos's poetry and, like the other two, created a space of its own, mysterious and surprising.

Festivals On and Off

In 1995, one of Edinburgh's Fringe First prizes and the Critics' Award was given to Poznan's Biuro Rodrozy, whose work had also been recognized at a variety of festivals in Poland.

Poland abounds in theater festivals. The international festival, KONTAKT, is held annually at the end of May in Torun. KONTAKT 95 included plays directed by Anatoly Vassiliev and Valery Fokin, productions of Theater '89, Vilnius LIFE and Cracow's Stary Theatre. Another festival, **Malta**, in Poznan, last year welcomed 38 companies.

In 1994, the Ministry of Culture granted equal to $360,000 to theater festivals. There are annual festivals of Street Theater, One-Actor Plays, Gombrowicz's Dramas, Theater Schools, Puppet Theater, and even of Little Garden Theaters. Among the experimental theater festivals are Cracow's **Reminiscencje**, **Encounters** in Lodz, and **Off held** in Bydgoszcz.

Intellectuals and Athletes with a Vision

A frequent participant in the festivals throughout Poland and abroad is the intellectually sophisticated Mandala Theater Company, which as its very name suggests, arose from oriental inspirations via Carl Gustav Jung's theories. Consequently, it devoted its *Threetwoone* to the idea of modernity in the esoteric vein, reconstructing and commenting on the *Large Glass* of Marcel Duchamp. For a change, Mandala's director, Katarzyna Deszcz, staged Chekhov's *Three Sisters* at the Scarlet Theater at the Young Vic.

The background of Theatr Ekspresji's actors is sports. Their productions, which blend dance, pantomime, and living pictures, celebrate the body (often presented in the nude) whereas their subject matter seems archetypal: love, jealousy, freedom. One of the troupe's hits was *The Passion* with the navy's guard cast as extras.

A Newer Wave

A different tone resonates in a young troupe started by a secessionist from Ekspresji: its name Dada von Bzdulow (Dada von Nonsense) explains everything. A kindred grotesque spirit is that of the Wififi Company, which succeeded in doing a send-up of Polish sexual politics. Liverpool's Red Star Brouhaha Festival invited Z Lublina – a company of teenagers who were squatters on a housing estate. Their first show, set in that very estate, developed a humorous story of no exit from a titular *Tower Block*. Applause from young spectators followed a monologue by a knight in paper armour who said after Bulatovic, "Oh! Fatherland, my curse, my apple! Let me, a worm, out, and you grow, develop, be the biggest and the most beautiful of apples." Equally sarcastic was Z Lublina's adaptation of *Round the World in Eighty Days*, a subtle satire on attitudes, mimicking an aggressive capitalism. Meanwhile, *A European Voodoo Doll* dealt with the growth of intolerance and violence. The company's director, Ela Bojanowska, has suggested Flann O'Brien's *Third Policeman* as a point of departure for Z Lublina's next production.

A Variety of Communities

Recent years have witnessed a development of theaters inspired by their immediate geographical or linguistic context. Simultaneously, they arrive at Universalist conclusions. An out-of-the-way village in the north eastern province of Vermia is where a company is based which researches not only local folk traditions but also medieval liturgical drama. Named after their village, Wegality reconstructed the founding piece of modern theater: the Easter Eve visitation of Christ's empty grave, as well as the Christmas celebrations of Ordo Stellae, following a manuscript from the St. Benoit Abbey on the Loire. Their meticulous preparations include coaching in Gregorian chant, philological and musicological seminars, and making copies of period instruments. The company's objective is to produce mystery and miracle plays, at the same time exploring the "local color" of their home town which is situated at the cross-roads of Poland, Lithuania, and Belarus.

Tom Bork, an erstwhile star in Polish TV series who settled down in Edinburgh to get involved in the Festival, was instrumental in starting the English Theater Company in Warsaw. Its objective is to mount plays in English for the growing English-speaking community in this country as well as to open English language drama workshops with Polish children. Alongside this professional company, theatricals abound among English language students who convene every year for a festival of drama in English.

In Lublin, NN Theater runs a cultural program for secondary-school students, by publishing a literary periodical and organizing lecture series, conferences, and exhibitions. The emphasis is laid on the multiculturalism of the city of Lublin which contains Jewish, Ukrainian, and Polish communities. Their most recent project is a presentation and discussion of TV theater plays, which reveal multiple modern identities.

TV Drama – "Poland's National Theater"

With its National Theater burnt down, Poland – according to one critic – has its national stage on the TV screen. This runs parallel to Denis Potter's diagnosis that British "true National Theater" is television drama. As a matter of fact, TV plays directed by Andrzej Wajda in the 1970s became classics of Polish theater. In the 1990s, *Balladyna*, a romantic tragedy directed by Janusz Wisniewski in his mannerist style, was among the best. It is remarkable that the stagings of Heirich von Kleist's dramas proved to become the hits of TV theater: *The Prince of Homburg*, a syncretic version of *Kathchen of Heilbronn* by Jerzy Jarocki, and *Amphitryon* with a strong cast of Jan Frycz, Krystyna Janda, and Krzystof Globiesz.

The Polish Radio boasts a rich tradition of theater. In the 1930s it broadcast in installments a radio novel written by Maria Kuncewicz, the then nominee for the Nobel prize. Outstanding playwrights wrote radio-plays. One of the most controversial modern dramas, *Two Theaters* by Jerzy Szaniawski, originated as a wireless production in 1937. Nowadays, the radio continues to commission original dramas (published in *A Quarterly of Radio Dramaturgy*) as well as to produce literary adaptations and documentaries. Every month about 250 actors play in them.

Cracow, the Capital of Polish Theater

The majority of actors who appear in TV dramas come from Cracow, which is no longer Poland's capital city but remains its most beautiful and most polluted city. The Higher School for Theater is based here. Its entrance exams attract each year hundreds of candidates competing for 20 available places. Its rector is Jerzy Stuhr, who played Hamlet in Wajda's 1981 production at the courtyard of the Royal Castle of Wawel. The unorthodox Father Tischner, philosopher of dialogue, lectures at the academy. Among the classes, there are voice workshops taught by Olga Szwajgier whose bel canto career included playing the role of the Queen of the Night and performing at the hundredth anniversary of Carnegie Hall. However, Szwajgier's main preoccupation is giving theatrical recitals of contemporary music. At the school, she not only teaches singing technique (of an artistic as well as healing function), but also helps the students discover their inner riches and articulate them on stage. Szwajgier awards prizes to students for excellence in their philosophy of life.

Who's New at the Old Theater?

Cracow's Stary Old Theater is one of the 14 companies in the Union of European Theaters alongside the RSC, Odeon, Piccolo, and St. Petersburg's Maly Theater. The Stary began to flourish in the early 60s when Andrzej Wajda and Konrad Swinarski were exploiting the open form of the Polish romantic drama. Nowadays, Krystian Lupa presents his productions at the Stary. Using Austrian plays as a starting point, which formerly had been thought unadaptable, his marathon-length productions analyze contemporary psychological issues, staged in atmospheric settings and the costumes of the decadent Danube Monarchy. Music, either by Mahler or Jacek Ostaszewski, also contributes effectively to the mood. Lupa himself operates the light and sound equipment at his shows so as to encourage his actors to improvise. His favorite actors were joined in a recent production by a Stary star, Anna Polony. Other directors associated at present with the Stary are Jerzy Jarocki, Rudolf Zio, Marek Fedor, and its current manager, Tadeusz Bradecki.

Playwrights Wanted

Although Cracow has been chosen as an European city of culture for the year 2000, it already welcomes international projects. In April, 1994, young Polish playwrights took part in a *Waiting For the Theater* conference sponsored by the Mandala Theater, the Slowackiego Theater, the magazine *Dialog*, and Stage International, who brought together Tom McGrath, Winsome Pinnock, Steve Gooch, and Clare McIntyre to lead playwriting workshops. Ever since, a center for fostering new dramaturgy has been active in Cracow.

Some early work by established playwrights has stood the test of time, proven by Kazimierz Rutz's TV productions of works by Slawomir Mrozek, Janusz Glowacki, and Tadeusz Rozewicz. Rozewicz, the outstanding author of *Post-Auschwitz Impossible Poetry*, wrote a new version of his drama *The Card Index*. Mrozek, a native of Cracow, presented in as grotesque a vein as ever *Eastern Europe under the Tsar, Stalin, and Post-Communism*. Mrozek's play *Love In the Crimea* was staged at the Russian Moscow Art Theater as well as at a number of Polish theaters. A different although equally witty examination of contemporary Europeans and their language is made by Boguslaw Scheffer, a Cracow composer. Professor at the Salzburg Mozarteum, he turned to writing drama. His plays constitute precise scores which give actors multiple parts.

Foreign plays rapidly reach Poland: only a couple of months after its first-night at the Lyttleton, Tom Stoppard's *Arcadia* was mounted in Gdynia and shot for TV. The same company staged *Angels In America* by Tony Kushner and the text was published in the monthly *Dialog*.

Small Companies Stage Big Spectacles

Tadeusz Slobodzianek is another young playwright. Together with Piotr Tomaszuk he founded the Wierszalin Association Theater, inspired by the mystical Russian Orthodox sects in eastern Poland. The company's impassioned style is best represented by Joanna Kasperek – an actress trained in puppet theater. The actors of Poland's first private company 3/4 – Zusno are also with a puppet theater background. Their show consists of what the actors do with their hands, feet, arms and calves in order to represent the life of a postmodern "everyman", an eponymous Gianni, Jan, John, Johann, Juan, Ivan, Jean.

Jolanta Lothe, who belonged to the avant-guarde company Szajna and then played at the National Theater, formed a "chamber" company with writer Piotr Lachmann. What it presents are live and video images of the actress combined with text in different languages. The eminent singers, Jadwiga Rappe and Artur Stefanowicz were invited to participate in these multi-media spectacles.

Since the turn of the century, a resort town in the Tatra mountains, Zakopane, has attracted bohemians. One of them was Witkiewicz, whose "metaphysical cabaret" is revived by a Zakopane company led by Andrzej Dziuk.

The Jewish Theater presents plays in Yiddish and runs its own Actors' Studio. Its tradition goes back to the Purim plays and to nineteenth century troupes. In the 1930s, Warsaw had six Jewish companies.

The Languages of Warsaw

Warsaw attracts many foreign companies. Following the 1956 Thaw, it hosted Peter Brook's *Titus Andronicus* with Laurence Olivier and Vivien Leigh. In 1996 a return visit by Forced Entertainment is expected. There are plans for foreign and Polish guest directors to stage Shakespeare at the Royal National Theater.

Hamletesque Catharsis in Jail

Hamlet has not left the Polish stage after the lifting of the Iron Curtain and Jan Kott's formula, "Shakespeare – Our Contemporary" is fresh in the Polish peculiar and diverse theater. The Theatrum Gedanense, where English players put on Shakespeare's dramas during his lifetime, is being reconstructed under the auspices of Prince Charles, Sir Peter Hall, and Andrzej Wajda. A supporter of the project, Günther Grass, native of multicultural Gdansk, diagnoses contemporary reality as not lacking Elizabethan tragedies. Sharing that view, but hopeful for an equally Shakespearian reconciliation, skinheads and punks played the two families of *Romeo and Juliet* at the Cracow's Ludowy Theater.

Poland had 18 translations of *Hamlet*. Another was added in 1994. In the Opole prison, *Hamlet* was mounted by convicts who commented that they felt liberated at the very moment of performing. The drama proved then far from a "bodiless creation" as the new Polish Hamlets, although "bounded in a nutshell" were free as a "king of infinite space".

1996

ROMANIAN THEATER

FIRST FOREWORD

Andrei Serban

My interest in returning to Romania after 20 years was to try to find a thread, a connection, that had been interrupted by my exile.

Theater is the place where one needs others, because one cannot do theater alone. That's why I thought the happy occasion after the events of 1989 would give me the chance to share a new experience with old friends. I imagined, I desired to experience this new moment in history together, like Christopher Columbus animated by the passion to explore new territories. The big mirror that is our theater would no longer be condemned to reflect reality indirectly only through metaphors, but freed from censorship and cleansed of the old and no longer needed metaphors, the mirror could reveal the truth of our present human experience.

When I took over the direction of the National Theater in the summer of 1990, everything seemed to meet my expectations: there I was, home again, searching for a vision, no longer in solitude. For a while, everything developed in the right direction: explosive projects, enthusiasm, the wonderful realization that theater can make history – shaking the bones of the political marionette-machine. What seemed new was that Art was feeding history, rather than the other way around.

This new affirmation of the spirit was in total contrast to the old, heavy crystallization of the forces that had opposed evolution for 50 years. For me, the permanent question, "What is the Romanian heritage?", could be addressed in a new light. As everywhere in Eastern Europe, there is a danger of a raising of nationalism – a slogan in the name of which one is allowed to kill. The opposite would be to find what is both ancestral and universal to our situation. Being born between two worlds – the Orient and the Occident, between Christianity and paganism, one could find the link between an old and a new cultural and mental landscape. That was my dream: an interpenetration of influences operating at different levels.

But after three years, what had started with passion and hope changed direction and turned into the opposite. After hope – crisis, the return to the same level of reality as in the past; history repeating itself: the old nomenclatura faces wearing western suits and smiles, censorship returning in subtle ways and with it – chaos and fear.

I had to leave for a second exile in order to escape being suffocated by the same sleepy bureaucratic elephant. The shock needed to wake the beast up had not gathered enough momentum. For sure it was too early.

Still, the question remains: what is to be presented on stage? Which reality? All over Eastern Europe should one show the ghosts of the unfinished buildings, the absent and down-cast eyes of the passers-by, the lack of spirituality, or the fake esotericism? The reality of the black market, the dirt, the Coca-Cola, the absurdity of a world that has lost contact with the higher, or exactly the opposite – the real hunger and thirst for something else?

The possibility to try to illuminate a particular aspect of the immense territory that opens now in this period of transition is extra-ordinary. In a country like Romania now, the theater could be the most effective instrument with which to reveal the levels, both known and unknown, of what life is like. Artistically, it could be a very creative moment. But curiously, for the time being, the infernal circle of the history-machine repeats itself.

SECOND FOREWORD

Nicolae Manolescu*

In the foreword to the first anthology of folklore published in Romania almost a century and a half ago, a great romantic poet said that Romanians were born poets. However, in my opinion, Romanians have also an indisputable vocation to the theater. I shall not say that they are all born actors or directors, but I do not consider it incidental that the theater in Romania has always been the most sensitive gauge of the national frame of mind. At the beginning of the last century, before the birth of modern poetry or prose, attempts were made with the support of the ruler's daughter to create a theater and memorable performances. In our century, the first signal of the intellectual thaw of the 1960s was seen in the theater – not so much in the content of the plays, but in the performances. The small cultural revolution, which was inspired by Ceausescu's trip to China in 1971, began in the theater. After 1989, when poets and novelists preferred politics to art, it was again the theater which awoke first from its dogmatic sleep. And, once again, the regression resulting from the present political regime is producing negative effects in the theater.

There is a verse dedicated to the Romanian theater at the dawn of its apparition. As the verses cannot be translated, I shall quote them in prose: "take care of the theater, as it will make you known all over the world."

---

* Translated by Horia Florian Popescu.

ONCE UPON A TIME IN ROMANIA ... FIVE YEARS OF POST-COMMUNIST ROMANIAN THEATER

*Marina Constantinescu**

Before the Revolution

During the communist period (1948–1989), the Romanian theater stayed alive through outstanding performances which sustained the tradition of the genre and simultaneously permitted the renewal of artistic expression. This might seem quite natural to an audience outside the communist stage, but for those within it who created theater, it was not so natural. During this period, the theater struggled continuously to maintain professionalism and to fight censorship and the ideological pressure of the authorities. Throughout the most difficult years (after 1948), the flame of legitimate theater continued to burn thanks to an extraordinary generation of actors who had been educated and trained before the war. Playwrights paid the heaviest dues because socialist realism did not allow them any opportunities, and directors, who were actually the creators of the productions, were stifled by dogmatism and routine. Only after the first signs of the Krushchev's ideological thaw, the directors came into the spotlight. It seemed to them that the curtain had been raised (though not yet the Iron Curtain!): they now had the possibility to show off those expressive forms and modes that they had been thinking about for a long time, but that they had been obliged to suppress. In the 1960s and 1970s, there was a theatrical movement in Romania led and supported by great directors who succeeded in creating a new artistic mentality: David Esrig, Radu Penciulescu, Liviu Ciulei, Lucian Pintilie, Lucian Giurchescu, and Aureliu Manea among others. The plays that they staged – *Troilus and Cressida* and *Le Neveu de Rameau*, directed by David Esrig; *King Lear*, directed by Radu Penciulescu, and *The Government Inspector*, directed by Lucian Pintilie – were major events, claimed as such not only by specialists and the public, but by the authorities as well. Nevertheless, soon the same authorities would ban them. Many of these directors exiled themselves. Some younger but no less gifted directors and designers followed their example: Andrei Serban, Miruna and Radu Boruzescu, Iulian Visa. All of them, without exception, proved

* Translated by Horia Florian Popescu.

their abilities and today are appreciated as leaders of world theater and creators of theater schools. The theater never died out in Romania. After the creative boom of the 1960s and 1970s, the communist regime resumed its instinctive hostility toward the arts. People working in theater searched for ways of survival through performances (some very important) that could elude the vigilance of the censors.

Then it was December, 1989. The Communist regime collapsed.

The Three Phases

In my opinion, from 1989 to date, the Romanian theater has passed through three phases. I see this passage linked closely (almost as a baby is linked to its mother by its umbilical cord) to the moral and spiritual liberty which we seemed irrevocably to have retrieved. The first phase can be considered *euphoric*, or *revolutionary*. Real performances took place in the street. A living theater, an enormous Happening, History was played out by common people who, in the course of events, became great actors. There followed the second phase, which I call that of *professional euphoria*. Liberty, in which we then believed and which seemed to us naturally and forever ours, made possible a genuine theatrical phenomenon. Andrei Plesu, the first Minister of Culture and a remarkable personality, appointed qualified individuals as managing directors of the theaters. The Romanian theatrical movement expanded to new horizons and developed a new form that was both representative and competitive. We witnessed the return of famous directors who had left the country for one reason or another. Productions were developed at solid institutions. These productions quickly traveled around the world, renewing traditions through their prestigious participation in tours and festivals, and reviving international interest in the new Romanian theater. New contacts, correspondence, exchanges, workshops, programs, and projects were established and consolidated. This professional euphoria also made possible the foundation of UNITER (the Theatrical Union of Romania) and a new national theater festival. We believed that the most enduring investment was culture.

Liberty, however, remained an ideal for which, little by little, we began pining. The moment of creative euphoria, when an artist focuses on his vocation and his gift, has been spoiled by the appearance of pressures and restrictions of another type of censorship. This represents the third phase, through which we are now passing, not of theatrical crisis, but of *moral crisis*. We are in a slump of bitterness, confusion, lack of values, and ambiguity. And again, quality is stifled and cannot manifest itself in a normal and harmonious way. Now, quality is compelled to twinkle here and there in quick gleams where ever the circle has not yet been completed. The theater can shape only an independent spirit because the theater itself is the product of such a spirit. The theater cannot be understood by those who out of impotence, ignorance, or self-importance consider it to be something intangible and consequently without any practical function. Once again, artists in Romania have become mere servants of the officials of power. But I have "theatrical" reasons to consider it a simple moment, a phase. Things are in quest of new forms, a new order, a resettlement, and we are sure we shall not fail to winnow the chaff from the wheat. This crisis is perhaps necessary in order to challenge us and charge us with new energy.

The Phase of Professional Euphoria

Almost four of the five years since the revolution coincide with an exceptional renewal of the Romanian theater, characterized by the institutional resurgence and the outburst of quality that I referred to above. It is difficult to offer a comprehensive picture of the situation and it would exceed the present purpose of this treatise. However, I will present, with inevitable approximation, the main data, i.e. the most significant in terms of the outcome of the Romanian theater phenomena between 1990 and 1994.

Early in 1990, Andrei Plesu was appointed Minister of Culture. One of the most important aims of his program for theatrical matters was to call back the great Romanian stage personalities to the country. At the same time, the new Minister tried to rethink the theatrical institutions. Taking into account criteria of talent and ability, he appointed remarkable men of theater as managing directors of the theaters. Andrei Plesu's invitation was accepted unhesitatingly by Andrei Serban, who became the director of the National Theater in Bucharest; by Lucian Giurchescu, appointed director of the Theater of Comedy in Bucharest; by Vlad Mugur, director of the Odeon Theater in Bucharest: by Iulian Visa, director of the Theater of Sibiu; and by Liviu Ciulei, honorary director of the Lucia Sturza Bulandra Theater in Bucharest. The directors Alexander Hausvater and Petre Bokor came back to work as well. Among the young directors who were offered leading positions in the theater were Alexandru Dabija, who followed Vlad Mugur at the Odeon, and Victor Ioan Frunza, who was appointed director of the National Theater in Cluj. The destiny of the Romanian theater has never been led by such an outstanding team. I should also mention the actor/director Ion Caramitru, managing director of the Bulandra Theater; the director Nicolae Scarlat, director of the Piatra Neamt Youth Theater (one of the cradles of Romanian theater); the director Adrian Lupu of the Drama Theatre in Galati; the actor Emil Borogina of the National Theater in Craiova; and Tompa Gabor of the Magyar Theater in Cluj. This was the moment of the rebirth of Romanian theater, of its opening up to another type of repertoire, artistic mentality, and audience. It was a period of thaw, from which a genuine *théâtre sans frontières* would emerge. It was the first spiritual release from censorship, cliche, and that Aesopian language which had been almost the sole means of artistic resistance during the communist era. Classical and modern plays were reinstated into the repertoire. Directors were no longer hampered by artificial ideology.

For the artists returning from American or European exile who had been trained under the conditions of the Romanian theater before 1989, experiences varied enormously. It was almost hallucinatory to see these experiences translated into productions which differed so much, belonging to different dramatic schools and traditions. Early on, *The Ancient Trilogy* was staged by Andrei Serban at the National Theater in Bucharest. The production consisted of three extremely difficult texts selected from the Greek classics, massive parts of which were in ancient Greek and took the form of incantations. I should also mention the way in which the director selected the actors and how he worked with them in preparing the performance. Competition for employment in a theater or for a specific role had long been abandoned in Romania. In this case, the whole troupe was selected individually. Then, all the actors followed special physical and mental training: calisthenics, concentration drills, and rhythm and diction exersises. But what a difference between *The Ancient Trilogy* and *Ubu Rex with Scenes from Macbeth!* The latter was a combination of texts by Shakespeare and Jarry, staged by Silviu Purcarete at the National Theater in Craiova. By means of another method and a different style, Purcarete gave a new start to the theater in a provincial town and raised it to an exceptional level. The National Theater in Craiova won almost all the top prizes at national festivals over the following two years. The productions staged there by Silviu Purcarete traveled around the world. *Ubu* is a parable about power and dictatorship, and, at the same time, a parodic and grotesque portrayal of the Ceausescus. Against sketchy scenery suggesting isolation, we witness the development of a tragi-comedy about a sick political regime led by lunatics. The text had been chosen to emphasize the crimes and absurdity of a totalitarian system, a frightening game with peoples' lives and souls.

The appearance of such productions implied also an institutional and managerial effort, technical accomplishment, and very high costs. It would have been necessary to radically change the entire body of the theater in order to continue that kind of revival. In Romania, the theater generally has been granted financial aid by the State. Subsidies for the National Theaters (in Bucharest, Timisoara, Cluj, Iasi, Craiova, and Targu Mures) are granted by the Ministry of Culture, and those for the local theaters (which are quite numerous: seven in Bucharest and over 60 throughout the rest of the country including puppet theaters), by the municipalities.

Private theatrical companies disappeared in Romania before the war. After 1989, attempts in this area were rather hesitant, due mainly to the absence of a sponsorship law. Also, spaces were not available and actors were not willing to risk their zealless but lifelong contractual agreements with the State theaters for productions and roles which had not been legislated. Under such circumstances, private companies are still few, and they are compelled to resort to some State subsidization. Except for Masca (the Theater of Movement and Pantomime, managed by the actor Mihai Malaimare), no private company has its own troupe. Both the Levant Theatre, run by the actress Valeria Seciu (who is herself employed by the State-run Teatrul Mic in Bucharest), and the Excelsior Children's Theatre in Bucharest, managed by the actor Ion Lucian, depend on directors and actors from the State theaters. Masca and the Levant do not possess their own auditoriums and perform their productions in unconventional spaces: parks, streets, show rooms, museums, etc.

In February 1990, Ion Caramitru initiated the founding of the Theatrical Union of Romania, UNITER, the only professional organization for people working in theater (actors, directors, designers, and critics). UNITER is an autonomous, non-subsidized organization whose purpose is to stimulate creativity in the Romanian theater, and promote theatrical exchanges between Romania and other countries. Its activity is based on projects and programs in which both Romanian and foreign specialists participate. The Romanian Center of the International Theater Institute (ITI), the Romanian Section of the International Association of Theater Critics (IACT), and the Romanian Center of the International Organization of Scenographers, Technicians and Theater Architects (OISTAT), all function within the framework of UNITER. Since January 1993, UNITER has organized an annual presentation of theater prizes, awarded by nomination, that has become one of the most important in the country. As of 1990, they have sponsored an annual contest for the best Romanian play of the year. UNITER also initiated the founding of the French-Romanian Theater, the Romanian-Irish Theater, and the Inopportune Theater.

The national theater movement has met with growing interest. This interest is expressed in the increasing number of national and international festivals. In recent years, old festival traditions have been revived and new festivals have been created. The most important is the I. L. Carajiale National Theater Festival, organized for the first time in 1991 by the Ministry of Culture, UNITER, and the Municipality of Bucharest. The festival selects and awards prizes to the season's most remarkable productions from all over the country, as well as to the best actors, directors, and designers. The week-long festival is held in Bucharest.

In 1990, Lucy Neal, the director of the London International Festival of the Theater (LIFT), arrived in Bucharest intending to select a Romanian production to participate in the famous London festival. She selected Shakespeare's *A Midsummer Night's Dream*, staged by Alexandru Darie from the Theatre of Comedy in Bucharest. The play was met with great success at LIFT – the director and actors were literally assailed by the journalists. Soon after, Declan Donnellan invited Silviu Purcarete's *Ubu Roi* to participate in the Edinburgh Festival. This marked the beginning of a long period of foreign exposure for the Romanian theater – performances abroad, tours, participation in major international festivals, invitations to directors to stage abroad or organize workshops, exchanges of professional experience, and joint programs. As it is impossible to list all, I shall mention only the most noteworthy of these events.

The Odeon Theatre from Bucharest made an important tour through Great Britain, performing Mihai Maniutiu's production of *Richard III* in Brighton, Leicester and at the City of Drama Festival in Manchester. The production received nominations there for Best Foreign Production, and Marcel Iures in the role of Richard was nominated for Best Actor. Commentary in the British press was telling: "Happy is Manchester where this astounding production from Bucharest's Odeon Theatre is performed," *The Times* wrote. One could read in *The Guardian*, "A charismatic, admirable, inconceivable *Richard*."

The Bulandra Theater in Bucharest became the first Romanian theater to be included into the Union of European Theaters, alongside the Royal Shakespeare Company, Maly Theatre of Saint Petersburg, Piccolo Teatro di Milano, the Odeon in Paris, and the Katona Jozsef in Budapest.

In 1991, Andrei Serban and UNITER, with the assistance of the French Association of Artistic Action (AFAA), invited Peter Brook to Romania. On this occasion, the great director presented *Woza Albert* and the short film version of *The Mahabharata*. He had several important meetings with those dedicated to the theater in Romania. It was an extraordinary event for the new Romanian theater, but only the quality of this new theater of Andrei Serban and his colleagues could explain why one of the most overwhelming personalities of the theatrical world came to Bucharest. Peter Brook was concerned with what had happened to the theater of the former communist countries. He had already conceived of a workshop project in Vienna within the framework of the Wienerfestwochen for which he had selected 20 to 30 young directors from Poland, the Czech Republic, Slovakia, and Russia. From Romania, he invited Felix Alexa, a recent graduate of the stage management department at the Academy of Theater and Film. The Viennese workshop was only the first stage of the project. After eight days of strenuous work, Brook chose Alexa and one other person out of 30 or so candidates to assist him on *Impressions de Pelléas*, an adaptation of the opera *Pelléas et Mélisande* by Debussy, which was performed at the Parisian Bouffes du Nord theater.

Other important visitors to Romania have been Garry Hynes (managing director of the National Theater in Belfast), Christopher Barron (the managing director of the Edinburgh Festival), British playwright David Edgar, Neill Wallace (the managing director of Glasgow's Tramway Theatre), and Richard Pulford (managing director of London's Royal Festival Hall).

Many renowned theatrical companies from all over the world came to Romania. In 1991, The Royal National Theater toured Romania, and on this occasion Richard Eyre (the then managing director of the theater) and the actors Ian McKellen and Brian Cox, among others, met with their Romanian colleagues and had an interesting professional dialogue. In 1994, at the invitation of the British Council, the famous British troupe Théâtre de Complicité performed Bruno Schulz's *The Street of Crocodiles* in Bucharest, directed by Simon McBurney. After a first tour with *The Tempest* and *Philoctetes* in 1989, Cheek By Jowl returned to Romania in November, 1994 with *As You Like it* (directed by Declan Donnellan), giving several performances at the Shakespeare Festival in Craiova and at the National Theater in Bucharest. The presence of this truly exceptional London company was a real theatrical event, one which was duly and widely noted by the Romanian press. Among other foreign guests, the young French director Jean Deaussoy produced Antonio Onetti's *La Punala*, and Dominic Dromgoole (the director of the Bush Theatre in London) staged *The Demonstration* by Marcel Tohatan, a young Romanian playwright, at the Odeon Theater in Bucharest.

Romanian directors were also invited to stage plays abroad and to take part in workshops. Many directors worked and are still working overseas: Ion Caramitru, who staged *Carmen* and *Eugene Onegin* at the Belfast Opera House in 1993 and 1994 respectively; Alexandru Darie; Tompa Gabor, who staged *Waiting for Godot* in Freiburg, as well as many productions in the United States and Australia; Alexa Visarion; Mihai Maniutiu, who directed *The Taming of the Shrew* in London; Alexander Dabija, who has held workshops in Great Britain; and Silviu Purcarete. Andrei Serban, Liviu Ciulei, Vlad Mugur, Alexandru Hausvater, Petre Bokor, and Petrica Ionescu have all long been recognized internationally and have well established reputations abroad.

Eleven Plays that Revived the Romanian Theater

The professional euphoria felt after the political changes could not have been better embodied than in the stage productions themselves. I have chosen to discuss eleven key plays from the innumerable productions of that period which are most responsible for the creation of a new Romanian theater. Of course, any selection is fatally subjective, but, as it would be impossible to provide an exhaustive description, this may be considered a calling card which might attract the attention and curiosity of theater lovers all over the world.

The most memorable theatrical event of this period was Andrei Serban's *The Ancient Trilogy*, produced at the National Theater in Bucharest. This was the miraculous "switch" that sent the Romanian theater off on a new path. Serban had tested this kind of spectacle before his return to Romania with a production of *The Trojan Women* in the United States that met with enormous world-wide public and critical acclaim. *The Ancient Trilogy* is comprised of three texts: *Medea, Electra*, and *The Trojan Women*. While each text stands on its own, taken together the three of them form a whole, one enormous performance as visualized by the director, a show performed in three different auditoriums that nevertheless maintains a mysterious unity based on the tragic stories of these women. The public can watch these plays separately on different days, or all on the same day, one after another. As in other productions of his, such as *The Cherry Orchard* (his last production in Romania at the National Theater in Bucharest), Serban created two complementary casts, because in his opinion, no matter how gifted the actor, he can never convey the complexity of the great characters. The audience should take in as completely as possible the mystery and the inner universe of each character and the network of his relations with the other characters. If we had been accustomed to rather static performances confined to the traditional stage, Serban broke this habit. During his grandiose production, everything is in full movement – actors swirl, swarm, and dynamically embrace the whole playhouse, the stage, the auditorium, the corridors: mixing with the audience, throwing the audience into the story, pulling them out of their contemplative passivity, perplexing them second by second so that they don't have time to recover. *The Trilogy* creates a colossal emotional whirl, sweeping away the traditional boundaries between those who watch and those who perform, the boundaries between life and theater, between reality and fiction. Perhaps for the first time, the Romanian spectator became aware that drama is simultaneously word, movement, mimicry, and gesture. Each of these elements is important in and of itself and in its relationship to the others, the stress shifting from one to the other according to artistic intention. *The Ancient Trilogy* proves the universality of the dramatic message which transcends the barrier of language. It shows off as never before the great magician of the theater: the director, the real creator of the spectacle. This production shook the foundations of both the act of creation and its reception. It brought the audience back to the auditorium by convincing them that theater is a dialogue, a mutual shaping, a purified form of communication.

In 1991, Liviu Ciulei came back to the Bulandra Theater (to which his career had been closely tied and on whose stage he had produced many unforgettable performances) to direct *A Midsummer*

Night's Dream. The production was in fact a performance exercise, and his concept seemed to have been formed in order to show off his new troupe of actors. Almost every character became the protagonist at some point during the performance. Ciulei's staging was a veritable character study. The play within the play scenes were fantastic: delightful, hilarious, intelligent – a combination of farce and wit. The comedy was conceived of as a humorous and diaphanous fairy play in which the frontiers between dream and reality evanesced, only to suddenly become clear again. There was no scenery on stage. The nature of the space was suggested through the use of large, colored scarves (obviously symbolic, the red suggesting sensuality, the white the purity of juvenile love) and by the amazing costumes.

Titus Andronicus, staged by Silviu Purcarete at the National Theater in Craiova, won most of the prizes awarded at the Carajiale Festival in 1992. In fact, the first two years of the festival were dominated by Purcarete's presence, who, in addition to the above-mentioned *Ubu Roi*, was responsible for an original and controversial *Phaedra* at the same theater, based on texts by Euripides and Seneca. He also directed *The Comic Theater* by Goldoni at the Bulandra Theatre, and a fascinating and mysterious version of Boccaccio's *Decameron 645* at the Anton Pann Theatre in Ramnicu Valcea with a troupe of amateur actors. *Titus* was visualized as a massacre. The director dispensed with classic scenery and instead defined the scenic space with huge draperies that suggested movement and change of locale through lighting effects. Similarly, the costumes were not individualized and were not character-specific. The characters surrounding Titus made up a sort of chorus that made speeches and reacted to events. The plasticity of the performance was remarkable as the image could regenerate itself, breaking up and then reassembling, relying on the protagonist as the center of the dramatic universe. Titus was the dictator, the manipulator, and the author of the massacre. Everything was defined in relation to him; the movement was directed at him, the characters marched past him in columns, tipping and rocking across the stage to different rhythms. The dictator's face and voice were repeated like a leitmotif on mobile television screens, which extended his sovereign presence to its maximum. The origins of this concept resided, perhaps, in a peculiar Romanian obsession resulting from having seen Ceaucescu's image, the unique face, for hours daily on every television screen. Thus, Titus's sickness acquired a grotesque form in which even humaneness was feigned. The white of the curtains and costumes turned gradually into red. A murderous universe in every sense, with, at its center, a cruel, beastly, unnatural character: a lunatic who relished both the hunt and the kill, savoring his prey as at a horrible and morbid feast.

Arrabal was presented on the Romanian stage for the first time in 1992 when Alexander Hausvater directed a production of *And They*

Put Handcuffs on the Flowers at the Odeon Theater. Two decades ago this play would have been considered an experiment, but it remained interesting to Romania of the 1990s where this type of production was completely unknown. The hypocritical sense of decency of the censors during the communist period would not have allowed such liberties. The Romanian public appreciated the originality of this performance for three reasons. First, the theatrical space of isolation and terror extended all the way to the door of the theater. The spectator was assaulted from the entrance, harassed, pushed, compelled to walk along a dark, winding, and seemingly endless corridor, finally to be thrown into a seat at the mercy of the "guides". Second, the nature of events on stage was cinematographic. Several nuclei of action operated simultaneously and vied for the attention of the audience. The scenic events seemed to compete with each other. The rhythm was rapid and exhausting for the actors who had to exert themselves physically and rely on varied forms of physical and verbal expression. This type of theater was unknown to Romanian actors. Third, this production compelled the actors to shed an old prejudice: the shame of exposing the naked body to the audience. Traditionally, the nude on stage appeared as exhibitionism, never in a dramatic context. Here, the audience was shocked by the movement of the nude. Their only experience with the contemplation of the naked body had been in sculpture and painting where the immediacy of the contact is suppressed and abstracted. With *And They Put Handcuffs on the Flowers*, Alexander Hausvater achieved one of the most radical changes in actors' attitudes: a total elimination of inhibition on stage.

Each of us has one or more performances stored in our emotional memory. I have Tompa Gabor's production of Ionesco's *The Bald Prima Donna*, which premiered at the Magyar Theater in Cluj on February 13, 1992. Over the following three years, the production was performed 108 times in Romania and abroad. Lack of communication and dialogue between people, the propensity to void discourse, the large gamut of verbal cliche, these are some of Ionesco's themes. The amalgam of situations, typology, absurd phrases, and the concerns of contemporary theater, all found an ideal solution in Tompa's rigorous and perfect production. The world of Ionesco's play was seen as a mechanism wound up with a key. The characters looked like huge puppets, walking and speaking jerkily, automatically. The interruptions in dialogue appeared to be a syncopation in the functioning of these automatons, as if someone had forgotten to turn the key. The performance was mechanically choreographed within a space that suggested the stage of a puppet show or a child's toy box. The absurd story of Smith and Martin seemed to have been created by these big puppets, which descended at night from the shelves where they had been aligned, enjoying their liberty, mocking it, and being hurried by the pressure of a time whose duration was unknown and beyond which they ceased to exist. Tompa understood that the story in *The Bald Prima Donna* has a recurring pattern which is ceaseless, as each of us discovers in his own life. Can we stop the cycle of senseless movements, gestures, and words which are nevertheless adjusted as finely as the parts of a clock? Yes, but only if the mechanism is accidentally or deliberately damaged. Thus proceeded Gabor, and in the final scene of his production, the puppets' time began to flow backwards, the whole performance unwinding in reverse at an extremely quick pace, condensing into only eight minutes of action. Having completed the cycle, the puppets returned to their shelves. Pause. Silence. At any moment they could have resumed their play from the beginning. Which beginning? It didn't matter.

In Cluj, at approximately the same time, Mihai Manuitiu staged another play by Ionesco, *The Lesson*, and found an extremely interesting solution which had never occurred to me although I had carefully studied the script. In his production, the English teacher's lesson was no longer a language lesson, but a lesson in political ideology, and the instruction was not aimed at the western world, but at eastern communism. The stage was dominated by a gigantic panel, similar to a blackboard. The teacher instructed the schoolgirl with a slightly erotic slideshow, tinged with a fanaticism which grew increasingly difficult for him to contain as the rhythm of the production approached a military cadence. The act of teaching seemed to be like the act of joining a political party. The teacher instilled his lesson into the girl's head subliminally. The schoolgirl was innocent and assumed that this game was part of the teacher's original teaching method. In the end, the teacher's fanaticism exploded. He wrote and painted the symbols of communism (the hammer and sickle, the five cornered star) on the panel/blackboard with red dye, using an enormous pencil/brush. The delirium was absolute. The teacher looked like an ideological maniac who, contemplating his own work, was so deeply absorbed in his demonstration that it had no importance if the pupil followed her lesson through to its end or not.

The premiere of *Decameron*, adapted by Alexander Hausvater and directed by Iulian Visa, took place at the Radu Stanca Theater in Sibiu in 1992. Visa returned home from Denmark and was, until his untimely death, the managing director of the Sibian theater. During his short activity there, he directed two other productions, *Chang Eng*, by Guren Tunstrum, and *The Card Index*, by Tadeusz Rozewicz. Both were real revelations for the new Romanian theater. Unlike Purcarete, Visa was a very versatile director, and there was hardly any similarity between his productions. The novelty of this adaptation of *Decameron* consisted in setting the action in a jail. Contact with the outer world was completely broken. The stage was a manège in which the well-raked sand awaited the beginning of the stories. The production portrayed the prisoners as actors who had to entertain their warden-tormentor at his command. The prisoners were obliged to choose those short stories by Boccaccio that could satisfy their jailer's wicked and obscene tastes. The forced impromptus increased the humiliation of people who were not only deprived of exterior reality, but even of the magic pleasure of the stories. The prisoners imaginatively remade a life they no longer lived, and their effort was distressing and frustrating to behold. The warden pretended to be an artist and ideologue, giving directions to emphasize those moments of the performance which intensified the frustrations of the interpreters, but which enhanced his "aesthetic" pleasure. In fact, he was the impotent one who exerted his power only to dominate and humiliate defenseless people who were at his mercy. The game was a perverse form of torture. Art, a living thing under conditions of liberty, became here an instrument of punishment, and its fundamental constituent, happiness, changed into unhappiness under these conditions. *Decameron* was a play within a play: a circus show enacted on the stage of a prison with a ringmaster who struck the people-animals with an invisible whip. The show ended with a revolt by the prisoners and a desperate need for spiritual liberation.

We come across the world of concentration camps again in *Ghetto*, by Joshua Sobol, directed by Victor Ioan Frunza at the National Theater in Bucharest in 1993. The pretext of the play was inspired by events (probably real ones) from everyday life in the ghetto in Vilna. The protagonists are a troupe of actors who are rescued by the Jewish commander of the ghetto and who must unexpectedly justify their existence. As in Visa's *Decameron*, the situation is paradoxical: to perform theater in a place of decimation and death, where everyone is struggling to survive and there appears to be no place for art. The characters in the play are the ordinary inhabitants of the ghetto, who strive to live by any means, and the artists, who rehearse and act in a command performance under the menace of death which is there, nearby, and watching them from all corners. Frunza's production was grandiose, and intensively exploited the stage machinery of the National Theatre which had never been fully used before. The spectators sat on the ghetto stage, on the immense stage of the National Theatre itself, where colossal tableaux took place. Dozens of actors were lowered, raised, and slid across the stage to the rhythm of ghetto life. Frunza knows how to build vivid, dynamic, broad compositions. Live music and the Chagallian scenery devised by Adriana Grand (a great Romanian designer) helped create an atmosphere in keeping with the director's vision. For three hours, the people of *Ghetto* sang, danced rehearsed, acted, lived, and died.

In Shakespeare's tragedies, violence does not only function as a catalyst for catharsis. *Richard III*, staged by Mihai Maniutiu at the Odeon Theater in Bucharest, was set under the badge of violence. The premiere took place on February 28, 1993. Maniutiu's version did not alter the text of the play, but he changed the order of its development, starting with the final part and cutting several scenes, characters, and lines. The center of the production was Richard, Duke of Gloucester whose only ambition is the crown of England. Like Shakespeare, the director disclosed the mechanism of power in a straightforward manner. Everything was focused on this point, which made Richard seem even more cruel and aggressive. Urged on by his thirst for power, Richard set up a network of diabolical relations. However, traps he set for others were in fact waiting to ensnare the greatest prey of all: Richard himself. The executioner undone by his own victims. There was no scenery, the stage was bare. The actors wore splendid costumes resembling samurai attire, designed by the remarkable Doina Levinta and individualized by symbolic details specific to each character. Maniutiu created a character – half man, half wolf – who played the part of the Fool but who represented at the same time the inarticulate double, the shadow, the embodiment of Richard's bestial instincts. The performance was driven by the fool-wolf, Buckingham, and Richard. Enjoying the game of power and the cruel play with others, Maniutiu's Richard set the game above all. A narcissistic game, it raised Richard to the top, only to throw him down to Death.

This Evening Lola Blau, written by Georg Kreisler and directed by Alexandru Dabija, premiered at the Jewish State Theater in Bucharest in 1994. *Ghetto, Richard III*, and *The Ancient Trilogy* were all grandiose spectacles with dozens of actors, ample scenic developments, and complicated scenery. Unlike them, *Lola Blau*, a one woman show, represented a refined salon theater and created an intense atmosphere of direct communication and intimacy. Dabija rewrote Kreisler's script for one character (played by Maia Morgenstern, one of the greatest Romanian actresses) accompanied throughout on a piano. The piano player in fact became a character without ever saying a word, taking on the roles of partner, witness, friend, and confessor. For an hour and a half, the audience witnessed a political-show-turned-cabaret: a jazzy, sexy, American-style variety show. The scenes – played, sung, or danced – were closely linked to Lola's struggle to survive. The words of the songs told her story. With the exception of the songs, which were in German, the text was in Yiddish. On stage, there was only a trunk, full of the actress's clothes for the performance and for everyday life, which was also used as a screen for her costume changes. Dabija built into his production (with a certain pedantry) a complex relationship between words, gesture, music, action, and choreography.

The Winter's Tale, translated, adapted and directed by Alexandru Darie at the Bulandra Theater, was one of the most remarkable productions of 1994. This western production tended towards ludicrous, gushing vitality. The relationship in the text between the verbs "to be" and "to appear" (in other words, between "reality" and "illusion") was essential to the production. The circular structure of the production clearly emphasized the characters' coming in to and going out of illusion. Darie also created a special relationship between three central characters in the play: Mammilius, Perdita, and Time were all played by the same actress. The swing between the two dimensions, the alternation of seasons and locations, the tension between hatred and love, the presence of life and death, here are the antithetical elements which created the vivid world of the production, a world of images where dreams could be at any time reality, and reality a dream. Dramatic moments alternated with frolic-some moments, such as a joyous snowfall, silly little songs, and dances with strange steps. The euphoric mood dominated that of anxiety and despair. The nightmares were effaced, Purcell's Elizabethan music flooded the auditorium. All's well that ends well.

The Regression

Unfortunately, beginning in 1994, the Romanian theater began to regress. Andrei Serban's resignation from the National Theater in Bucharest and subsequent departure from Romania sounded the alarm. All the managing directors appointed by Andrei Plesu have been replaced by his successor at the Ministry of Culture. The new managing directors are no more competent than their predecessors. Political agendas have taken priority over issues of ability. A series of abusive measures followed that have reinstated centralized, government control over the arts. Former nomenclatura, again in charge of our cultural destiny, are blocking creative initiatives and reestablishing the old ideological and financial bureaucracy. The quality of productions and the value of experimental projects has rapidly declined. It seems that we are witnessing a crisis, a moral and institutional one, not a creative one. The bureaucracy hinders noteworthy theatrical experimentation. The legislative vacuum surrounding the theater, compensated for by governmental regulations, hampers the theater's normal development which had begun so promisingly back in 1990. Old officials bring back old mentalities. However, the Romanian theater will survive these times. Creative artists have not disappeared and original ideas have not diminished. But the effort will be tremendous – out of proportion. And it is a pity. All had begun so nicely.

Final Remarks

Price of a theater ticket: 1,000 Lei (=US$0.50)
Average actor's salary: 200,000 Lei (US$100.00)
Average production cost: 15,000,000 Lei (US$7500.00)
(As of June, 1995)

RUSSIAN THEATER

FOREWORD: AN INTERVIEW WITH YURY LYUBIMOV

Nina Velekhova

During a rehearsal break, while his actors had a quick breakfast, I had the opportunity to ask director Yury Lyubimov for his insights regarding the state of Russian theater:

Nina Velekhova: Yury Petrovitch, what are your thoughts about the modern Russian theater, about the changes it is going through today?

Yury Lyubimov: I've always supported activity and search. I'm troubled by many things about the state of theater in general. I see a deterioration in the work of many formerly well regarded, famous theaters. Even some master directors have had the ground shaken under their feet and have become disoriented. Not all, of course. But even at my theater, not all is perfect, even though we are working our fingers to the bone.

N.V.: In 1964, the Taganka Theater became a real Mecca for audiences who wanted to experience free theater. On the stage there, you dared to tell the truth about our lives. That was not so easy.

Y.L.: For us, that was a happy time of complete communication with our audiences and a surprising feeling of undying creative insight. We had freedom in our work and yet did not want to compromise our high principles regarding life and human relations, as we see happening around us today in every sphere of the arts. Do I miss the past? I would say yes, if it had not been for those obstacles that prevented us from moving forward. Nowadays, everyone understands that one need not censor artists, deprive them of citizenship for disobedience, or publicly reprimand them (as I was for my production of *The Queen of Spades*). I suffered much by staying away from this country, but did not lose faith in my vocation. Traveling around the world, I saw many good things from which our theater could learn a great deal: not everything in Russian actors' education is OK; traditions are being lost; the work of geniuses like Meyerhold, Stanislavski, and Vakhtangov, which has been recognized all over the world and which has shaped theater everywhere, is being wasted. We have to think about these problems. All our national disasters are tied to common, world disasters.

N.V.: What do you call a disaster? What prevents art from prospering today?

Y.L.: Human separation. But we mustn't despair. One of my idols, Vakhtangov, produced the cheerful *Princess Turandot* during the most tragic of times, and the way was opened by only one performance.

N.V.: And what about contemporaneity?

Y.L.: *Turandot* is contemporary. She isn't getting any older.

THE STATE OF RUSSIAN THEATER
IN THE 1990s

Nina Velekhova

The theatrical scene in Russia today combines seemingly incompatible phenomena. On the one hand, it is full of life: the creative expression of artists' ideas, godsends, and discoveries; while on the other, it is superficial and goes no further than to satisfy the basest needs of an uncultured audience. Of most interest to the researcher is the fact that Russian culture currently manifests itself at both of these extremes, ranging from ascetic strictness to unlimited freedom. Nonetheless, both of these trends seem to be following a single common course.

In the late 1980s on a trip abroad, Mikhail Gorbachov stated that artistic censorship simply did not exist in the Soviet Union. And with those words, it in fact did cease to exist. From that moment on, the arts in Russia were freed from the control and supervision of any special organizations. The theater now chooses which plays to produce, stages them on its own, and answers to no one except those critics and publicists who participate in the creative process itself and interact directly with the theaters.

A stream of truth flowed into the arts following the disappearance of censorship. Mikhail Shatrov's plays subsequently vanished from the theaters. Shatrov had written about Lenin, but wrote according to official sources which were now publicly pronounced inauthentic. Plays about the fairness of the "great proletarian revolution" disappeared, as did those about the perniciousness of Czarist Russia. The truth could now be told about pre-Revolutionary events and the Revolution itself. Many works appeared which dealt with the annihilation of the royal family, such as the novels of Edward Radzinsky, articles by film director Gelia Ryshov, Stanislav Govorukhin's film *The Russia We Lost*, and Kuznetsov's play *And Elements of Retribution*, splendidly staged by Boris Morozov at the Moscow Maly Theater with Yury Solomin as Nicholas II.

The Russian theater reached its highest spiritual level in the past, during the most arduous of times, despite obstacles, prohibitions, and conditions adverse to the full development of one's own personality – not to mention the interpersonal relationships which make up society as a whole. Today, although the theater has preserved its artistic originality, not everything has moved along a favorable path. Over the last six years, theatrical trends have changed along with changes in the very essence of the culture of a country that has now become the Commonwealth of Independent States (CIS). CIS is no longer the USSR, and this must be kept in mind when discussing the state of the arts.

The 1990s have been years of a changing country and a changing people with changing attitudes towards every aspect of life. Goals have changed. The country had to change from a Soviet state with all its economic and political peculiarities into a capitalist one in a most primitive form, forced to accumulate initial wealth in a manner lacking in productive activity. Inflation, which had long been kept at bay, broke in, and art ceased to occupy the important status it had hitherto rightfully enjoyed. The ground was, in fact, knocked out from underneath art's feet. This was manifested in a sharp drop in subsidies. The government had always supported the theaters: suddenly it was not in a position to do so. The fact that theaters depend on aid from the state should not surprise anyone – they had always existed through government subsidization and operated knowing that no chance occurrence could cause their failure. Theaters are turning to their patrons for assistance, that is, to the Ministry of Culture or to the municipal cultural committees.

Theaters, Funding, and Sponsorship

Over 200 theaters are registered in Moscow. One third of these are State theaters – either federally or municipally supported (the majority falling into the latter category). Several of these theaters have been officially recognized as National Property: the Bolshoi Theater, the Maly Theater, the Moscow Art Theater (both the Chekhov and Gorky theaters), and the Mariinsky Theater of Opera and Ballet in St. Petersburg among others. While the Moscow Municipal Department of Finance pays its share of funding in full, the Russian Ministry of Finance meets its financial obligations irregularly, which explains why many of these theaters are often in difficulty. An annual subsidy can, in some cases, amount to as much as two billion rubles. This sum, however, is still not enough (the Mayakovsky Theater for example, receives only 40 percent of the financing it needs) and a theater must therefore either be able to raise money by itself or earn as much as it needs through box office receipts (which hardly ever happens). This is why sponsorship arose. Sponsors are sought out primarily from among the so-called "new Russians", a group of rich, prosperous people from various backgrounds. These new patrons of the arts are not to be confused with the more noble Maecenas[1] of the

---

[1] The Maecenas were a group of generous merchants and entrepreneurs who gave money to talented artists, buying their supplies, maintaining their theaters, and at times saving them from a hungry death. The future would prove that these sponsors never erred in their choice of deserving protégés.

late 19th and early 20th century. Today it is very difficult and frequently impossible to convince potential sponsors that it is a matter of honor and valor for citizens of impoverished Russia to help the theater. As one *Izvestia* newspaper reviewer wrote, "support of the dramatic arts is [...] an absolutely special form of sponsorship. Unlike film, opera, and the music industry, in the theater there is no hope of recovering losses, and even less hope of making a profit." And so, the theaters have been liberated, but there is no money.

Private sponsorship of theater has existed in Russia for approximately ten years now, during which time it has gone through several stages of development. In the beginning, money poured into the theater as if from a horn of plenty. The names of general sponsors appeared repeatedly on playbills and programs. "Friendship Evenings" (benefits) were held in the theaters. Those times have passed. Today, the practice of single investments in a play or touring production is most popular, but the general unreliability of sponsors' generosity together with the country's changing economic situation has poisoned theatrical life. Only very large, stable organizations can help theaters today, although they too are becoming increasingly difficult to find. Large banks are not interested in funding theaters and there are very few instances of large corporations assisting theater companies (the Koleso Studio Theater in Tolietti is a notable exception). Russian bankers and rich "new Russians" are often illiterate and uncivilized, preferring to spend their millions at the casino, on TV game shows, and on other frivolous pursuits. Slowly but surely the theater has begun to ingratiate itself to their low tastes. For example, sex has burst into the theaters, onto TV screens, and into movies. Pornography is demanding a place alongside legitimate freedom of expression on stage with an aim to replace it altogether.

Masters of the Russian Stage

In the late 1980s, everyone felt that, finally, favorable conditions existed for artistic creativity. Writers rushed to their desks, theaters staged quality plays, and audiences filled the houses – dying to see all that had lain hidden for so long. Russia's 70-year-long Soviet history suddenly became an open book. Works by poets and novelists like Mandelshtam, Zamyatin, Nabokov, and Olesha which had been forgotten or read in secret were returned to the people. Paintings by modern artists were hung in galleries and every manuscript from libraries and warehouses was displayed. Ordinary librarians, selfless people as it turned out, had preserved nearly all that had been doomed to destruction in their day. Alexander Vampilov's plays, previously banned, began to be staged everywhere. He was probably the first playwright who, as early as the 1970s, would deal with the theme of the modern young man. He had alarmed us with his world in which emptiness, egotism, and nihilism were the result of the disparity between reality and its representation in literature, the visual arts, and the media. New directors took over from those who for many years had served our Soviet theater, sustaining its high artistic principles. Many writers, actors, and directors such as Stanislav Govorukhin, Oleg Basilashvilli, and Mark Zakharov, went into politics. Beginning with *You Cannot Live Like That*, Govorukhin's films became catalysts for social change. Many people, influenced by his criticism of the country's moral, economic, and cultural state, left the Communist party. The frankness of his revelations called for the exposure of corruption and for contrition, as did Tengiz Abuladze in his internationally acclaimed film, *Repentance*.

What happened in the dramatic theater? A sensation: Yury Lyubimov returned to Russia having spent six years abroad and almost losing contact with his theater, Taganka. He resurrected the play *Alive*, an adaptation of a Boris Maghaev story about Soviet village life and the hopelessness of the collective farm system which had been banned for 25 years. He also staged Pushkin's *Boris Godunov* and *The Covetous Knight*, Euripides's *Medea*, and a version of Pasternak's *Doctor Zhivago* (also formerly banned). These productions represented a new style for Lyubimov: classical and calmly realistic.

Lyubimov's tireless spirit of search, discovery, and modernization along with his ability to make everything on stage topical quickly influenced others to continue the kind of experimentation he had begun at the Taganka. His return brought a surge of energy to the theater, which, while it did not last long, was of essential importance.

Andrei Goncharov, another theater veteran, took over the Mayakovsky Theater after Okhlopkov's death and salvaged its influential status and high standards. A person of dynamic character, Goncharov possesses the strong will and self discipline that distinguished Okhlopkov. His work, which tends toward romantic-realism, includes a brilliantly modernized version of Ostrovsky's *The Last Sacrifice*, a production of Babel's *Sunset*, and many other plays by both Russian and foreign playwrights.

Goncharov's disciples have actively stepped out into theater life and are proving themselves to be directors of a strong and multifaceted realistic school. Tatiana Abramkova stands out among them as she is responsible for a renewed interest in the formerly banned plays of Arkadi Averchenko. Also of note is her production *A Comedy About Hamlet, the Danish Prince*, a collage of plays by Ionesco, Beckett, Vlas Dorosevich (a topical satirist of the beginning of the century), and the modern writer Muza Pavlova.

A director of Goncharov's magnitude is Boris Lvov-Anokhin. His remarkable New Theater is best known for its production of *The Aspern Letters* and an interesting version of Bruckner's *Heroic Comedy*.

Serso by V. Slavkin was for some time the number one play in Moscow thanks to Anatoly Vassiliev's brilliant production. Slavkin is a writer of rash and cocky plays which resemble stylistically those in the western absurdist tradition. *Serso* is a factual account of how the young Soviet generation strove toward a meaningful, active life and how, more often than not, this aspiration was tragically broken off. The play deals also with the theme of rejecting revolutions in general, their destructiveness and anti humanism. In his philosophically cryptic production, Vassiliev compared the Russian and the French revolutions and examined their negative impact on human psychology. After the success of *Serso*, Vassiliev set up a "laboratory", the School of Modern Dramatic Art. Unfortunately, he shut himself up in his narrow professional experiments and was unable to sustain public interest in his work.

The Moscow Art Theater split into two: the Chekhov, lead by Oleg Efremov, and the Gorky, lead by Tatiana Doronina. The Gorky Theater is extremely popular, known primarily for its brilliant acting. One of its best productions is of Edward Radzinsky's *An Old Actress in the Role of Dostoyevsky's Wife*, directed by R. Viktiuk. Efremov's theater is not as popular, despite a sufficiently serious and varied repertoire. Its rehearsal space functions as a small stage as well. There, one can see Bulgakov's *Days of the Turbins*, and a play about the friendship and subsequent estrangement of Maxim Gorky and Leonid Andreyev. Efremov himself directed Griboyedov's classic comedy, *Woe From Wit*, Pushkin's *Boris Godunov*, and M. Roshchin's *Mother-of-Pearl Zinaida*, in which he attempted to define moral and social signs in present day Russia.

For years prior to *perestroika*, Anatoly Efros, the former director of the Moscow Art Theater, and Yury Lyubimov, the director of the Taganka Theater, were considered to be the major figures of Russian theater. Efros died before the changes in 1989 and Lyubimov left the country for six years. Thus, the Russian theater was for some time without out a leader. But did this destroy the theater? I think not. Students of the older generation of masters have taken over positions of leadership quite successfully. For example, the gifted Sergei Yashin now runs the Gogol Theater, Pavel Khomsky now leads the Mossovet Theater, and Pyotr Fomenko staged the highly successful and influential *Guilty without Guilt* by Ostrovsky. At the St. Petersburg Bolshoi Drama Theater, the talented Temur Chkeidze has replaced the late Georgi Tovstonogov. A newcomer to St. Petersburg, Chkeidze is a Russian-Georgian whose mastery of both form and content is remarkable. He is well known for his productions in Tbilisi. He staged a most interesting performance of Schiller's *Cabal and*

Love in St. Petersburg. Yury Eremin, another young director of note, staged many brilliant productions at the Theater of the Russian (formerly Soviet) Army before moving to the Pushkin Theater. Eremin is a profoundly realistic director who knows how to develop characters and deepen dramatic conflicts. Recently he has gained recognition for his adaptations of Hamsun's *At the Gates of Paradise*, Dostoyevsky's *The Possessed*, Gogol's *The Government Inspector*, and Chekhov's *Ward Number Six*. He is best known, however, for his version of Andrei Platonov's *The Ivanov Family*, pulled at long last out of oblivion. Alexander Burdonsky stands out among the directors of his generation for his production of *Mandate*, by N. Erdman, as well as for his version of the modern play *Your Sister and Your Niece*, about Elizabeth Tudor and Mary Stuart and featuring the gifted actress Ludmila Kasatkina, a Soviet film and stage star of the 1950s and 1960s. *Brilliant Orchid*, translated from the Spanish and dedicated to the famous Eva Peron, also aroused great interest.

The Maly Theater, still the most tenaciously loyal to tradition, is a theater of great historical value. Its leader, actor/director Yury Solomin, firmly decided that only classics (Russian and foreign) would be produced there and he does not deviate from his agenda. Among the Maly's most noteworthy revivals have been Aleksey Tolstoy's *Czar Feodor Ioannovitch* and Pushkin's *Boris Godunov*. Boris Morozov, a director of a critical nature, stands out among the directors at the Maly. His work there includes productions of Ostrovsky's *The Ardent Heart*, Chekhov's *The Wood Demon*, and Beaumarchais's *A New Tartuffe or The Guilty Mother*, the latter never before seen in Russia. Today Morozov is the director of the Theater of the Russian Army.

On the basis of the productions discussed above, one can see that the Russian theater continues to search for means of expressing the "life of the human soul" (Stanislavsky). The most shining example of this is the above mentioned play, *An Old Actress in the Role of Dostoyevsky's Wife*. This play reflects modern Russian society so profoundly and exerts such a powerful influence on the audience that I can find no analog to it at any other theater today. The actors, Tatiana Doronina and Aristarkh Livanov, deserve the highest esteem. They realize the great goal to which Russian theater and literature have always aspired: they elevate man, keeping the heavenly light in him from dying out, keeping him from pitifully battling for a "sweet life" limited by biological needs.

The Traps of Freedom

Our theater's path today is a complicated one. Absolute freedom without selection, without taking into account mankind's experiences, turns into a situation where everything is permissible. The powers of instinct are breaking free, trying to overcome the powers of reason. The Russian theater, having crossed the boundary of censure but not always able to handle the process of emancipation, has fallen into a state of stress and landed in a swamp of sin. For example, there is an obsession with the portrayal of sexual acts on stage. Orgasm, masturbation, and every kind of deviant sexual act has now been performed on stage. A sort of coronation of primitive feelings took place in the theaters. Most likely, the director Kama Ginkas is to blame for starting this trend with his work, ironically, at the Theater For Young Spectators. Subsequently, an actor playing the lead in a version of Ostrovsky's *Wiseman* at the Lenkom Theater was stripped of all his clothes too. Rather than being hooted off the stage, these types of productions often meet with critical acclaim. However, theaters are beginning to awaken, as if from a coma, and come to their senses. And now, even if you can still see naked women in Mark Zakharov's *Marriage of Figaro,* or men without trousers at the Moscow Art Theater, interest in revealing intimate parts of the body has noticeably diminished.

An Outburst of Ideas: New Theaters, Trends, and Repertoires

The 1980s and 1990s have brought new ideas, new problems and new points of view. A new hero has also appeared in contemporary plays, reminiscent of the British "angry young man" of the 1950s: critical and unrecognizing of authority. The problems of the discontented individual have come to the forefront.

George White, president of the O'Neill Theater Center in the United States, finds a resemblance between new Russian playwrights and their American colleagues. He aptly notes, "Russian playwrights now carry out functions other than those of their predecessors. Unfortunately, most playwrights themselves don't know what they want. Apparently, this is connected to processes taking place in society. There is a kind of general incomprehension of what is happening in society, a feeling of hostility towards one's surroundings, a negative internal energy in people. [...] This strongly influences playwrights. Hence their rejection of reality."

These new trends in Russian drama and directing are mainly apparent in the young, informal theater companies that are springing up everywhere. The 1980s dazzled us with new theater companies which resembled roaming troupes, gathering for agitational performances rather than for academics or schools. Some of these have since matured and become established theaters, such as Morozov's Mannequin Theater in Chelyabinsk, Anatoly Vassiliev's School of Dramatic Art, the Chelovek Studio Theater, and On the Boards. These new theaters violate tradition: they do not want to continue or develop anything – they want to start completely anew and discover everything all over again. The list of newcomers is still growing. There are too many noteworthy new theaters to mention within the scope of this chapter. Small new theaters can be found in practically every city across the country: in the Urals, in the Komi-Permyatsky region, in Khabarovsk, Barnaul, Vladivostok, Bratsk, etc. However, strange as it may seem, none of these new theaters influence the broad picture of Russian theater. They do not lead major movements, as did Meyerhold, Vakhtangov, Tairov, or Okhlopkov. At times they disappear as quickly as they came, or reform into rock groups, variety acts and other smaller, more commercially viable ensembles. They survive by merging into private enterprises or troupes for one show. On splitting up, they soon reunite, because among the many traditions of our theatrical life, collectivism still reigns. Organizations such as the Gosconcert and Philharmony inspired the creation of traveling actors' collectives that call themselves "concert reciting teams" because they do not have the appropriate license to qualify for theatrical status.

Among the most popular of these recently formed young groups is the Trifonovsky Experimental Theater in Moscow, organized in 1988. It has produced 15 plays, some of which have received awards. The Trifonovsky Theater also gives concert performances. Not partial to any one genre, this theater's repertoire is diverse, ranging from Anouillh's *Medea* to children's fairy tales. It is subsidized by various major firms. It seats 70 people and it employs 25, seven of whom are actors.

Another young theater is the Versia Drama Theater, which was organized in 1986 in Saratov as an actors' association. It is lead by V. Sergienko. While production styles vary, leaning toward the experimental, plays performed here are always highly acclaimed. The Versia is a privately sponsored, three hundred seat theater.

The municipal theater, School of Modern Plays, in Moscow was set up in 1989. It is lead by I. Reikhelgause and Marin Druzhina and employs 30 people. One can see such famous actors as S. Yursky, L. Durov, and L. Polishchuk on the stage of this very contemporary theater, as well as productions by the prominent film director Marlen Khutsiev. A. Kanensky's Musical Troupe performs here from time to time as does P. Fomenko's Masterskaya Group. This theater is well known in Russia and abroad.

Anatoly Ledukhovsky's Model Theater opened in Moscow in 1987. This is a private theater which is also already known internationally. The repertoire here is diverse and does not include plays which can be seen at other Moscow theaters.

The Klim Masterskaya at the Meyerhold Creative Center is an older group. Formerly V. Mirzoev's group, Domino, it is now under the leadership of V. Klimenko (from whom it derives the name Klim).

In 1991, O. Shevedova, the former head of the literature department at the Pushkin Theater, gathered together a group of creative young actors to form an association named "OK". They are a touring company with a broad repertoire, ranging from a rock opera, *Salome, Jewish Empress*, to a dramatization of Leonid Andreyev's story, *Poor, Poor Judah*.

The Vedagon Theater in the city of Zelenograd performs a repertoire based primarily on revivals of ancient Slavic poetry (the word "vedagon" symbolizes the life and soul of the ancient Slavs). Here, audiences become familiar with ancient Slavic rituals as well as modern, realistic plays. Teachers from the Maly Theater's Shchepkin School cooperate with the Vedagon whose directors are Pavel Kurrochkin and Elena Shurpeko.

The Tembr Studio-Laboratory was also created within the last few years. According to its director, N. Kosenkova, it exists on the brink between music and prose. It is one of the most varied and original theaters, synthesizing music and drama. The Tembr's repertoire consists of staged poems by Velimir Khlebnikov (a Russian Futurist of the 1920s), Foma Akvinsky's *Lessons*, ancient mysteries, and the old Russian tale *The Lay of Igor's Host*.

The Formal Theater is also quite original. This 15-person touring group performs outdoors. It is famous for its spectacular use of sound and light in its stagings of various myths and legends. It experiments with realism, providing concrete images of abstract ideas. It performs lesser known plays like *People, Lions, Eagles, and Partridges* by Tom Stoppard, and Sam Shepard's *Fulfola*.

The oldest of all these theaters is the Mannequin Theater. It has already staged about 40 plays. Its productions are serious and successful, without trying to be terribly original.

The Tericose Theater in the resort town of Gelendzhik is led by Anatoly Slyusarenko. Set up in 1992, it is quite successful. They play to full houses and the repertoire is interesting.

Finally, it is worth noting that special theaters of pantomime and clowning were created in 1989 and 1993 respectively. The Pantomime Theater is headed by A. Plyushch. It seats 120 people and the company (of two to five people) loves to tour. The Clown Theater, under the direction of Teresa Durova, unites principles of dramatic theater, circus, variety shows and mime. It does not stage conventional plays. Famous actors such as Y. Nikulin, A. Petrenko, and A. Filozov perform here frequently.

* * *

The period in which we are living can be described in two words: shock therapy. The repercussions of this era will inevitably be felt in all areas of culture, in art's very essence, and primarily in the theater arts: the art of the live actor, who moves and responds to the conditions surrounding him. Changes in the life of this country have been so unexpected and so profound that it is difficult to speak about the consequences without alarm. We are no longer those Russians whose ideas and emotions have gone down in the history of mankind as components of the "mysterious Slavic soul." The modern poet Vladimir Vysotsky was the first in 70 years to express the truth about Russia in his songs. He said:

> "I stand as if before an eternal enigma,
> before a great, almost legendary country,
> before a salty, bitter-sour-sweet land,
> with its blue skies, spring water, rye,
> and squashing through greasy, almost rusty mud
> Into which horses sink up to the stirrups,
> But it draws me, my drowsy land,
> that has soured and swollen from sleep ... "

Art's task is to solve this enigma, and the best talents and most lucid minds are beginning to think it over. George White describes the Russian nature in a very interesting way: "The Russian soul cannot be happy. One wants to pray for the Russian person, to suffer and pray – he has no confidence in the future. A tranquil flourishing is strange to him, he finds himself with difficulty. He, the Russian, does not acknowledge reality. This culture with its searching, its tossing about, is dear to me". "So what?" one could perhaps ask me, "Do you think that Russia has perished and that it is time to bury her body and soul, her geniuses and her simple folk, her ability to rise from the ruins, her ability to be patient without losing her dignity, and her unique ability to portray the human soul in art?" No, we still have our resurrection, our inevitable renaissance. Today, we are all witnessing, as well as participating in, the growth process of the integrity of the country and of the famous Russian theater, which at present is still searching for its true self.

1995

SLOVAK THEATER

FOREWORD

Darina Karova

For many people in Slovakia, life after the fall of the Iron Curtain became more diverse, funnier, even easier. However, many were stricken by poverty, depression, and disappointment. Due to stormy changes, barriers fell – real ones in the form of barbed wire fences as well as imaginary social and ethical ones. New possibilities for understanding, inspiration, and the realization of different skills and abilities opened up, but at the same time we were overwhelmed by crime, prostitution, and drugs. It became clear that under the former regime, people's sense of ethics and responsibility had not developed adequately. We suddenly found ourselves thrust into the wilderness of a new reality without sufficient survival skills. Our hierarchy of values had been destroyed. Commercial values took their place instead of the real values of a free and cultured society. It is now time for "soul ecology." And what could be a more appropriate means of accomplishing this than through art? Recent history demonstrates that neither education nor religion protect people from negative new influences, but I am sure that art can. Even at the worst times under communist totalitarianism, it was art that opened up new experiences, consoled, kindled a sense of community, and elevated ethics and aesthetics.

I think that art and culture above all else need special help today – more than ever before. Artists are right to ask for more money, but this is not the essential problem. The problem lies in the relationship between society and art. When a work of art is made only to be popular, it without exception ends by serving either business or an ideology. In countries where technocrats are in power, art is given short shrift. One of the fundamental duties of the State is to create optimal conditions for the development of art and culture in general. A free society needs pure, independent art just as our planet needs forests.

CLOSER TO THE "SEWER" ...
A VIEW OF SLOVAK THEATER

Anna Gruskova

Because of its numerous tours abroad, the Stoka (Sewer) Theater is perhaps the best-known Slovak theater. This Bratislava-based company is
well known at home and in the neighboring Czech Republic, which
despite three years of independence (the division of Czechoslovakia took
place on January 1, 1993), is still considered by many to share a common
cultural heritage with Slovakia. When I reflect on the changes in Slovak
theater life after the collapse of the totalitarian regime, when I peruse
theatrical yearbooks, magazines, and programs, and when I talk to theater people, all the remarkable events of the last few years somehow con-
dense themselves in my mind into the experience of the Stoka Theater.
In 1993 at a conference about the once influential Slovak theater, Theater
on the Corso, I attempted in my speech to persuade the audience that it
is necessary to search for parallels between what the legendary Theater
on the Corso represented in its time and what the Stoka Theater represents today. What both have in common is that both represent more than
just a theater. I chose to approach the topic of contemporary Slovak
theater from the view point of the Stoka Theater with which I am very
familiar, realizing that this perspective may be biased. I give up any
claim to objectivity in advance, although I will certainly try to be so ...

Closer to "The Sewer" ... through Politics

The name *Stoka*, or the Sewer, indicates the singular position of the theater, its specific place in the public space. *Stoka* disposes of the sewage
and hides it from the aggressively clean bodies that are used to showing
off and making an impression. But *Stoka* does not run under Moscow or
New York, it runs under Bratislava, the capital of Slovakia. Bratislava's
time of glory was in the 18th century as the coronation place of the
Hungarian royalty. After that, it became an Austro-Hungarian "town of
pensioners." In 1918, this pro-Hungarian suburb of Vienna turned into
a strategically important city in the newly formed Czechoslovakia. Nearly
80 years later, Bratislava's population has almost entirely changed,
along with the city's overall image. The number of inhabitants has multi-
plied five times, and stands currently at over a half a million people.

Originally, over two thirds of the residents of Bratislava were not Slovak, but mostly German and Hungarian. Today, Bratislava is almost 100 percent Slovak. Many people came to Bratislava from small towns and villages. Often these people were unaccustomed to city life and had little appreciation for the city's past. This is one reason why the architecture of Bratislava is not harmonious. Only a small historic center now remains after a large part was torn down 20 years ago and the old town is sliced in half by a highway.

The members of the Stoka Theater company represent a small cross section of the population of Bratislava. Many brought their individual concerns, hobbies, and tastes from their home towns and some have not even been changed by city life. At cast parties, 30-year-old Ingrid Hrubanicova from Presov likes to sing folk songs with great gusto. When she combined them with an eclectic mix of popular music and her own texts, the result was a revue entitled, *Only a Seagull Can Dip Its Feet in My Tears*. Blaho Uhlar, the director and manager of the Stoka Theater, brought a deep sensitivity for the Slovak language and for the Slovak nation with him from his Ruzomberok family. He had warmly welcomed the creation of the independent Slovak state in 1993, but ironically, it was then that the theater's greatest difficulties began. The Stoka Theater was actually created outside the structures controlled by the state, and to date the state does not know what to do with it. Even the theater's location is somewhat irregular – it obtained temporary premises between the Small Stage of the National Theater and the new National Theater building, then moved to a one-story building belonging to the Union of Transport Enterprises in the former industrial zone. There, among the new monumental buildings which have sprung up in a rather chaotic way, the Stoka Theater looks like an old village gymnasium.

Stoka Theater's Place in Slovak Theater

The Stoka Theater was founded by director Blaho Uhlar and designer Milos Karasek after the lifting of the Iron Curtain in 1991. Since then, it has produced 12 shows and given over 500 performances. Stoka's working methods have influenced many theater makers, old and young alike. Uhlar, an admirer of the experimental Czech theater of the 1970s and 1980s, has founded a school of fixed collective improvisation.

The state controlled and sponsored theater network, of which the Stoka is not part, has not changed much in recent years. In Slovakia there has traditionally been little possibility of mobility for actors. After graduating, they usually find permanent employment at one of the state theaters where they stay until they retire. Young actors are less and less willing to work outside Bratislava because standards as well as salaries at the regional theaters are, with some exceptions, relatively low.

It is unusual for regional theater companies to perform in the capital. There have been some attempts made at uniting artists for a single production (at Studio "S" in Bratislava, for example), but only here and there. Since the lifting of the Iron Curtain, the Stoka Theater is the only alternative theater to have become fully professional and to operate regularly. In spite of good artistic results, the Stoka still has to pay a price for independence in the incessant fight for survival and funding.

To date, Slovakian theaters are funded by the Ministry of Culture, which, with only rare exceptions, provides their main source of income. According to the director of the Slovak National Theater Center, Andrej Matasik, in 1995 half a billion SK, a quarter of the Ministry's budget, was given to theaters. Today in Slovakia, a country of five million inhabitants, there are 24 state theaters in 11 towns, along with 36 opera companies, puppet theaters, musical theaters, ballet companies, and youth and alternative theaters.

"If the state refuses to support you, why don't you find money elsewhere?" – ask foreign colleagues. Many western theaters do not receive state support. But in Slovakia, even the municipalities do not have money to support theater. The town of Zilina, a rare exception, supports a theater, but this may be linked to the fact that the mayor of Zilina is also the leader of one of the government coalition parties. Most theaters do not want to depend on town administrations and are satisfied with the Ministry's support.

It has been often stated that insufficient legislation restricts non-governmental support of the arts because the legal status of the so-called third sector (non-profit, endowment foundations) remains unresolved. In 1989, a State Fund for Culture, *Pro-Slovakia*, was created to finance certain projects, chosen by a special commission, that were eligible for support from the state. Unfortunately, from the very beginning, the Ministry of Culture had the right to veto the commission's decisions, and so the Fund became just another channel for Ministerial money. Originally, both the commission members and the grant recipients were publicly known. Later, the Fund's activities were kept hidden from the public, and new commission members were chosen according to unpublicized criteria. In 1994, the commission decided to fund the Stoka Theater, but the Minister of Culture at the time, who had a known dislike of alternative theaters, vetoed the decision. The Stoka's financial situation was later salvaged by a loan from the Ministry of Culture, which the theater had hoped to repay with its regular grant from the state, but the Stoka never received its grant and the loan is now being repaid by the Public Association of the Stoka.

Another similarity with the prerevolutionary era is the lack of published information about the amount of money theaters receive and how it is spent. Western theater-makers cannot believe that at the beginning of a season, some theaters do not yet know which plays they will be producing in the second half of the season, let alone what the opening dates will be. Slovak theaters can only dream of a situation in which they could publish a program before the start of the season, complete with strictly observed opening dates and financial data. In late 1995, a year-book of Slovak theater was published. It referred to the 1993/1994 season and contained information about theater artists, premieres, perfor-mances, and reviews, but no financial data. The Ministry of Culture also published a yearbook, but it didn't contain any financial information either. The Stoka Theater has repeatedly requested the disclosure of information regarding allocation of state funds. At press conferences, the Stoka regularly submits detailed reports of its activities and detailed information about its finances to the press and to any other interested parties. To my knowledge, the Stoka is the only theater to do so.

The Stoka as a Political Subject

> Traditional thinking in Slovakia, shaped by long years under the cen-tralism of the Austrian monarchy and later by the totalitarian regime, is extremely elastic. Even for this nation, the road to independence was not easy, and as it turned out, dependency was not as much of a prob-lem as was centralized power. Such a nation can hardly create anything without direct state control, and if it does come up with something on its own, the state will do its utmost to suppress it.
>
> – Blaho Uhlar

> ... What kind of idol do the hopeful eyes of the Slovakian intellectual, artistic, and scientific elite look up to? Is it not the state and its treasury? The thing is that the other side of state paternalism is citizens' infantilism.
>
> – Milan Sutovec[1]

With the growing public consciousness and the lessening dependence on the state as the only source of finances, the legislative activity of the present government is also increasing – not, however in order to encour-age alternative financing, but rather in order to restrict it. The present government has in fact begun the most radical process of centralization and strengthening of state power. It has proposed bringing the Slovak Academy of Sciences under state control, creating regional cultural cen-ters which would control all cultural institutions in their region through financial pressure, handing control of non-profit organizations over to the state, and concentrating theaters into smaller, easier to control groups. Dramaturg Darina Karova, the head of the International Slovak

---

[1] J. Puskas, "An Interview with Milan Sutovec", *Narodna Obrodna*, 21 March 1995.

Theater Festival Divadelna Nitra, summed up the need to discuss Slovak theater atter 1989 in conjunction with the political situation:

> The struggle for Stoka is not only the struggle for a concrete group, or even a person, as many theater-makers may injuriously think or interpret with a great deal of indifference. It is a struggle for principle [...]. I have in mind the unfavorable legislative and economic environment in which this type of creativity cannot prosper [...] and which kills all vital activity whatsoever. And the worst thing is that this all happens with the full knowledge of the Slovak (theater-going) public [...]. The liquidation of the Stoka will end nothing. On the contrary – a new era of vassal obedience of state theaters will begin.[2]

A Center for Alternative Art: Stoka Theater's Maturity

The Stoka Theater gradually moved from lamenting the state's stinginess to assuming a conscious citizen outlook: the private theater became a public association and a foundation was created to support the company. The Stoka Theater began working on its public relations by targeting an audience, by holding press conferences, by mailing out monthly programs to the public with commentaries, quotations, and company news. These steps, normal abroad, have been quite rare in Slovakia. Touring abroad more frequently has resulted in new contacts, and foreign troupes have started to come to the Stoka Theater. Also, local theater companies with no permanent space of their own have begun to perform at the Stoka Theater. Gradually, the Stoka Theater has become a kind of cultural center where new books are launched, and where intellectuals, artists, and students can relax and meet. It has come to realize its own importance as a political subject and has begun to fight publicly for its existence through public announcements and lobbying in Parliament. Protests against the liquidation of the theater have become protests against the legislative vacuum, growing centralization, and the willful subjective decision making of those in power. This self-realization has culminated in the theater hosting political discussions in cooperation with Radio Free Europe and the Foundation for a Civil Society, begun successfully in 1995 under the name *The Bugles Are Calling* and in which time is given to the whole spectrum of political opinion. From there it was only a short step to the creation of a center for alternative arts (and, I would add that given the current state of political division in society, a center for the alternative perception of life).

The Stoka Theater thus, in a kind of predestined way, has freed itself from state patronage. Why predestined? All public activity in Slovakia today is confronted with society's division into two camps: the

---

[2] Darina Karova, *Teatro*, June 1995.

coalition camp and the opposition camp. If an activity defies the state's control, it automatically falls into the opposition camp, regardless of the participants' intentions. For example, one declared priority of the present government's cultural policy is an adherence to national roots. Simply put, all activities pronounced "Slovak" or "national" get a green light. Blaho Uhlar is well known for his strong nationalist feelings, which he declared by signing the "Sixty-Six Steps to Slovak Independence" before the division of Czechoslovakia. In spite of this, he is viewed as a persona non grata. The Stoka has become a political theater even though this was not its original intention and seems to become more political with each production. But what kind of politics does it advance? The Stoka Theater's productions reflect the impact of politics on people, the hidden, officially secret face of politics. It holds up a mirror of social reflection to uprooted existence and decadent evil, but also to a touching cleanliness and humanity amidst the sewage.

Closer to "The Sewer" through Postmodernism

Fixed Collective Improvisation as a Guarantee of Diversity

In his interviews with the press, Blaho Uhlar has repeatedly emphasized that he no longer believes in a rational perception of the world. In his productions, he breaks with realist narrative, heralds the death of unified characters, decentralizes the subject matter, and shatters conventions of perception. It may not be coincidental that the actors at the Stoka are so different from one another in their creative and physical characteristics. This alone promises diversity. A method of using a fixed collection of improvisations based on a series of "meta-texts", which become increasingly detached from life, is considered by the Stoka to guarantee an end to the theater of "mimesis" or imitation, which tries to represent the text by enriching, or impoverishing, it through interpretation. The subject of the improvisations is not determined, but only roughly indicated, either by a common setting, or general topic, like "childhood" in *Blind Man's Bluff*. The Stoka Theater's productions have no beginning and no end, their structure is free. In a way, they are never-ending stories, a series which at any moment we can switch on or off, without missing any part of the plot. By preparing a production in this way, talented artists have a better chance of attaining the kind of theater Artaud desired.

The Midwife and the Medium

When I write the word "actor" in discussing the company of the Stoka Theater, I always hesitate. For me, "actor" is too closely knit with names such as Laurence Olivier or Ursula Hopfner ... What is ultimately meant by the word "actor" does not apply here. Some actors at the Stoka Theater actually lack what is known as technique and are sometimes reproached for that. Vocal range and its cultivation, for instance, allow an actor at a repertory theater to control a large auditorium and to express a wide range of emotions. The actors at the Stoka Theater have a much smaller space at their disposal (they can actually reach out and touch the audience) and they play themselves for the most part. Technical virtuosity is somehow superfluous here and would even seem almost untrustworthy. An actor at the National Theater portrays a character within the context of the text, the direction, and the design concept. He also represents the character to the best of his ability while keeping his own individuality in the background. Thus, the actor in this situation becomes a medium for the expression of the theatrical piece, a part of a whole. At the Stoka Theater, every actor is an island, a microcosm. Each actor is an author of the piece: simultaneously the work's creator and its instrument. At this theater, the director is not a dictator, but a kind of "midwife" who assists at the birth of a new, relatively independent entity. In *The Heather*, a girl crawls from behind a dark curtain on her elbows. She clenches a box of matches in her teeth, and rattles them, shaking her head. To question dramatic character here would be ridiculous and pointless.

Not a single Stoka company member was trained as an actor. This is not a priority. A performance thus is similar to a séance in which the actor assumes the role of medium. If the medium goes into a trance, then he can receive and relate a message from a higher sphere, a message which can reward all the participants with an Artaud-like experience of transcendence.

Closer to "The Sewer" … through Gender Characteristics

The recurring themes of family, safe haven, and community with which the Stoka Theater works, along with the name of the theater itself (in Slovak, the word *stoka* is of feminine gender) and all the connotations it conveys represent a strong feminine element. I have already mentioned that as a director, Blaho Uhlar is a kind of midwife. "I have never been capable of forcing contexts on people," he says. His staging is very feminine. His approach is primarily emotional, intuitive, agnostic: the world cannot be understood, the work of art cannot be interpreted – we can only approach it, "surround" it. This approach, of course, can be extraordinarily difficult to understand. A critic with preconceived rational criteria can miss the whole point of a production, as was the case with the excellent French theater theoretician Patrice Pavis when he attended a performance of *Eo Ipso* at the Stoka Theater in the spring of 1995.

Poor, Weak Form: Patrice Pavis and the Stoka

Patrice Pavis maintained that one cannot claim to be searching for new theatrical forms when one is working on a level already attained elsewhere. Though interested in the contrast between high culture and the proletarian world in the production, he commented on the insufficient use of music, light, and space. He considered the form to be too poor and too weak to "withstand an audience." This is how Pavis, who understands Slovak and who is interested in Slovak culture evaluated the performance which many Slovak critics had referred to as the "event of 1994." *Eo Ipso*, written collectively by the company of the Stoka Theater, was published in the leading Czech theater magazine, *World and Theater*, and many consider it to be the best contemporary Slovak play. Why did Pavis miss the point of the production? Why is there such a discrepancy between his opinions and those of the local critics? Perhaps it is because of the production's above-mentioned detachment from rationality, which from the logical, masculine point of view is an incomprehensible feminine approach. In addition, in the work of the Stoka Theater, a typically Slavic spirit of innate sorrow, a certain self-absorption, and a slightly different set of values from those understood and respected in western countries are always present. In this particular case, the intercultural transfer did not occur.

She – Stoka; *He* – Pitinsky

Perhaps Stoka's production of *The Pantry* would have appealed to Pavis more because it was staged by a strongly opinionated director with a rational approach to staging theater. The meeting between the feminine Stoka Theater and the masculine working methods of the Czech director J. A. Pitinsky signaled a host of problems and hopes from the very beginning: for the first time, the company was influenced by a "foreign element." Pitinsky's approach is entirely different from that of Uhlar. Pitinsky uses written texts, always respecting the authors. He maintains a calligraphic direction book and is very thorough in his preparation of a complicated concept for the play. His productions are intricate structures, full of well-crafted connections and refined artistic sensibility, overloaded with expressive details and often almost obsessively ornamental stylization. As a director, he approaches the actors as a governing and moving force. He sees them as a means of achieving a detailed vision founded on the text and adjusts their work in order to precisely fulfill the concept. In this respect his method of directing is very classical. Judged from the viewpoint of gender characteristics, it is a typically dominant male approach.

On opening night, I could see a form of acting in which the "oppression" of the direction was apparent. The actors did not appear to feel free in their roles. As it turned out, a solid structure was hidden under this somewhat uncertain appearance, a structure which did not collapse even after Pitinsky left Bratislava and the typical "post-opening night process" of adaptation, improvement, and relaxation of form began. This process, which is also feminine in nature, has culminated recently in a balancing of the masculine and feminine principles within the production which as a whole has moved into a more relaxed state while retaining its ingenuity and depth.

In Conclusion

The first professional theater in Slovakia was founded in 1920, but the real development of professional Slovak theater did not start until after World War II. As the independent Slovak Republic was created only recently, some self-absorption is understandable to a certain extent. However, I am convinced that it is not in our best interest. As far as I know, what all Slovak artistic achievements of any value have in common is a deep understanding of the national phenomenon combined with outstanding inspiration from abroad. I am convinced that the denigrated, troubled waters of the Stoka, the Sewer, long polluted by experimental foreign influences, reflect the whole Slovak universe.

1996

UKRAINIAN THEATER

FOREWORD

Les Tanyuk

European civilization is only now recognizing Ukraine as the new state in its center. With a territory of over 60 million hectares and a population of approximately 52 million, of the former Soviet republics, Ukraine is second only to Russia in size. Only the fall of the Kremlin "monster" has made it possible for Ukraine to become an independent state.

During the Soviet occupation, the conservatism of the Ukrainian villages was the guardian of the Ukrainian nation as the proletarianized socialist cities had not withstood the pressure of Russification, amorality, and ruthlessness. The spiritual vacuum of post-communism is slowly being filled by culture and religion. In Ukrainian theater, as in Ukrainian art in general, two tendencies can be discerned. The first is connected to Ukraine's return to Europe. The second is connected to the return to our own sacred national values. In fact, Ukraine is a heiress to Kievska Rus, to the traditions of Ukrainian Cossacks, to the golden days of Ukrainian Baroque. It assimilates the achievements of the modern twentieth century Ukrainian art (Malevich, Kandinsky, Les Kurbas) and the achievements of Russian, Baltic, Polish, and Czech drama. The State Center of Les Kurbas was recently created in Ukraine with the goal of uniting the above mentioned tendencies and of developing alternative projects on contemporary culture, above all in the realm of theater.

Nowadays in Ukraine, the interest in mass manifestations has abruptly changed to an interest in the individual. Theater is modeling life on its own, in an experimental way. Now, new drama studios are working here, Ukrainian productions were presented at the Torun and Edinburgh festivals as well as in New York, Avignon, Paris, and Moscow. The new Ukraine greedily familiarizes itself with the works of Artaud, Grotowski, Barba, and Strehler, and explores the cultural traditions of Japan, Africa, the Middle East, and Latin America.

Certainly it is much more difficult to come out from under psychological slavery than to declare a new state. Old artistic ideas still show through new dramatic forms. Many talented people had to emigrate from Ukraine in the days when the pressure of communism was especially strong. Nowadays, there is still a lack of bright, creative individuals in Ukraine, but the overall brightness of the theater scene, the variety of plays, performances, temperament, and quantity compensate for this deficiency. One can say that despite the difficulty with which the arts exist during this transitional period, the Ukrainian theater has overcome the crisis and survived. It has survived by mustering all of its strength and continues its never-ending battle against routine, stagnation, and falsehood.

UKRAINIAN THEATER: ON AN UNEASY PATH TO SELF-AWARENESS

Anna Lypkivska

"Kiev is not Moscow, and Ukraine is not Russia!" read huge banners hung on every street corner in Kiev on the occasion of American President George Bush's visit to the newly independent Ukraine. This slogan contained not only a political message, but a cultural one. Over the last few years, the arts in Ukraine have been searching for their identity, roots, and role in European culture with great difficulty. The search has been taking place under trying circumstances at a time when everything, from simple daily routine to the highest of ideals, has been shattered. These times have shaken the ground under our feet. The past has become unknown, the present diminished, and the future problematical. Besides, the fall of the Empire is coinciding not only with the end of the century, but of the millennium itself: we are suffering from mini-apocalypses. Freedom, which we now have, is still "freedom from" rather than "freedom to." Artists at present do have more opportunity to express what they had once only cherished inside, but having escaped the rigid ideological regimentation of the past, they are now caught in an economic trap. There is little possibility for the kind of serious creative activity that has nothing in common with the loud, commercial productions that are currently enjoying success. Most theater professionals prefer to keep silent or turn to other fields. Nevertheless, in comparison with the early 1980s, recent years have brought with them many more interesting and, more importantly, varied cultural events. Many young people have turned to drama, and they are the ones who will lead us into the third millennium.

The Ukrainian theater certainly has much to offer the rest of the world. Its history dates back 400 years. The first examples of "academic drama" appeared in the late sixteenth/early seventeenth century. At approximately the same time, Vertep (the original national puppet theater) also began its development. Professional theater has existed in Ukraine for almost 200 years. The twentieth century has been characterized by a strong avant-garde movement. Unfortunately, the vitality of the Ukrainian national character is not, and cannot be, fully revealed in the arts today due to the country's many social and economic problems.

Independent Theaters: Key Features of
the New Theatrical Landscape

From the mid 1920s through the late 1980s, only government-run theaters existed in Ukraine. Prior to 1987, when the first independently run
theaters were formed, there were over 50 state-run drama theaters alone.
The oldest, most powerful of these were the "academic theaters", founded
in Kiev during the first few years following the Revolution, 70 to 75 years
ago. Professional theaters also existed, all organized and run by the government. In the realm of theater, as in all others, any private initiative
was forbidden during those years. The arts could exist only within the
framework of official ideology and the rigid structure of government
institutions. By nature a public and collective art, the theater especially
was unable to sustain any kind of "underground" life. Although there
were amateur drama groups that had more freedom than their professional counterparts, they too were attached to corresponding government institutions and were under their control. After the political changes
in the late 1980s and early 1990s, many new, professional, black-box
type theaters appeared in most major cities (such as Lvov and Odessa)
and in some smaller towns (such as Sevastopol and Uzhgorod). They
were all founded as privately managed, independent ventures, created
for the most part by ambitious theater professionals. How many of these
theaters opened is impossible to determine, but an unofficial count
would seem to indicate over one hundred in Kiev alone. Some of these
theaters never in fact produced anything. Some produced only one or
two shows, while others are already securely established. These theaters
were created in a variety of ways. Most grew out of amateur collectives.
Others were formed by actors and directors who could not find their
place in the state-run theater system, or who were not satisfied with the
type of work they were doing and were looking for creative freedom.
New theaters also appeared to serve those theatrical genres for which no
professional theaters had existed before, such as pantomime, variety
revues, and folk drama. Theaters also opened that are available on
a rental basis to directors with independent productions, or to groups
with special limited-run projects. This assimilation of western theatrical
venues is very new to Ukraine. Few people are old enough to remember
the non-regulated drama of the 1910s and 1920s.

Thanks to these new theaters, cultural life brightened somewhat,
but unfortunately, no great changes occurred. Many independent theaters failed to survive. Having been founded more on personal ambition
than on original ideas, most simply could not compete with the state-run
theaters. Often working out of basements and other cramped, inadequate
spaces, they were unable to profit financially. Under the prevailing
circumstances of economic instability and galloping inflation, it was next

to impossible to find sponsors. Traditionally, Ukrainian audiences have consisted primarily of intelligentsia and young people. Unfortunately, these sectors of the population have fallen well below the poverty line and can no longer afford the cost of theater tickets. The nouveau riche on the other hand, have other leisure-time priorities. This explains why the independent theaters are now "backpedaling", trying once again to receive state support. Some of the better established ones have already succeeded in doing this. The government is constantly trying to cut expenditure on the arts, sciences, and education. Considering the deplorable state of the economy, this is not surprising, however, it is very shortsighted. Theaters and other cultural institutions are waiting in vain for changes in tax laws, but in the meantime, it is simply unprofitable to sponsor the arts. A system favorable to those who are in a position to support the arts must be created. Still, theaters are happy to get scanty subsidies from the government. These grants more or less cover operating costs and salaries.

It is understandable that under the pressure of so many difficulties, only the strongest theaters have survived. At the most recent Festival of New Theaters in Kiev (held every two years), 17 independent drama theaters were accounted for. Only nine of them are still in business. This means that only 16 drama theaters (including state theaters), are currently operating in Kiev, a city of almost 3 million inhabitants.

Aleksey Kuzhelny's drama studio, Constellation, is located in the center of Kiev, in a Secession-style building with marble stairs and oak-paneled rooms. During the winter, fireplaces are kept ablaze. There is no permanent acting company here. Different actors, directors, designers, and composers from various theaters are brought in for each production. Constellation is best known for the brilliant work of famous Kiev actors, for its staging of the plays of the Hungarian president Árpád Göncz, and Pope John Paul II, and for hosting festivals of chamber theater and one-act plays.

The Kiev Experimental Theater, under the leadership of Valery Bilchenko, first opened with a production of A. Shypenko's play, *Archeology*. The theme of this production was nostalgia for lost illusions. The characters wandered about amidst sand and old newspapers, mouthing empty dialogue, in a world where their only memories of the past were preserved on washed-out clips of film. *And B Says* ... was a production based on two other plays by Shypenko. A very different type of performance, it used abrupt, grotesque combinations of genres and languages. Bilchenko and his company have also created a cycle of street performances, a form which they are continuing to experiment with. Their production of Chekhov's *The Cherry Orchard*, entitled *Shot in the Autumn Garden*, was voted Best Production of 1994 in Kiev. Staged in a suite of rooms in an old house, it united lyricism and eccentricity.

A little girl played with a spaniel amidst apples hanging from the ceiling, people came and went, a cuckoo clock ticked away, comic skits were performed while waiting for the results of the auction, and in the final scene, Gayev shot himself in the empty house. The Experimental Theater does not have its own permanent premises. It currently performs at the Kiev-Moglylianska Academy and the most recent premiere of *The Eastern March* was staged in the recreation hall where bookshelves line the walls.

Young Kiev theater-goers fondly recall the white walls of the cellar of the Drama Club. Under the guidance of Oleg Liptsyn, it became famous for its productions of works by Cocteau and Mrozek among others. Especially noteworthy were its productions of *Antigone* by Sophocles, and of *Dyushes*, based on James Joyce's novel, *Ulysses*. The building and its famous cellar are currently closed for renovations, and with Liptsyn living and working abroad, plans for future productions are on hold.

The arts association Budmo! (Let's Be), led by Sergey Proskurnya, is a group of young, creative administrators who produce works by contemporary Ukrainian authors, such as Lina Kostenko (the first Ukrainian poetess), the American-Ukrainian B. Boychuk, and the avant-garde poet O. Lysega. They arrange open-air happenings. They have done two joint projects with the Yara Arts Group from New York's experimental LaMama Theater. They are currently working on *To Be the Child in Europe*, in conjunction with British, German, and Italian theater groups. Budmo! is associated with Mystetske Berezillya, an annual international festival of avant-garde theater. In 1995, it was held for the fourth time and attracted 46 theaters from 7 countries. During the 32 day long festival, 103 performances and artistic events took place. Berezillya is currently the most important theater festival in Ukraine.

Vladimir Kuchinsky at the L. Kurbas Youth Theater in Lvov works with classic works from national and international literature and drama. Only here can one see on stage the dialogues of G. Scovoroda, a famous Ukrainian vagrant philosopher of the baroque era, side by side with a trilogy of performances based on Dostoyevsky's novel *Crime and Punishment*. Kuchinsky experiments with different states of consciousness, physical space, and emotional atmosphere. Based on the teachings of Jerzy Grotowski, his work is the primary example of the Europeanized side of intellectual Ukrainian culture.

The cafe-theater Koleso, under the guidance of Irina Klischevska, is a kind of Kiev version of the burlesque theater. Koleso is based in a small house on the famous Andrejevki Uzviz Street (almost opposite the museum house of M. Bulgakov). A richly imaginative company, it manages to produce diverse, high quality performances on its tiny stage.

There are several other small independent theater companies worth mentioning. Olexandr Balaban's Studio Theater is best known for staging plays by Maeterlink, Gelderode, and Lovinescu among others – works which were formerly almost unknown in Ukraine. Vera Mishneva's Creative Drama Theater of Kiev performs imaginative adaptations of such philosophically rich works as Racine's *Phaedra* and Anatole France's *Thaïs*. The Actor Theater was founded by the wonderful Kiev actor Valentin Shestopalov. It is best known for its passionate production of Gogol's psychological tale, *Diary of a Madman*. The Kiev Podol Theater, under the guidance of Vitaly Malakhov, is a pioneer among the new theater companies. Rarely seen at home, his productions tour widely abroad. Most recently, his production of *Iago* (based on Shakespeare's *Othello*) was staged in a swimming pool for the Edinburgh Festival, but has never been performed in the Ukraine. The very first private theater established after the political changes was the Bravo Theater. Its sponsor, Lubov Tytarenko, gambles on productions with big box-office appeal, casting famous, popular actors in every major role.

Due to current economic conditions, no new theater companies have been formed recently. Instead, the practice of producing shows with a limited run is becoming more widespread. The most notorious and expensive of these projects was *Who's Afraid of the Gray Wolf?*, based on Edward Albee's *Who's Afraid of Virginia Wolf?* and directed by Andrey Joldak. Among the sponsors were Philip Morris and the Fund for the Development of the Arts in Ukraine, headed by former Ukrainian president Leonid Kravchuk. Because the idea of theater management as a separate profession is still relatively new in Ukraine, all organizational, administrative, and financial responsibilities fall onto the shoulders of the directors. In addition to their creative duties, they must also find their own sponsors, funding, actors, etc. While the enormous advertising campaign for *Who's Afraid*... far outshone the actual performance, if nothing else Joldak certainly proved his managerial abilities. And although other Ukrainian directors have not yet been so enterprising, no doubt other projects will be realized in this way in the future.

Today, many artists and directors do not want to be tied to any one theater and prefer to free-lance. The resulting dilemma is how to preserve the repertory theaters which have their own advantages and traditions. It is obvious however, that the coexistence of all the various types of theater companies is most conducive to the realization of many different kinds of projects.

Reviving Multiculturalism in the Theater

There were times when not only was Ukrainian theater being performed in St. Petersburg, but Polish, Jewish, German, and Romanian theaters were all in existence in Ukraine. All of them closed sooner or later, but during the last few years of the Soviet regime, people again began searching for their national roots. A few Jewish theaters opened in Ukraine (the best known being the Mazltov Theater in Kiev, under the direction of G. Melsky), a Tartar theater opened in Crimea, a Hungarian theater opened in Zakarpattya, and *Roma*, a gypsy theater, opened in Kiev under the direction of I. Krykunov. The problems facing these theaters are the same as those facing all Ukrainian theaters, but with some peculiarities: most noticeably a shortage of trained personnel with the appropriate ethnic background. For example, although courses in Hebrew have been started at the Drama Institute in Kiev, there are still few actors who speak the language. Only the Hungarian Iyesha Theater operates on a fully professional level. The others are viewed more as exotica, seen, if you will, as the "color on Ukraine's dramatic palette." They must still mature and must attract broader audiences than the ones they currently address, which are united by common language, but not by any sense of national pride or community. Until they do so, their future is uncertain.

In contrast, none of the Russian theaters in Ukraine have closed. They exist side by side with Ukrainian theaters and have their own audiences. However, Ukraine is very rural, and the promotion and development of Ukrainian culture is of central importance to the government. Therefore, only theaters producing Ukrainian plays and plays performed in Ukrainian are eligible for state subsidies.

Cleaning the Augean Stables

For decades, the Ukrainian theater was bound by the narrow framework of Socialist Realism. Theater had to be "nationalist in form, but socialist in content." The theater must now rid itself of the stereotypes and bad habits it acquired under that system in order to face its future. The past few years have been like "cleaning the Augean stables" and the theater, not so resolute as Hercules, is proceeding slowly.

True national identity, cultural roots, and genuine traditions must be separated out from stereotypes resulting from excessive socialization. Essentially all of Ukraine's history was rewritten under the Soviet regime and falsified. National literary works that were formerly taboo are now of special interest to the theater as a result of a renewed interest in reassessing Ukrainian history.

Until recently, performances of Ukrainian national drama relied heavily on superficial portrayals of picturesque ethnic life. Peter Brook's definition of "dead theater" was a very apt description of this kind of Ukrainian theater. In these productions, there was no real understanding of ethnic reality or understanding of the original ideas underlying traditional staging conventions. Ukrainians' special musical talents were often touted as an excuse for inserting ridiculous and badly performed musical divertissements into dramatic productions. In general, a lack of aesthetic experimentation and conceptual thinking predominated.

The most successful theaters today are trying to shake off the burden of these old habits and start anew with a fresh perspective. Successful productions are now characterized by their unexpected approach to familiar situations and characters. Young directors are attempting to shake clean classic plays from their rigid traditional staging in order to lay bare their mythological core and to find the universal theme which binds them to audiences of all ages. To meet the need for new approaches to history, many new historical plays have been written and produced, such as *Dictate of Consciousness* by M. Shatrov, and *Children of Arbat* by A. Rybakov. Over the last few years, many brilliant period plays have also been staged successfully.

A New Repertoire

Before the breakup of the Soviet Union, all Ukrainian theaters were repertory companies: permanent acting troupes producing approximately 15 plays per season. Every play was performed at least once a month. New plays were performed four to five times a month. Every season, three to six new plays would be staged. Shows could stay in the repertoire for many years, as was the case with *The Stolen Happiness*, which opened in 1979 at Kiev's I. Franko Theater and has been performed 300 times since. The repertoire of the new black-box type theaters is not so extensive as this of the larger state theaters, and they produce fewer new shows. Another major change is that old thematic restrictions are little by little being overcome. Repertoire was formerly under severe governmental control, with quotas for producing classic Russian and Ukrainian plays, contemporary plays, western plays, etc. The pool of permissible authors was rather limited. The repertoire of the provincial theaters duplicated the repertoire of the Kiev theaters, which in turn copied the repertoire of the theaters in Moscow and St. Petersburg. Except for very slight differences in the national plays being produced, playbills from different theaters were practically indistinguishable from one another.

Today, staging Ukrainian plays is extremely important. Unfortunately, there are almost no new plays being written by Ukrainian playwrights. Old Soviet-style playwrights are either dead or not working anymore. Ukrainian versions of Russian plays from the "new wave" of the 1970s and 1980s belong to that era and are not called for by today's audiences. Those authors no longer write for the theater, dealing mostly nowadays with film scripts and adaptations, or working for the government.

Plays by younger playwrights seem to be in the shape of postmodern literary games, approaching a "stream of consciousness" style which is then chopped up into dialogue. Most of these plays contain witty turns of phrase, precise observations, and original philosophical maxims, but are not so much dramatic works as they are literary ones, and provide few possibilities for scenic interpretation.

Because of the scarcity of good new Ukrainian plays, in their search for new diverse repertoire theaters have turned to classic national and foreign drama, or to shows with no real story line, like the "street actions" by V. Biltchenko's Experimental Theater and the open air happenings organized by S. Proskurnya. Formerly, there was a set of ten or fifteen plays which were considered national classics. Recently, this set has been expanded to include works by V. Vinnichenko, Lesyia Ukrainka, O. Oles, S. Cherkasenko, and I. Kocherga among others. Some of these plays are waiting to be staged for the first time. Paradoxically, while theaters now have the freedom to choose their own repertoire, they are now restrained by the fact that many foreign plays have not yet been translated into Ukrainian. Nevertheless, theaters have begun to fill the holes in their repertoires with formerly prohibited plays by writers such as Nabokov, Berberova, Averchenko, and Voynovich. The names of Harold Pinter, Sam Shepard, Tennessee Williams, Beckett, Joyce, Prévert, Wilder, Ionesco, and Büchner are appearing in playbills for the first time. Initially introduced to the public by new theaters and young directors, these authors are now included in the programs of the older state theaters as well. Most theaters have certain plays in their repertoire that can only be seen there. For example, Salinger's *The Catcher in the Rye* can only be seen at the Chernigov Youth Theater.

Directing in Ukraine: An Ongoing Intrigue

The director Les Kurbas was the most remarkable figure of twentieth century Ukrainian theater. His influence can be compared to that of Gordon Craig, Stanislavsky, and Meyerhold. The Ukrainian school of directing is still suffering the consequences of his devastating defeat in the mid 1930s. Kurbas's followers continued their work and went on to train another generation, but their spirit was broken. Ukrainian drama, although always maintaining a tradition of high professionalism, never produced another Kurbas, or even a director like Sturua in Georgia or Efremov in Russia. Bright young artists with original ideas were excluded from the theater for so long that dull, mediocre productions became the norm.

Now, however, for the first time it is possible to speak not only about talented individuals, but about an entire generation of creative young directors. The directors of the new generation are between 25 and

35 years old and include, among others, Valery Bilchenko, Oleg Liptsyn, Vladimir Kuchinsky, Andrey Zholdak, Andrey Krytenko, Olexandr Balaban, Sergey Klyapnev, Stephan Pasichnyk, and Dmitro Bogomazov. Their shows are the most brilliant products of the free, post-Soviet theater. Essentially post-modernists in approach, their productions deny social engagement of any kind. Their theater stays aloof from life's realities and irrationality prevails. One extreme leads to another: decades of imposed realism and collectivism have led to this backlash of subjective, individualist, and sometimes egocentric theater. These directors use the text only as a kind of creative springboard. Their aim is not so much to support the text as to create a unique, self-contained world on stage. Borrowing text and symbols from wherever they want, their performances are not comedies, farces, or dramas, but dreams, hallucinations, and recollections. This kind of theater destroys all stereotypes, for actor and audience alike. This is a theater of white and black boxes, endless chairs, and monochrome costumes. A theater of long coats and rumpled hats – of things from grandmother's attic, and of civilization's waste: styrofoam, empty bottles, old newspapers. A theater of extremes, where Gregorian chants can accompany half-forgotten folk tunes, it seems to be simultaneously mystery and hoax. This type of theater is obviously transitional in character, but is clearing a path for these directors. Young directors with a more harmonious (although still somewhat pessimistic) approach to the world include Roman Markholia, Atilla Vidniyansky, and Dmytro Lazorko. It is still difficult to say what the future will hold for this generation of directors and it will be an ongoing intrigue.

Of course, it cannot be claimed that this new generation appeared out of the blue. V. Opanasenko, I. Molostova, V. Gripich, A. Novikov, A. Barsegyan, and A. Sytnik are representative of a senior generation of directors: imaginative, inventive, and knowledgeable about contemporary drama, they come from the older, realist school of theater that is tinged with conventionalism. Sometimes successful, sometimes not, their shows are essentially museum pieces which time has left behind. There are however notable exceptions to the rule.

Sergey Danchenko, currently the head of the I. Franko Theater, is a member of the senior generation of directors whose work is of special interest. The critic Olexandr Sakva accurately described Danchenko's directorial style as "epic commentary." Over the last few years, Danchenko has experimented with mixing serious drama and musicals. Together with the ingenious designer D. Lider, he staged the most popular Ukrainian show of the last decade, *Tevie-Tevel*, by G. Gorin, based on Sholom Aleichem.

Eduard Mitnytsky, the founder and director of the Drama and Comedy Theater in Kiev, is responsible for one of the most extraordinary and controversial productions in recent years: *The Seagull*, by Chekhov, produced at the Lesyia Ukrainka Theater. Mitnytsky is a precise director, capable of ruthless psychological analysis through sometimes excessively eccentric means. His shows are always characterized by brilliant acting, and are at once traditional and contemporary.

Alla Babenko from Lvov and Mikail Reznikovich are two other masters of directing. Babenko is the original "impressionistic" director who prefers plays from the so-called Silver Age, while Reznikovich is a firm mathematician and moralist.

Igor Borys, head of the T. Shevchenko Theater in Kharlov, is one of the youngest directors. He is a master of large scale scenic shows. In his productions, the hero's fate always correlates with general universal laws. For example, the Fool in his production of *King Lear* climbs up an enormous mechanism on stage and swings on a huge pendulum.

Mykola Yaremkiv is a follower of R. Viktiuk, and in many ways he carries on his teacher's methods of working with actors and staging productions. He builds his shows on contrasts: mixing masks with bare faces, burying serious concepts and experiences inside capricious external designs. His best work was a production of *Largo Desolato*, by Václav Havel in Kharkov.

Finally, Genady Kasyanov is responsible for creating one of the youngest and most promising theaters in Ukraine, the Chernigov Youth Theater. This theater grew out of a puppet troupe and has come a very long way from the modest but sincere productions of its past to its present performances of classical plays and adaptations by Nabokov, Salinger, Shakespeare, and Ukrainka.

Many Ukrainian directors work abroad. Only one has come back home: Valentin Kozmenko-Delinde has returned to Kiev after working for many years in Moscow and Pryashev. He attracted audiences' attention at once with his adaptation of *Kobzar* by T. Shevchenko, produced at the I. Franko Theater. As *Kobzar* is a collection of poetry, a sort of Ukrainian Bible, the director was taking a considerable risk. However, he gambled and won. He now runs the Kiev Youth Theater.

Ukrainian Actors: The Pride of the National Theater

In spite of all Ukraine's problems, past and present, the theater has always had indisputable achievements, and the main one is probably the high quality of its actors. Among Ukrainian actors, one can find highly educated intellectuals; individuals of spontaneous emotions and gentle humor; philosophers and pragmatists; wilful actors, emotional actors, and intellectual actors; actors who have perfected their technique to such a point that their hold over the audience is absolute, but intangible.

For many years, actor training in this country was rather one-sided. Simple, straightforward interpretations of roles were all that were expected from performers. Nowadays, the variety of theatrical styles and genres, and directors' unleashed imaginations all require actors with more technical skill. Les Kurbas had a system for the multifaceted training of actors. According to his vision, the actor was like an "intelligent Harlequin." Today, rigorous training, like that which A. Vidniyansky puts his actors through, forecasts an optimistic future for Ukrainian performers.

Because acting is not a very prestigious profession in Ukraine, there is not much sympathy for unemployed actors. It is a pity, but some of Ukraine's best actors and actresses simply don't have the opportunity to appear on stage very often. However, on a more optimistic note, conditions seem to be improving, and every evening, actors still appear on stage, live and die there, and allow the audience to forget their problems and look for the beauty, sense, and harmony in their own lives.

The Great Potential of Ukrainian Scenic Design

After an impressive boom in the late 1970s and early 1980s, Ukrainian scenic design is in a crisis. Before, scenic designers appeared to be well ahead of the times conceptually. Now, however, it is an epoch of compulsory "poor theater." Many productions are forced to use stock costumes and props. The task of achieving the maximum visual effect every time through tremendous effort and minimal facilities has apparently lost its appeal to designers. On the other hand, when a theater does find funds, many designers immediately create lavish sets and costumes, regardless of the fact that the expensive solution might not always be the most appropriate one.

Danylo Lider, the father of Ukrainian scenography, recently celebrated his 75th birthday before retiring from theater. The design for *Tevie-Tevel*, by G. Gorin, directed by S. Danchenko, was Lider's masterpiece. In this production, one little candle on the proscenium turned into a seemingly endless scattering of stars, and throughout the performance the stage was surrounded by lights. When asked about his design, Lider replied, "I am an accidental guest on Earth... . There are no signatures on my work and there never have been. What for? There is no point to the work. It is never finished. I live with it. I only search for originality. *Tevie* is about exactly this. I don't know who created the world, or how, but it is always surprising to me. I believe in God's existence, you know, because I myself have created my own world on the stage. Skovoroda, Gogen, God – they were all wise men, wanderers. Ever since I was small, I've wandered about alone, thinking. My mother would swear at me – 'Where did you vanish to?'. 'To the woodshed.' 'And what did you do there?' 'I was hitting the wood and listening to the sound float away into space...'." Lider left the theater after *Tevie* on purpose, believing that one should leave while at one's peak. However, he still teaches future designers at the art academy and paints. Lider's stories about his imaginary productions are more interesting and alive than many real productions.

Many designers make a living by working in film, selling paintings, or working abroad. Nevertheless, the strongest are still working in theater. These include Andrey Olexandrovych, a pupil of Danylo Lider who became the resident designer at the I. Franko Theater after Lider's retirement; Alexander Semenyk; and the very young Yury Larionov who has become very visable due to his strong work in Kiev and Beregovo. Other working designers include Natalya Rudyk, Olena Bogatyryova, and Lyudmyla Kovalchuk. Ukrainian scenic designers have enormous potential which could be fully realized if only there were more funds at their disposal.

Problems Facing Theater Critics

In Ukraine there has always been a small but strong vanguard of theater critics. For many years, critics had to be "ideologically consistent", extolling certain events and remaining silent about others. Critics had to pay more attention to the ideological content of a show than to its aesthetic aspects. In the past, critics received a rather broad education and, from the very beginning, were closely tied to theater institutions and schools throughout the USSR. Certainly, no school for drama criticism existed in Kiev as it did in St. Petersburg. Despite this, professional Ukrainian critics do exist who can analyze and express ideas well, and who have a clear understanding of drama and of culture in general. Most critics live and work in Kiev. The situation in the provinces is more complicated. For the most part, outside Kiev and other major cities, local journalists review theater productions, and since they have no theatrical training, their approach is quite different from that of a trained critic. Many regional theaters are upset at this situation. They feel deprived of sophisticated, professional commentary about their work. There are simply not enough critics to cover all the professional theaters spread out through 35 cities and towns in Ukraine. The reasons behind the insufficient number of critics are a general lack of regard for the profession and low salaries. Nevertheless, this is slowly changing and more and more young people are turning toward careers in drama criticism. This is due in part to the increase in non-government controlled media. Arts programs are being broadcast on new television channels and radio stations, and are gaining popularity. However, there is still a need for theatrical press in Ukraine. At the moment, only one bimonthly theater magazine exists and only one weekly newspaper, *Culture and Life*, which reserves one column for theater reviews every other week. Many critics dream of serious theatrical magazines and newspapers, but under today's economic conditions, they are not likely to become a reality. A much more serious problem is Ukraine's isolation from outside information. The old communication networks within the former USSR have broken down. New connections with colleagues abroad are only beginning. Travel abroad and advertisement in foreign press is unaffordable. Foreign scripts are simply not being translated. Information about theatrical activity outside Ukraine only trickles into the country sporadically. Directors, actors, designers, and critics all devour whatever information they can find: little clips of video tape, bits of printed reviews, or verbal accounts by the occasional eye-witness.

The Ukrainian Theater and the Rest of the World

Despite its informational isolation, Ukraine is slowly beginning to integrate itself into world theater. Not only are certain theater companies traveling abroad and participating in international festivals, but foreign professionals are also coming to Ukraine. Ukrainian directors working abroad (either permanently or on special grants) include G. Glady in Canada; O. Liptsyn in Austria, Germany, and the United States; A. Krytenko in the United Kingdom and Germany; A. Furmanchuk and I. Opanasev in the United States; and M. Nnarodnetsky in Israel. A. Zholdak staged a performance in Paris, Kozmenko-Delinde worked in Pryashev for many years, and A. Vidniyansky produced his thesis performance in the former Yugoslav Republic. Budmo! and the L. Kurbas Youth Theater in Lvov participated in several joint projects with the Yara Arts Group from the United States, the Del Solo Theater from Italy, Snap from Great Britain, and Spielwerke from Germany. The Grotowski center's *Slavonic Pilgrims* program sent a group of young actors from Lvov to continue their education in Pontedera. Foreign visitors to Ukraine included E. Bez from Germany who participated in a production at Budmo!, and K. Kolstrupp from Denmark who collaborated with V. Bilchenko. *Terra Incognita* by G. James was staged by the American Neil Simon at the Koleso Theater in Kiev. A theater troupe from Turkmenestan performed in Lvov. Five years ago, such events would have been considered extraordinary, but today they are accepted without surprise.

On its Way to the 21st Century

While members of the older generation of theater makers have been working abroad, it is primarily members of the younger generation who have been out actively trying to "conquer the world." This new generation with its completely different psychological make-up and understanding of their profession is coming of age and, in the process, allowing the Ukrainian theater little by little to adapt to international culture. The educational level, abilities, and creativity of today's Ukrainian theater-makers allow them to take their place in this process. There may still be a lack of communication with the rest of the world, but in the words of former Soviet leader Gorbachov, "the process has begun, and it is irreversible." The Ukrainian theater is overcoming the inertia of its Soviet past. It is trying to find its own identity and to compare itself to the rest of the world. It is trying every day to find answers to many questions: How to become integrated into European culture without losing national cultural integrity? How to present Ukrainian plays and artists to the rest of the world? How to preserve professional standards and produce beautiful, passionate productions under extremely difficult economic conditions? Only one thing is certain: our theater will survive. There is constant talk, in every age, of the "crisis of the theater." But the theater lives according to its own inscrutable laws. Its real treasures sometimes reveal themselves when least expected. So, the Ukrainian theater is not experiencing a post-Soviet crisis. It is only experiencing life, with all its problems, defeats, and victories. And that is not easy in and of itself.

1995

NOTES ON CONTRIBUTORS

Valda Carake, Ph.D. is an Associate Professor at the Department of Latvian Literature at the University of Latvia where she has been teaching since 1983. She is the author of many articles in Latvian magazines, journals and almanacs. Her research and publications concentrate on theater and drama. She was a recipient of a five-month Fulbright research grant at the University of Wisconsin, Madison, USA in 1993.

Leonid Chemortan, Ph.D. is a Moldavan theater critic and theater historian. He is the author and coauthor of many books and publications on theater and culture. Since 1991 he has been head of the Institute of Art History and Theory at the Moldovan Academy of Arts and Science. He is a corresponding member of the Moldovan Academy of Arts and Science.

Mihai Cimpoi is a Moldovan writer and theater critic. Since 1991 he has been president of the Moldavan Writers' Union and a member of the Moldavan Academy of Arts and Sciences. He is a member of Romanian Writers' Union as well. He is the author of many articles on theater and books on literature.

Marina Constantinescu is a Romanian drama critic, editor of *Romania Literara* magazine, and drama critic for Radio Free Europe.

Krisztina Galgoczi is a Hungarian freelance theater critic. She is mostly interested in contemporary Hungarian and British drama, and international theater life.

Árpád Göncz is a leading figure in the Hungarian literary and political life. After the Hungarian revolution of 1956 he was sentenced to life in prison and was released from jail only after the amnesty of 1963. From 1963 to 1990 he worked as a freelance writer, translator, and playwright. He is the author of many plays, short stories, and a novel. He has translated authors like William Faulkner, Sam Shepard, and John Updike. Since 1990 he has been the President of the Hungarian Republic.

Anton Donchev is a an internationally renowned Bulgarian writer. He is a nominee for the Jane and Irving Stone award for best historical novel. His novel *Time of Parting* has been published in 26 languages.

Anna Gruskova, Ph.D. is a Slovakian theater critic, theater historian, journalist and a lecturer in the Slovak Academy of Music and Dramatic Arts. She is editor-in-chief of the *Meantime* journal devoted to the young and innovative culture. She is a member of the artistic jury of the Divadelna Nitra International Theater Festival in Slovakia.

Václav Havel was born in Prague on October 5, 1936. Because of his "bourgeois" background, his education options were limited. Havel studied at the Economics Faculty of the Czech Technical University from 1955 to 1957, and after compulsory military service began working in theater. He joined Prague's Theater Na Zabradli in 1960, where his plays enjoyed their first international success. From 1962 to 1966, Havel studied dramaturgy at the Academy of Performing Arts in Prague. He was active in the Prague Spring era of reforms which ended with the Warsaw Pact invasion in August 1968. Havel actively opposed the invasion and the resulting hard-line Communist policies and in 1969 his work was banned in Czechoslovakia. In 1977 Havel became a co-founder of the Charter 77 human rights initiative. He was under house arrest in 1978–79 and was incarcerated several times for his beliefs. In November 1989 Havel became one of the leaders of Civic Forum, the opposition movement that helped bring about the end of Communist rule. On December 29, 1989 he was elected president of Czechoslovakia. The new freely elected Parliament re-elected him on July 5, 1990. Havel resigned on July 20, 1992 as the country headed for dissolution. On January 26, 1993 Havel was elected the first president of the Czech Republic. Havel's plays have been performed around the world and, along with his essays and speeches, have been translated into many languages. Books in English include *Letters to Olga, Disturbing the Peace, Open Letters: Selected Writings 1965–1990, Selected Plays,* and *Summer Meditation.* Václav Havel is the recipient of numerous international awards.

Ismail Kadare is a world-famous Albanian writer and poet. He is a Nobel-prize nominee. Most of his works are translated into many languages. He now lives in France.

Zofia Kalinska is a Polish actress and theater director. For 20 years she was a member of Tadeusz Kantor's company Cricot 2. Later she found an all-women company in Poland. Her Polish productions have toured Poland, France and England. She has directed shows in Britain and Norway, and has taught masterclasses in Britain and Australia. Her show *Plaisirs d'Amour* is a winner of a 1991 Edinburgh Fringe First Award.

Darina Karova is the head of the Divadelna Nitra International Theater Festival in Slovakia, part-time dramaturg at the Slovak National Theater and head of the Association of the Slovak Theater Professionals. She is a lecturer at the Slovak Academy of Music and Dramatic Arts as well.

Tomasz Kitlinski is a Polish theater historian and performance artist. He is the author of essays, prose and poetry published in Poland, France, and England. He has presented his performance art throughout Poland and in Scandinavia, and Britain.

Theodor Laco is an Albanian writer, playwright and scriptwriter. His books of short stories have been published in France, Russia, Italy, Greece, Bulgaria, Turkey. He was accused of liberal viewpoints and was transferred from Tirana to Fier city where he worked in the theater for seven years. In 1991–1992 he was head of Albania Filmstudio. Since 1994 he has been the Albanian Minister of Culture, Youth and Sports.

Anna Lipkivska, Ph.D. is a Urkainian drama critic, professor of Theater Criticism and Drama Arts at Kiev State Institute of Drama Arts, and drama correspondent of the weekly newspaper *Program*. She is the author of over 150 articles on theater.

Yury Lyubimov is a Russian theater director, famous at home and abroad for his theater innovations and courage. He started his career as an actor at the Vachtangov Theater where he worked afterwards as a theater pedagogue as well. In 1964 he created his famous Taganka Theater out of a class of his students. He is considered the pioneer of the poetic theater movement which was an overt opposition to the dogmas of the official theater in the USSR. In 1982 he was forced to leave Russia. For the next seven years he staged theater and opera in Western Europe. In 1989 he returned to Russia and his theater.

Jana Machalicka, Ph.D. is a Czech theater critic and theater historian. For ten years she worked at the Theater Institute in Prague, first as a musical theater specialist, then (after 1989) as a specialist of Czech theater in big cities and regions as well. She was subsequently promoted to a head of the Theater Department and became an editor for the Institute's magazine. She reviews theater for Czech daily papers, well known magazines and the Czech Radio. At present she is the theater editor for the daily paper *Lidove noviny.*

Nikolae Manolescu, Ph.D. is a professor of Romanian literature at the faculty of Letters in Bucharest, literary historian, theater critic and author of twenty books. Since 1989 he has been a senator. At present he is president of the International Festival of Professional Young Theater in Sibiu as well.

Ramune Marcinkeviciute is a Lithuanian theater critic and theater historian teaching at the Department of Theater and Film at the Academy of Music in Vilnius, Lithuania. She is the author of many articles and TV programs on Lithuanian theater. She works as a theater expert at the Ministry of Culture as well.

Eimuntas Nekrosius is a Lithuanian theater director internationally famed for his bold imagination and original interpretations of literary texts. He graduated from the Moscow State Institute of Theater. From 1979 to 1993 he worked as a director at the State Youth Theater. His productions have been performed to rave reviews in Poland, Finland, Italy, USA, Switzerland, Russia, Israel, Sweden, Slovakia. In 1991 the Taormina Art Committee and the European Theater Union awarded him with a special prize for his contribution to the theater. In 1994 he received the award of the Baltic Assembly and the Grand Prixes at the festivals of Saint Petersburg and KONTAKT, Poland. At present he collaborates with the Lithuanian International Theater Festival (LIFE).

Raimonds Pauls is an internationally renowned Latvian composer of popular music. His compositions include musicals, ballets, and instrumental music for concerts and theater productions. He has conducted the Riga Light Music Orchestra of the Latvian State Philharmonic Society (1964–1971) as well as other professional groups (1972–1983). In 1988 he became the chairman of the Latvian State Culture Committee. At present he is the culture councillor of the president of Latvia.

Andrei Serban is an internationally renowned Romanian theater director who has worked with inspiring range of international artists – from opera companies and traditional Japanese theater-makers to experimental performers. From 1990 to 1994 he was the artistic director of the Romanian National Theater in Bucharest. Since 1993 he has been head of the Oscar Hammerstein Center for Theater Arts at Columbia University in New York as well.

Krassimir Spasov is a leading Bulgarian theater director famous for his detailed work with his actors and for the extraordinary psychological exquisiteness of his shows. He has directed over 80 theater productions and two feature films over the last 30 years. From 1990 to 1995 he was one of the staff directors at the National Theater in Sofia. He is a recipient of many national awards for directing, including the most famous one – ASKER. Some of his most popular recent productions are: *Vassa Jeleznova* by Gorky, *The Seagull* by Chekhov, and *The Night of the Tribads* by Ber Uluv Enkvist. Spassov is also a professor of directing and acting at the National Academy of Theater and Film Arts in Sofia.

Kalina Stefanova, Ph.D. is a Bulgarian theater critic and theater historian. She is the author of three books (two published in Bulgaria and one in England) and more than 100 publications in Bulgarian and foreign periodicals. She is an editor of the first ever Bulgarian-published anthologies of contemporary American and British theater criticism and of an issue of *Contemporary Theatre Review* on contemporary Bulgarian Theater. From 1990 to 1992 she was a Fulbright Visiting Scholar at the Department of Performance Arts of the New York University, USA. In 1996 she won a five-month British Council Visiting Scholarship at City University of London. At present she is an Assistant Professor of Theater Criticism at the National Academy of Theater and Film Arts in Sofia.

Les Tanyuk is an Ukrainian producer of more than 50 theater shows, author of scripts and film producer of 15 films, writer, composer, editor of 12 books, poet, publisher, translator. Since 1992 he has been head of The Union of Drama Activists of Ukraine. At present he is a deputy of the Supreme Council of Ukraine and vice head of the parliamentary commission of culture.

Kudret Velca, Ph.D. is an Albanian drama critic and a Professor of Theater History and Theory of Drama at the Academy of Fine Arts in Tirana. From 1965 to 1969 he was exiled for his dissident views. His writings were banned from publication for 10 years (1973–1983). He has written many books and articles on theater, literature and culture.

Nina Velekhova is a Russian writer, journalist and theater critic. She is author of many articles and books on modern theater, playwriting, cinema, poetry, ballet, and culture.

Ann Waugh is an American set designer. She has been working as Broadway and Hollywood designer Tony Walton's associate since graduating from New York University (major Set and Costume Design), as well as pursuing her own freelance design career. With Mr. Walton, she has collaborated on feature films, opera, ballet, dramatic plays and several Tony award-winning musicals, including *Guys and Dolls* and *She Loves Me!*. She has personally designed over twenty theatrical productions over the last five years in the US and in Bulgaria, working with directors such as Christopher Durang, Woodie King, and Liviu Ciulei. She has twice won the Princess Grace of Monaco Foundation award for excellence in design.

INDEX

A. Mateevitch Theater, Moldova, 160
ABC Theater, Czech Republic, 51
Abramkova, Tatiana, 206
Abramov, Fyodr, 2
Abuladze, Tengiz, 206
Academic Theater, Moldova, 158, 159
Academy of Fine Arts, Albania, 10
Academy of Music, Lithuania, 104
Academy of Theater and Film,
    Romania, 190
Academy of Theater Arts, Albania, 10
Actor Theater, Ukraine, 235
Actors' Hall, Latvia, 90
Actors' Studio, Poland, 178
Adalbert, St., 52
Adashev, A., 82
Aesopean, language, 30, 83
Akademia Ruchu Theater, Poland, 173
Akolli, Dritero, 16
Akvinsky, Foma, 211
Albec Edward, 31, 235
Aldwych Theatre, UK, 1
Alexa, Felix, 190
Alexander Moisiu Drama School,
    Albania, 10
Alexandri, Vasile, 153, 159, 160, 163,
    164
Aleykhem, Sholom, 239
Alfea, 21
Alive, 206 i
Alternativa 2000 Theater, Albania, 17
Amadeus, 161
America, 172
Amphitrion, 175
Anatoly Vassiliev, 70, 173, 207, 209
Ancient Trilogy, The, 188, 192
And B Says …, 233
And Elements of Retribution, 203
*And They Put Handcuffs on
    the Flowers*, 194

Andersen, Hans Christian, 161
Andreyev, Leonid, 207, 211
Angels In America, 177
Anouilh, Jean, 109, 210
Antigone, 172, 234
Anton Pann Theatre in Ramnicu
    Valcea, Romania, 193
Arcadia, 177
Archa Theater, Czech Republic, 49
Archeology, 233
Ardent Heart, 208
Aristophanes, 159, 163
Arrabal, Fernando, 14, 193
Art Theater in Panevezys, Lithuania,
    108
Art Theater, Hungary 70
Art Theater, Latvia, 82
Artaud, Antoan, 161, 223, 229
As You Like It, 191
Ascher, Tamas, 68
Askenazy, Ludvik, 44
Aspern Letters, The, 207
At the Gates of Paradise, 208
Augean stables, 21
August, August, August, 50
Auskaps, Karlis, 84, 85, 86
Averchenko, Arkadi, 206, 238
Awakening, The, 104
Azarjan, Krikor, 34

B. Shchukin Theater School, Russia,
    156, 157, 162
B.P. Hashdeu Theater in Kagul,
    Moldova, 159
Babel, Isak 206
Babenko, Alla, 240
Balaban, Olexandr, 235, 239
Bald Prima Donna, The, 14, 15, 75, 162,
    163, 194, 195

Balladyn, 175
Baltic Spring Theater Festivals, Latvia, 88
Barba, Eugenio, 17, 229
Barber of Seville, 53 i
Barbukov Theater, Bulgaria, 29, 30
Baron Otto von Futtinghoff, 82
Barron, Christopher, 191
Barsegyan, A., 239
Basilashvilli, Oleg, 206
Bathhouse, The, 106
BBC, 1, 2
Beaumarchais, 208
Beauty of Amherst, The, 109
Beckett, Samuel, 7, 14, 15, 32, 70, 104, 162, 172, 206, 238
Bednarika, Jozef, 56
Beggar's Opera, 44
Belfast Opera House, UK, 191
Bennent, Anne, 69
Bennett, Alan, 53
Berberova, 238
Bergman, Ingmar, 109, 111
Bernhard, 172
Bertolds, Janis, 89
Betrayal, 93
"Bible '94 Festival, The", Finlandia, 92
Bilchenko, Valery, 233, 238, 239, 243
Bishop, David, 163
Black Stretched Theater of Frantisek Kratochvil, Czeck Republic, 50
Blaumanis, R., 89
Blazing Darkness, The, 95
Blez, 109
Blumbergs, Ilmars, 84
Boccaccio, 193, 196
Bogatyryova, Olena, 242
Bogomazov, Dmitro, 239
Bogosian, Eric, 36
Bojanowska, Ela, 174
Bokor, Petre, 187, 191
Boll, Heinrich, 68
Bolshoi Drama Theater, Russia, 207
Bolshoi Theater, Russia, 203
Bonjour, Madame …, 111
Book of Ruth, The, 91, 92
Bora, Armando, 15
Borchert, Wolfgang, 107

Boris Godunov, 206, 207, 208
Bork, Tom, 175
Borogina, Emil, 187
Boruzescu, Miruna, 185
Boruzescu, Radu, 185
Borys, Igor, 240
Boychuk, B., 234
Bozsik, Yvette, 68
Bradecki, Tadeusz, 176
Bravo Theater, Ukraine, 235
Brecht,Bertolt, 1, 31, 53, 107
Brilliant Orchid, 208
British Council, 191
Brno National Theaters, Czech Republic, 55
Brook, Peter, 173, 178, 190
Brothers and Sisters, 2
Brothers Grimm, 161
Brouhaha International Festival, Liverpool, UK, 17, 174
Bruckner, Anton, 207
Buchner, Georg, 72, 238
Budapest Chamber Opera, 72
Budapest Spring Festival, 74
Budmo! Theater, Ukraine, 234, 243
Budzisz-Krzyzanowska, Teresa, 171
Buero-Vallejo, A, 95
Buffes du Nord, France, 190
Bugles Are Calling, The, 221
Bulatovic, 174
Bulgakov, Mihail, 164, 207, 234
Bulgarian Army Theater, 26, 32, 34
Burdonsky, Alexander, 208
Buresova, Hana, 53
Burien, Jan, 44
Bush Theatre, UK, 191
Bush, George, 231
Busuiok, Aureliu, 159
Butnaru, Valeriu, 160, 163

Cabal and Love, 207
Cabaret, 54
Cabinet of Dr. Cagligary, The, 172
Cacahuite, Turbo, 111
Cafe Theater 1, 16
Caks, A, 85, 86
Calderon, de la Barca, 53

Caligula, 106
Camus, Albert, 55, 106, 112
Cantemir, 153
Carajiale Festival in Bucharest,
    Romania, 162
Carajiale, Ion, 153, 159, 161, 164
Caramitru, Ion, 187, 189, 191
Card Index, The, 177, 195
Caretaker, The, 93
Carmen, 191
Carmina Burana, 173
Carnegie Hall, USA, 176
Carreri, Roberta, 17
Cassandra, 172
Catcher in the Rye, The, 238
Cats, 73
Ceausescu, Nikolae, 183, 188, 193
Celetna Theater, Czech Republic, 49
Central Bohemian Theater, Czech
    Republic, 49
Central European Dance Theater,
    Hungary 72
Central Theater, Albania, 10
Cerha, Jiri, 52
Cerny, Jindrich, 45
Chagall, Marc, 97, 196
Chamber Theater, Czech Republic, 49
Chamber Theater, Hungary, 71
Chang Eng, 195
Chapek, Karel, 161
Charms, 112
Cheek By Jowl, 191
Chekhov Theater, Russia, 204, 207
Chekhov, Anton, 34, 45, 54, 68, 82, 87,
    90, 95, 101, 107, 111, 112, 161, 163,
    172, 174, 208, 233, 239
Chekhov, Mikhail, 82, 105
Chelovek Studio Theater, Russia, 209
Cherkasenko, S., 238
Chernigov Youth Theater, 238, 240
Cherry Orchard, The, 34, 45, 107, 192,
    233
Chesky Krumlov, 48, 49
Chibotaru, Ion, 163
Children of Arbat, 237
Chinese, The, 66
Chinoherni Klub, Czech Republic, 43,
    44, 45, 49

Chinoherni Studio, Czech Republic, 43
Chinoherni Studio in Usti nad Labem,
    Czech Republic, 49
Chkeidze, Temur, 207
Chodakowska, Anna,
City of Drama Festival in Manchester,
    UK, 190
City Stage, Czech Republic, 48
City Theater of Zlin, Czech Republic,
    54, 56
Ciulei, Liviu, 185, 187, 191, 192, 193
Civic Forum, 41
Claudel, Paul, 52, 55
Clavijo, 50
Clown Theater, Russia, 211
Cmurosja, 15
Cocteau, Jean, 112, 234
Columbus, Christopher, 181
Comedie Francaise, 173
*Comedy About Hamlet, the Danish
    Prince, A*, 206
Comic Theater, Hungary, 65
Comic Theater, The, 193
Constant Prince, The, 1
Constellation Drama Studio, Ukraine,
    233
Country, Wait!, 160
Covetous Knight, The, 206
Cox, Brian, 191
Cracow's Theater School, 172
Cracow's Witkiewicz Festival, Poland,
    172
Craig, Gordon, 238
Craziness of Grandeur, The, 14
Crazy For You, 73
Creanga, 153
Creative Drama Theater of Kiev,
    Ukraine, 235
Creditors, The, 106
Cricot 2 Theater, Poland, 169, 172
Crime and Punishment, 234
Critics' Award, Edinburgh, UK, 173
Crucible, The, 73
Csaba, Antal, 67, 69
Csakanyi, Eszter, 69
Csanyi, Janos, 72, 74
Csongor and Tunde, 69
Cupchia, Valeriu, 156

Cyrano, 50
Czar Feodor Ioannovitch, 208

Dabija, Alexandru, 187, 197
Dada von Bzdulow Theater, Poland, 174
Daile Theater, Latvia, 84, 85, 87, 97
DAMU Acting Studio, Czech Republic, 49
Danchenko, Sergey, 239
Dangerous Liaisons, 161, 163
Daniel Leon, 32
Darie, Alexandru, 191, 197
Daubeny, Peter, 1
Daugava, The, 85 i
Daugavpils Theater, Latvia, 93, 95, 96, 97
Dautartas, Julius, 108
David, Karel, 56
Day Over a Hundred Years, A, 108
Days of the Turbines, 207
Dead Class, The, 171, 172
Death and the Maiden, 105
Deaussoy, Jean, 191
Debussy, Clod, 190
Decameron 645, 193, 195, 196
Dejvice Theater, Czech Republic, 49
Del Solo Theater, Italy, 243
Delirium for Two, 52
Demons, 55
Demonstration, The, 191
Deszcz, Katarzyna, 174
Dialogue Theater, Bulgaria 28, 29
Dialogue Magazine, 177
Diary of a Madman, 235
Dictate of Consciousness, 237
Dobchev, Ivan, 35
Docekal, Michal, 49, 50, 54
Doctor Zhivago, 206
Dodin, Lev, 2
Dodov, Nikolai, 30
Dog, The, 90
Dolmieu, Dominique, 16
Domino Theater, Russia, 210
Don Giovanni, 49
Don Juan, 45, 53, 69, 172
Don Quixot, 35
Donnellan, Declan, 190, 191

Dorfman, Ariel, 105
Doronina, Tatiana, 207, 208
Dorosevich, Vlas, 206
Dostoyevsky, Fyodor, 53, 55, 70, 83, 97, 208, 234
Dr. Herz, 73
Dracula, 56
Drama and Comedy Theater, Ukraine, 239
Drama Club, Ukraine, 234
Drama Institute, Ukraine, 236
Drama School, Albania, 10
Drama Theater in Galati, 187
Drama Theater of Klaipeda, Lithuania, 106
Drama Theater of Panevezys, Lithuania, 106
Drama Theater, Lithuania, 105
Dream Play, The, 107, 109, 111
Dream, The, 67
Dromgoole, Dominic, 191
Drutse, Ion, 159
Druzhina, Marin, 210
Duchamp, Marcel, 174
Dullin, Charles, 106
Dumb Waiter, The, 93
Duras, Marguerite, 94
Durov, L., 210
Durova, Teresa, 211
Durrenmatt, Friedrich, 15, 44, 107, 164
Dyushes, 234
Dzene, Lilija, 89
Dziuk, Andrzej, 178

E.F. Burian Theater, Czech Republic, 48, 49
Eastern Europe under the Tsar, Stalin, and Post-Communism, 177
Eastern March, The, 234
Edgar, David, 191
Edinburgh Festival, UK, 173, 190, 191, 229, 235
Efremov, Oleg, 207, 238
Efros, Anatoly, 91, 207
Eftimin, V., 159
Eglitis, Anslavs, 89
Eight and a Half (and a half), 54
Eight and a Half, 54

8 Persons Plus, 16
Electra, 192
Elephant, The, 106
Eminescu, M, 153, 160
Eminescu, Nicolae, 160
Encounters Festival in Lodz, Poland, 174
Endgame, 104
Engelova, Lida, 51
English Theater Company, Poland, 175
Eo Ipso, 223, 224
Erdman, Nikolai, 208
Eremin, Yury, 208
Esrig, David, 185
Estates Theater, Czech Republic, 49, 55
Eszenyi, Eniko, 72, 73
Eugene Ionesco Theater of the Absurd, Moldova, 159, 160, 162, 164
Eugene Onegin, 191
Euripides, 107, 193, 206
European Voodoo Doll, A, 174
Evening Theater, Czech Republic, 48
Excelsior Children's Theater, Romania, 189
Exiles, The, 54
Exit The King, 162, 163
Experimental Theater, Ukraine, 238
Eyre, Sir Richard, 191

F.X. Shalda Theater, Czech Republic, 48
Fando and Lis, 14, 15
Fanko, Serafin, 15
Faulkner, William, 96
Faust, 44, 53
Festival of Theater Schools, Poland, 174
Fedor, Marek, 176
Feldmanis, Ernests, 82
Fellini, Federico, 54
Fernando Krofti Wrote Me This Letter, 15
Festival of Experimental Theaters in Cairo, Egypt, 162
Festival of Gombrowicz's Dramas, Poland, 174
Festival of Hungarian Theaters from Neighboring Countries, 75

Festival of New Theaters in Kiev, Ukraine, 233
Festival of Street Theater, Poland, 174
Filippo, Eduardo de, 15
Filozov, A., 211
Fire and the Night, The, 95
Flowers for Algernon, 50
Fokin, Valery, 173
Fomenko, Pyotr, 207, 210
Forced Entertainment, Poland, 178
Forefathers' Eve, 1
Formal Theater, Russia, 211
Forman, Milos, 46
Foundation for a Civil Society, 221
Four Days in June, 84
France, Anatole, 235
Free Theater, Bulgaria, 29
Frehar, Jiri, 52
Freibergs, Andris, 84
Freibergs, Edmunds, 89, 90
French Association of Artistic Action (AFAA), 190
French-Romanian Theater, Romania, 189
Fringe First Award, Edinburgh, UK, 172, 173
Frycz, Jan, 175
Fulfola, 211 i
Fund for the Development of the Arts in Ukraine, 235
Funny People Theater, Lithuania, 108
Furmanchuk, A., 243
Fust, Milan, 71
Fusu, Mihai, 162, 164

Gabor, Tompa, 187, 191, 194
Gadilich Theater in Belts, Moldova, 164
Gaidys, Povilas, 106
Galileo, 107
Gallerova, Vlasta, 52
Garas, Dezso, 70
Garden Party, 44
Gardzienice Theater, Poland, 173
Geikins, A, 85
Gelderode, 235
Genet, Jean, 54, 172
Ghetto, 196, 197

Giants from the Mountains, 45
Ginkas, Kama, 209
Giurchescu, Lucian, 185, 187
Glady, G., 243
Glancova, Helena, 45
Globiesz, Krzystof, 175
Glowatcki, Janusz, 177
Goethe, Wolfgang von 50, 56, 96
Gogol Theater, Russia, 207
Gogol, Nikolai, 54, 71, 108, 112, 156, 208, 235
Goldoni, Carlo, 73, 159, 193
Gombrowicz, 69
Goncharov, Andrei, 206
Göncz, Árpád, 233
Gooch, Steve, 177
Goose On a String Theater, Czech Republic, 54
Gorbachov, Michail, 157, 203, 243
Gorin, Grigori, 239, 241
Gorky Theater, Russia, 204, 207
Gorky, Maxim 106, 207
Gotchev, Dimitar, 25
Government Inspector, 54, 185, 208
Govorukhin, Stanislav, 203, 206
Gozzi, Carlo 159
Grabbe, 53
Grand, Adriana, 196
Grass, Gunther, 178
Great Wonder, The, 15
Grecu, Sandu, 163
Griboyedov, 207
Grichuk, Dimitriu, 163
Gripich, V., 239
Grossman, Jan, 44, 52
Grotovsky Center, 243
Grotowski, Jerzy, 1, 96, 169, 171, 172, 173, 229, 234
Grupa Chwilowa, Poland, 173
Grusas, Juozas, 104
Grzegorzewski, Jerzy, 172
Guardian, The, 190
Gugutse Theater, Moldova, 164
Guilty without Guilt, 207

Halasz, Peter, 66
Half Past Six, 160, 163
Hall, Sir Peter, 178

Hamlet, 53, 68, 171, 173, 176, 178
Hamsun, 208
Handke, Peter, 107
Hashdeu, B.P., 159, 161
Ha-Theater, Czech Republic, 56
Hausvater, Alexander, 187, 191, 193, 194, 195
Havel, Václav, 45, 46, 240
Heather, The, 223,
Hello, Sonya New Year, 112
Hello, Tolstoy, 67
Hercules, 105
Hercules, 21, 236
Hermanis, Alvis, 94, 95
Heroic Comedy, 207
Herr Puntila and His Servant Matti, 31, 53
Higher School for Theater, Cracow, Poland, 176
Hila, Edi, 15, 16
Hodga, Enver, 11
Hodoronk-tronk, 160
Hoffmann, E.T.A., 96
Hofmannstahl, Hugo von, 45
Hollywood, 63
Hopfner, Ursula, 222
Horacky Theater, Czech Republic, 48
Horansky, Milos, 51
House by the Sea, 173
House of Bernarda Alba, The, 53, 90
How Pisar Tricho Didn't Marry Princess Kita, 32
Hrubanicova, Ingrid, 218
Hugo, Victor, 68
Hungarian Theater of Cluj Kolozsvar from Romania, 75
Hunting Scenes from Lower Bavaria, 53
Hyden, Michael, 110
Hynes, Garry, 191
Hysi, Ferdinand, 15

I. Franko Kiev Academic Theater, 237, 239, 240, 242
I.L. Carajiale National Theater Festival, Romania, 189, 193
Ibsen, Henrik, 54, 71, 83, 87, 90, 107
Idiot, The, 53
Iliev, Boiko, 29

Illegitimate Daughter, The, 56
Impossible Person, The, 45
Impressions de Peleas, 190
In Venice, Everything Was Different, 160
Independent Theater of Budapest, 75
Ines, Zofia de, 172
Inopportune Theatre, Romania, 189
Institute of Theater Arts, Russia, 108
International Association of Theater
    Critics (AICT), 189
International Merlin Theater, Hungary,
    67
International Organization of
    Scenographers, Technicians and
    Theater Architects (OISTAT), 189
International Slovak Theater Festival
    Divadelna Nitra, 221
International Theater Festival BITEF,
    Yugoslavia, 110
International Theater Festival of
    Chicago, USA, 108
International Theater Institute (ITI),
    189
Ioan Frunza, Victor, 187, 196
Ion Kryange Company, Moldova, 159
Ionesco, Eugene, 7, 16, 32, 52, 75, 104,
    162, 194, 195, 206, 238
Ionescu, Petrica, 191
Iures, Marcel, 190
Ivanov Family, The, 208
Ivanov, 112
Ivona, Princess of Burgundia, 69
Iyesha Theater, Ukraine, 236
Izvestia Newspaper, 205, 205

J. K. Tyl Theater, Czech Republic, 44
J. Myron Theater, Czech Republic, 48
James, G., 243
Jancevska, Zan. 90
Janda, Krystyna, 175
Jarocki, Jerzy, 175, 176
Jarry, Alfred, 106, 188
Jeles, Andras, 67
Jero, Minush, 11
Jesus Christ Superstar, 55
Jewish State Theater, Romania, 197
Jewish Theater, Poland, 178
Jinta Latine Theater, Moldova, 160

Joldak, Andriy, 235
Jonynas, Ignas, 112
Jordan, Tamas, 67
Joseph and His Concubine, 160, 163
*Joseph and the Amazing Technicolor
    Dream Coat*, 73
Joyce, James, 54, 234, 238
Judith, 17
Julliard School, USA, 110
Jung, Carl Gustav, 174
Jurasas, Jonas, 105, 106

Kacer, 43
Kacs, Arkadijs, 83
Kafka, 107, 172
Kafka's Dick, 53
Kagul Theater, Moldova, 160
Kalanovski, Veselin, 29, 30
Kalinska, Zofia, 172
Kaloc, Zdenek, 55
Kame, Gezim, 15
Kamra Studio, Hungary, 66, 72
Kandinsky, Vassily, 229
Kanensky, A., 210
Kanovicius, Grigorijus., 107, 111
Kantor, Tadeusz, 1, 2, 107, 169, 171, 172
Kapkov, 106
Kapolcs Art Weeks, 75
Kaposvar Theater, Hungary 69
Karasek, Milos, 218
Karova, Darina, 220
Kasatkina, Ludmila, 208
Kaspar Theater group, Czech
    Republic, 54
Kasperek, Joanna, 177
Kasyanov, Genady, 240
Kathchen of Heilbronn, 175
Katona Jozsef Theater, Hungary, 64,
    65, 66, 68, 69, 70, 190
Kaunas Drama Theater, Lithuania, 106
Kerare, Petrum, 159
Keys, Daniel, 50
Khlebnikov, Velimir, 211
Khomsky, Pavel, 207
Khutsiev, Marlen, 210
Kichinev Ionesco Festival, Moldova, 14
Kiev Experimental Theater, Ukraine,
    233, 234

Kiev Podol Theater, Ukraine, 235
Kiev Youth Theater, Ukraine, 240
Kiev-Moglylianska Academy,
    Ukraine, 234
Kimele, Mara, 83, 91, 92, 94
King Lear, 91, 173, 185, 240
Kishinev Art Institute, Moldova, 157
Kishinev Municipal Theater, 159
Kishinev Poetry Theater, Moldova, 156
Kistol, Igor, 163
Kitajevs, Marts, 84
Klaipeda Drama Theater, Lithuania,
    104
Klavina, Elita, 95
Kleist, Heinrich von, 68, 72, 96, 175
Kleist's Death, 68
Klicpera Theater, Czech Republic, 54
Klim Masterskaya Theater, Russia, 210
Klimenko, 210
Klischevska, Iryna, 234
Klyapnev, Sergey, 239
Kobzar, 240 i
Kocergo, 106
Koch, 11
Kocherga, I., 238
Kohout, Pavel, 44, 50
Koinakov, Yavor, 27, 28
Koleso Cafe-Theater, Ukraine, 234, 243
Koleso Studio Theater, Russia, 205
Kolowrat Palace Theater, Czech
    Republic, 55
Kolstrupp, K., 243
KONTAKT International Festival,
    Poland, 173
Korca Theater, Albania, 11
Korsunovas, Oskaras, 112
Kosenkova, N., 211
Kostenko, Lina, 234
Kott, Jan, 91, 178
Kovalchuk, Lyudmyla, 242
Kozmenko-Delinde, Valentin, 240, 243
Kracik, Petr, 53
Krapp's Last Tape, 104, 173
Kraus, Karel, 45
Kravchuk, Leonid, 235
Kreisler, Georg, 197
Krejca, Otomar, 45, 53
Krilovs, Peteris, 95, 96, 97

Kriz, Karel, 44, 52, 53
Krobot, Miroslav, 55
Kroders, Olgerts, 83, 90
Kronis, 85 i
Krushchov, Nikita, 185
Krusnohorsky Theater, Czech
    Republic, 48
Kryange, Ion, 160
Krykunov, I, 236
Krytenko, Andrey, 239, 243
Kublinskis, Mihails, 85, 89
Kuchinsky, Vladimir, 234, 239
Ku-Ku TV Show, 35
Kumbaro, Arben, 14, 15
Kuncewicz, Maria, 175
Kurbas, Les, 229, 238, 241
Kurrochkin, Pavel, 211
Kushner, Tony, 177
Kutaj, Z., 16
Kuzhelny, Aleksey, 233
Kuznetsov, 203

La Bottega del Caffe, 73
La Punala, 191
La Strada Theater, Bulgaria, 30, 35
Labyrinth Theater, Czech Republic, 43,
    46, 47, 49, 52, 53
Lachmann, Piotr, 177
Laclos, Choderlos de, 161, 163
Lacplesis, 83, 85, 86
Lady in the Country, 163
LaMama, USA, 234
Landovsky, Pavel, 44
Landsbergis, Algirdas, 104
Large Glass, 174
Largo Desolato, 44, 240
Larionov, Yury, 242
Last Night of Socrates, The, 31
Last Ones, The, 106
Last Sacrifice, The, 206
Latvian Academy of Culture, 84
Lay of Igor's Host, The, 211
Lazar, Kati, 67
Lazorko, Dmytro, 239
Le Neveau de Rameau, 185
Lebl, Petr, 51, 53, 54
L'Ecume des Tours, 51

Ledukhovsky, Anatoly, 210
Leeway Art Center in Kaunas,
    Lithuania, 104
Leigh, Vivien, 178
Lenin, Vl.I., 203
Lenkom Theater, Russia, 209
Leonce and Lena, 72
Les Kurbas Youth Theater, Ukraine,
    234, 243
Les Miserables, 55
Lesson, The, 195
Lessons, 211
Let's Live and See, 160
Levant Theater, Romania, 189
Levinta, Doina, 197
L'Homme Qui Rit, 68
Liberated Theater, Czech Republic, 51,
    56
Lider, Danylo, 241, 242
Liepaja Theater, Latvia, 86
Liepins, Zigmars, 83
Life is a Dream, 53
Likuritch Theater, Moldova, 164
Lilium Street Art Center, Hungary, 74
Liptsyn, Oleg, 234, 239, 243
Listener, The, 1
Literature and Art, Latvia, 84 i
Lithuanian International Festival LIFE,
    110, 111, 173
Lithuanian Piano, The, 105
Lithuanian State Academic Drama
    Theater, 104, 106, 107, 109, 111
Little Garden Theaters' Festival,
    Poland, 174
Little Room, 51
Livanov, Aristarkh, 208
Lominski, Tadeusz, 173
London International Festival of the
    Theater (LIFT), 189, 190
Lorca, Federico Garcia, 7, 53, 90
Lost Honor of Katharina Blum, The, 68,
    69, 72
Lothe, Jolanta, 177
Love In the Crimea, 177
Love Theater, USA, 66
Lovinescu, 235
Luarasi, Mihail, 11
Luce, 109

Luchaferul Theater, Moldova, 156, 159,
    164, 165
Lucia Sturza Bulandra Theater,
    Romania, 1, 187, 190, 192, 197
Lucian, Ion, 189
Ludowy Theater, Poland, 178
Lupa, Krystian, 169, 172, 176
Lupan, Emilia, 163
Lupu, Adrian, 187
Lurins, Valdis, 83, 86, 90
Lvov-Anokhin, Boris, 207
Lysega, O., 234
Lysistrata, 163
Lyttleton Theatre, UK, 177
Lyubimov, Yury, 1, 206, 207

M. Eminescu National Theater, 158,
    161, 164, 165
Maculevics, Valentins, 83, 85
Madzik, Leszek, 172
Maeterlink, Maurice, 235
Magdalena Festival in Cardiff, 172
Maghaev, Boris, 206
Magyar Theater in Cluj, Romania, 187,
    188, 194
Mahabharata, 173, 190
Mahler, Gustav, 176
Maids, The, 54, 172
Makovskis, Andris, 93
Malaimare, Mihai, 189
Malakhov, Vitaly, 235
Malevich, Kazimir, 229
Malta Festival in Poznan, Poland, 173
Maly Theater, Russia, 1, 176, 190, 203,
    204, 208, 211
Mandala Theater Company, poland,
    174, 177
Mandate, 208
Mandelshtam, 205
Manea, Aureliu, 185
Maneatsa, Calin, 163
Manie, C., 109
Maniutiu, Mihai, 190, 191, 195, 196,
    197
Mannequin Theater, Russia, 209, 211
Marai, Sandor, 71
Marat/Sade, 69, 71
Marcinkevicius, Justinas, 104

Mariinsky Theater of Opera and
    Ballet, Russia, 204
Markholia, Roman, 239
Markov, Plamen, 27, 32, 35
Marquez, Gabriel Garcia, 163
Madame de Sade, The, 94, 95, 109, 111
Marriage of Figaro, 209
Mary Stuart, 85
Masalskis, Valentinas, 104
Masca Theater, Romania, 189
Master Builder, The, 106
Masters of Time, The, 106
Masterskaya Group, Russia, 210
Matasik, Andrej, 219
Mate, Gabor, 72
Matei, Valeriu, 160
Mausoleum, 72
Mayakovsky Theater, Russia, 204, 206
Mayakovsky, Vladimir, 11, 106
Mazltov Theater, Ukraine, 236
McBurney, Simon, 191
McGrath, Tom, 177
McIntyre, Clare, 177
McKellen, Ian, 191
Medea, 107, 191, 206, 210
Medins, Janis, 95
Meetings Festival, 1
Mein Kampf, 52
Melis, Laszly, 68
Melsky, G., 236
Menshikova, Alla, 163
Menzel, Jirji, 44
Merlin Theater, Hungary, 75
Merta, Zdenek, 56
Metropolitan Playhouse, USA, 110
Meyerhold Creative Center, Russia,
    210
Meyerhold, Vsevolod, 87, 201, 210, 238
Midsummer's Night Dream, A, 56, 72,
    190, 192, 193
Migeni Theater of Shkodra, Albania,
    15, 16
Miller, Arthur, 7, 11, 73, 107, 108
Miltinis, Juozas, 106, 107
Mio, Sokrat, 10
Mirabeau, 86
Miraculous Story, A, 173
Mirzoev, V., 210

Misanthrope, The, 69, 72
Miser, The, 109
Mishima, Y, 94, 95, 109, 111
Mishneva, Vera, 235
Miss Julie, 163
Miss Saigon, 73
Mitkov, Zdravko, 32, 33, 35
Mitnytsky, Eduard, 239, 240
Mladenova, Margarita, 34, 35
Model Theater, 210
Modern Ballet Theater, Belgium
Mohacsi, Janos, 73
Moldavian Institute of the Arts, 164
Moliere, 45, 69, 109, 156, 159, 164
Molostova, I., 239
Monteverdi Birkozokor, Hungary 67
Mooncalf, 172,
Moonlight, 52
Moravek, Vladimir, 54
Morfov, Alexandar, 35
Morgenstern, Maia, 197
Morozov, Boris, 203, 208, 209
Mosa, Stanislav, 56
Moscow Art Theater, 82, 157, 177, 204,
    207, 209
Moscow Kamerny Theater, 82
Moscow Theater Institute, 91
Mossovet Theater, Russia, 207
Mother-of-Pearl Zinaida, 207
Mountain Language, 105
Mozart, W.A., 49
Mrozek, Slavomir 44, 177, 234
Mu Theater, Hungary, 74
Mugur, Vlad, 187, 191
Muller's Dancers, 68, 72
Mummy's Funeral, The, 111
Musical Troupe, Russia, 210
Mystetske Berezillya International
    Festival of Avant-garde Theater,
    Ukraine, 234

Nabokov, Vladimir, 205, 238,
Nagy's Mausoleum, 68
Nameless Star, 163
Narodna Obrodna, 220
National Academy Of Theater And
    Film Arts, 35

National Center for Theater, Bulgaria, 26, 27, 28
National Opera, Latvia, 84
National Theater Festival, Hungary, 75
National Theater in Cluj, 187
National Theater in Craiova, Romania, 187, 188, 193
National Theater in Iasi, Romania, 188
National Theater in Targu Mures, Romania, 188
National Theater in Timisoara, Romania, 188
National Theater, Albania, 10, 12, 14, 16
National Theater, Bulgaria, 26, 28, 34, 35, 36
National Theater, Czeck Republic, 44, 54, 55
National Theater, Latvia, 82, 84, 85, 87, 88, 89, 90, 91, 97
National Theater, Lithuania, 107
National Theater, Poland, 175, 177
National Theater, Romania, 181, 187, 188, 191, 192, 196, 198
National Theater, Slovakia, 218, 223
National Theater, Ukraine, 240
National Theatre in Belfast, 191
Neal, Lucy, 189
Nebesky, Jan, 54
Negrutsi, K, 160
Nekrosius, Eimuntas, 79, 105, 108, 109, 110, 111, 112
Nemeth, Akos, 68
New Riga Theater, Latvia, 84, 91
New Tartuffe or The Guilty Mother, The, 208
New Theater, Hungary 68, 69, 70
New Theater, Russia, 207
Nichols, P., 91
Nightmare Pains (Exodus), 17
Nijinsky, 67
Nikulin, Y., 211
NN Theater, Poland, 174
Nnarodnetsky, M., 243
No Exit, 16
No Man's Land, 67
Noah's Ark, 161, 162

Nobel, 55
Nominatae Filiae, 172
Nose, The, 108
Nottingham Meeting Ground, UK, 172
Novak, Eszter, 69
Novikov, A., 239
Noviks, Ivar, 90

O' Henry, 161
OBER, Russia, 112
O'Brien, Flann, 174
Odeon Theater, France, 176, 190
Odeon Theater, Romania, 187, 190, 191, 194, 196
Odin Theater, 172
Off Festival in Bydgoszcz, Poland, 174
"OK" Group, Russia, 210
Okhlopkov, 206, 210
Old Actress in the Role of Dostoevsky's Wife, An, 207, 208
Old Testament, 92
Old Woman, The, 112
Oles, O., 238
Olesha, Jury, 205
Olexandrovych, Andrey, 242
Olivier, Laurence, 173, 178, 222
On the Boards Theater, Russia, 209
On the Edge of the World, 107
Once Upon a Time There Was a Rider …, 85
One Hundred Years of Solitude, 163
One-Actor Plays' Festival, Poland, 174
O'Neill Theater Center, USA, 209
Onetti, Antonio, 191
Only a Seagull Can Dip Its Feet in My Tears, 218 i
Opanasenko, V., 239
Opanasev, I., 243
Open Forum, Hungary, 73
Orniflis, 109
Ostaszewski, Jacek, 176
Ostrauskas, Kostas, 104
Ostrava National Theater, Czech Republic, 55
Ostrava State Theater, Czech Republic, 43
Ostrovsky, Nikolai, 206, 208, 209

Othello, 235
Our Town, 106

Padegimas, Gytis, 106
Pantomime Theater, Russia, 211
Pantry, The, 224
Panzaru, Anatol, 163
Papyrus '94, 15
Paris Conservatory, 10
Parti, Lajos, 68
Pasichnyk, Stephan, 239
Passion Play, 91
Passion, The, 174
Pasternak, Boris, 206
Pavis, Patrice, 223, 224
Pavlova, Muza, 206
Pecale's Adventure, 160
Peer Gynt, 53
Pegasus, 21
Peleas et Melisande, 190
Pellea, 21
Penciulescu, Radu, 185
People, Lions, Eagles, and Partridges, 211
Peron, Eva, 208
Persona, 109
Petofi Csarnok Art Center, Hungary,
    66
Petrenko, A., 211
Petri, Gyorgy, 69
Phaedra, 193, 235
Philip Morris, 235
Philoctetes, 191
Piatra Neamt Youth Theater, 187
Piccolo Teatro, Italy, 176, 190
Picture of Dorian Gray, The, 95
Pilzen International Theater Festival,
    56
Pinnock, Winsome, 177
Pinter, Harold, 44, 52, 92, 104, 105, 238
Pintilie, Lucian, 185
Pirandello, Luigi, 7, 45, 68, 161
Pirosmani, Pirosmani, 108, 110
Pitinsky, J.A., 54, 224
Plaisirs d'Amour, 172
Platanov, Andrei, 208
Platonov, 68, 72
Plepis, Rudolfs, 93
Plesu, Andrei, 186, 187, 198

Plyushch, A., 211
Pocket Theater, Latvia, 84
Pocket Theater, Moldova, 163, 165
Polak, Roman, 55
Polishchuk, L., 210
Polony, Anna, 176
Poor Murderer, The, 50
Poor, Poor Judah, 211
Popa, V.I., 159
Pope John Paul II, 233
Possessed, The, 1, 96, 208
Post-Auschwitz Impossible Poetry, 177
Potter, Denis, 175
Prague City Theater, 46
Prague National Theater, Czech
    Republic, 55
Prevert, Jack, 238
Prince Charles, 178
Prince of Homburg, The, 175
Princess Turandot, 202
Prokofiev, Sergey, 95
Proskurnya, Sergey, 234, 238
Proteus, 52
Psychic Assault, 86
Pulford, Richard, 191
Pumpurs, A, 83
Punzaro, Anatol, 162
Puppet Theater Festival, Poland, 174
Puppet Theater, Latvia, 84
Purcarete, Silviu, 188, 190, 191, 193,
    195
Pushkin Theater, Russia, 208, 210
Pushkin, Alexander, 206, 207, 208

Qesari, Anton, 16
Qirjaqi, Agim, 14, 15
Quarterly of Radio Dramaturgy, A, 176
Queen of Spades, The, 201

Racine, Jean, 235
Radi, Ferdinand, 16
Radichkov, Yordan, 34
Radio Free Europe, 221
Radnoti Theater, Hungary, 70, 71
Radok, Alfred, 49, 52
Radu Stanca Theater in Sibiu,
    Romania, 195
Radzinsky, Edward, 203, 207

Radzobe, Silvija, 84
Rainis, 83, 87, 92
Rajmont, Ivan, 43, 55
Rappe, Jadwiga, 177
Realistic Theater, Czech Republic, 43
Redevelopment, The, 44
Reid Mayne, 32
Reikhelgause, I., 210
Reinbergs, Augusts, 88
Reinhardt, Max, 1
Reminiscencje Festival in Cracow,
    Poland, 174
Repentance, 206
Replica, 1
Res Publica I & II, 43 i
Revenge, The, 72
Reznikovich, Mikail, 240
Richard III, 14, 190, 196
Rijnieks, Juris, 86, 92, 93, 94
Rise and Fall of Comrade Zylo, The, 16
Ritsos, Janis, 173
Rodrozy, Biuro, 173
Romanian center of ITI, 189
Romanian Center of OISTAT, 189
Romanian Section of AICT, 189
Romanian-Irish Theater, Romania,
    189
Romeo and Juliet, 178
Rosencrantz and Guildenstern Are Dead
    68, 72
Roshchin, Michail, 207
Rossini, Joacino, 53
Rostand, Edmond, 50
Round the World in Eighty Days, 174
Royal Festival Hall, 191
Royal National Theater, UK, 178, 191
Royal Shakespeare Company, UK, 173,
    176, 190
Rozewicz, Tadeusz, 44, 173, 177, 195
Rubin and A-studio, Czech
    Republic, 54
Rudyk, Natalya, 242
Russev, Nikola, 32
Russia We Lost, The, 203
Russian Drama Theater, Latvia, 84
Russian Drama Theater, Lithuania, 107
Rustaveli Theater, Georgia, 1
Rutz, Kazimierz, 177

Rybakov, A., 237
Ryshov, Gelia, 203

S. K. Neumann Theater, Czech
    Republic, 44, 53
Saalbach, Astrid, 53
Sahlins, Bernard, 108, 109
Saka, Seraphim, 160
Sakva, Olexandr, 239
Sale of the Demonic Women, The, 172
Salinger, Jerome, 238, 240
Salome, Jewish Empress, 210
Salzburg Mozarteum, 177
Sapiro, Adolfs, 83, 87, 88
Saroyan, William, 163
Sartre, Jean Paul, 11, 16
Satin Slippers, 55
Satiricus Theater, Moldova, 160, 163,
    164
Scarlat, Nicolae, 187
Scarlet Theater, 174
Scene Studio-Theater, Latvia, 84
Scheffer, Boguslaw, 177
Schejbal, Milan, 51
Schikaneder, 71
Schiller, Friedrich, 85, 207
School of Dramatic Art, Russia, 209
School of Modern Dramatic Art,
    Russia, 207
School of Modern Plays Theater,
    Russia, 210
Schorm, Evald, 43
Schroffenstein Family, The, 72
Schultz, Bruno, 191
Scovoroda, G., 234
Seagull, The, 34, 54, 95, 163, 239
Sebastian, Mihail, 159, 163
Seciu, Valeria, 189
Secret Pictures, 94
Sedlenieks, Ints, 89
Sella, Robert, 110
Semafor Theater, Czech Republic, 46
Semenyk, Alexander, 242
Seneca, 193
Serban, Andrei, 185, 187, 188, 190, 191,
    192, 198
Sergienko, V., 210
Serso, 207

Seven Simpletons, The, 92, 93
Seweryn, Andrzej, 173
Sex, Drugs, And Rock'n Roll, 36
Shaffer, Peter, 161
Shakespeare Festival in Craiova, 191
Shakespeare, William, 14, 52, 53, 55,
    56, 83, 92, 156, 159, 178, 188, 190,
    196, 197, 235, 240
Shameless Old Men, The, 89
Shatrov, Mikhail, 203, 237
Shchepkin School, Russia, 211
Shepard, Sam, 211, 238
Shestopalov, Valentin, 235
Shevchenko, Taras, 240
Shevedova, O., 210
Shkuria, Ion Sandri, 156, 163
Shock, Shop, Show, 160
Shostakovich, Dmitry, 101
Shot in the Autumn Garden, 233
Show, 160
Shurpeko, Elena, 211
Shypenko, A., 233
Sidon, Karol, 44
Silesia Theater, Czech Republic, 48
Simon, Neil, 243
Skema, Antanas, 104
Slavkin, V. 207
Slavonic Pilgrims Program, 243 i
Slitr, Jiri, 46
Slobodzianek, Tadeusz, 177
Slovak National Theater Center, 219
Slovakian Academy of Sciences, 220
Slowackiego Theater, 177
Slyusarenko, Anatoly, 211
Small Theater of Vilnius, Lithuania,
    107, 111
Small Valentino, 67
Smile Upon Us, Lord, 107, 111
Smilgis, Eduards, 82
Smoking Room, The, 160
Snap, UK, 243
Sobol, Joshua, 196
Sokirke, Andrei, 163
Solomin, Yuri, 203, 208
Sonnets by Shakespeare, 52
Sophocles, 172, 234
Sound and the Fury, The, 96
Spalek, Jakub, 49, 50, 54

Spassov, Krassimir, 34, 35
Sperro, Martin, 53
SPHUMATO Theater Workshop,
    Bulgaria, 34
Spielwerke, Germany, 243
Spring's Awakening, 93, 94
Square, 108
Squat Theater, Hungary, 66
St. John's Eve, 105
Stage International, 177
Stanislavsky, 1, 10, 35, 66, 201, 208, 238
Staprans, R, 84
Stars On the Willow, 56
Stary Theater, Poland, 1, 171, 173, 176
State Center of Les Kurbas, Ukraine,
    229
State Fund for Culture, Pro-Slovakia,
    219
State Theater of Vilnius, Lithuania, 107
State Theater, Albania, 10
State Youth Theater, Lithuania, 108
Stefaniuk, Victor, 164
Stefanov, Vassil, 36
Stefanowicz, Artur, 177
Steigerwald, Karel, 51, 55
Stoichev, Valentin, 26, 28, 33
Stoka Theater, Slovakia, 217, 218, 219,
    220, 221, 222, 223, 224, 225
Stolen Happiness, The, 237
Stoppard, Tom, 44, 52, 68, 177, 211
Strambyanu, Michaela, 163
Stratiev, Stanislav, 31, 33
Street of Crocodiles, The, 111, 191
Strehler, Giorgio, 161, 229
Strindberg, August, 54, 71, 107, 109,
    111, 163
String with One End, 45
Strnisek, Vladimir, 44
Studio "S", Slovakia, 219
Studio Karlinek, Czech Republic, 46
Studio Theater, Ukraine, 235
Stuhr, Jerzy, 176
Stumbre, Lelde, 85, 90
Sturua, Robert, 238
Suchy, Jiri, 46
Sunset, 206
Sutovec, Milan, 220
Svoboda, Josef, 45

Swedish Royal Drama Theater, 111
Swinarski, Konrad, 1, 176
Sytnik, A., 239
Szajna Company, 177
Szajna, Jozef, 1
Szaniawski, Jerzy, 176
Szekely, Gabor, 68, 69
Szikora, Janos, 71
Szkene Theater, Hungary, 74
Szwajgier, Olga, 176

Tabori, Georg, 52
Taganka Theater, Russia, 1, 201, 206, 207
Tailor's Days in Silmaci, The, 89, 90
Tairov, A., 1, 82, 210
Talia Theater, Hungary, 70
Tamers of Troy, The, 53
Taming of the Shrew, The, 191
Tamuleviciute, Dalia, 108
Tankovska, Snejina, 35
Taras Shevchenko Theater, Ukraine, 240
Tashkent Theater Festival, 1
Taub, Janus, 70
Teatrul Mic Theater, Romania, 189
Technical University in Budapest, 74
Tembr Studio-Laboratory, Russia, 211
Tempest, The, 172, 191
Temptation, 44
Tender Women, 52
Tericose Theater, Russia, 211
Terra Incognita, 243
Tevie-Tevel, 239, 241
Thais, 235
Theater 13, Bulgaria, 29, 35
Theater 199, Bulgaria, 27, 33
Theater '89, 173
Theater and Life Magazine, Latvia, 84
Theater Bez Zabradli, Czech Republic, 50
Theater Faculty of the Moldova Institute of Fine Arts, 157
Theater Festival, The, Albania, 13, 14, 15
Theater For Young Spectators, Russia, 209
Theater Herald, The, Latvia, 85 i
Theater Institute at the Celetna Theater, Czech Republic, 49

Theater Komedie, Czech Republic, 50
Theater Na Vinohradech, Czech Republic, 43
Theater Na Zabradli, Czech Republic, 43, 44, 45, 51, 53, 54
Theater of Boleslav Polivka, Czech Republic, 50
Theater of Comedy, Romania, 187, 190
Theater of Cruelty, 83
Theater of Jara Cimrman, Czech Republic, 52
Theater of Satire, Bulgaria, 26, 27
Theater of Sibiu, 187
Theater of the Absurd, 83
Theater of the Eight Day, Poland, 173
Theater of the Russian (formerly Soviet) Army, 208
Theater of Vlora, Albania, 15
Theater on the Corso, Slovakia, 217
Theater Pod Palmovkou, Czech Republic, 53
Theater Rokoko, Czech Republic, 49
Theater Uhasicu, Czech Republic, 50
Theater Ungelt, Czech Republic, 50
Theater Za Branou, Czech Republic, 45, 48
Theater-Maker, 172 i
Theatertreffen, 1
Theater Ekspresji, Poland, 174
Theatre de Complicite, 111, 191
Theatrum Gedanense, Poland, 178
There To Be Here, 112
Third Policeman, 174
This Evening Lola Blau, 197
3/4—Zusno Company, 177
Three Minds on Auction, 15
Three Sisters, 34, 68, 111, 112, 174
Threetwoone, 174
Tidings Brought To Mary, 55
Time of Your Life, The, 163
Time When We Knew Nothing About Each Other, The, 107
Times, The, 190
Titus Andronicus, 178, 193
To Be the Child in Europe, 234
Today Is My Birthday, 172
Todorov, Ilie, 156
Tohatan, Marcel, 191

Tolstoy, Aleksey, 208
Tomaszuk, Piotr, 177
Tonight We Improvise, 68
Topol, Josef, 43
Torocsik, Mari, 70
Torun Festival, Poland, 229
Touched By Immortality, 85, 86
Tovstonogov, Georgi, 207
Tower Block, 174
Tramway Theatre, UK, 191
Trebicka, Alfred, 15
Trial, The, 107
Trifonovsky Experimental Theater, Russia, 210
Troilus and Cressida, 185
Trojan Women, The, 192
Tucci, S., 105
Tuminas, Rimas, 107, 111
Tunstrum Guren, 195
Turas, Jokubas, 112
Two Theaters, 176
Tyl Theater, Czech Republic, 49
Tytarenko, Lubow, 235
Tzanev, Stefan, 32, 33

Ubu Roi with Scenes from Macbeth, 188, 190, 193
Ubu Roi, 106
Uhde, Milan, 44
Uhlar, Blaho, 218, 220, 222, 223
Ukrainka, Lesyia, 238, 240
Ulmanis, Karlis, 84
Ulysses, 234
Uncle Vanya, 108, 112
Uncle's Dream, 70 i
Ungurianu, Ion, 156
Union of European Theaters, 68, 176, 190
Union of Theater Actors (UNITEM), Moldova, 156
Union of Transport Enterprises, Slovakia, 218
UNITER (the Theatrical Union of Romania), 186, 189, 190
University Stage, Hungary, 74
Upits, A., 86
Urski, Georgie, 160
Ursu, Niki, 163

V. Alexandri Theater in Belts, Moldova, 156, 159, 162, 163
Vaclav Lohnicky, 53
Vaidilos Ainiai Chamber Theater, Lithuania, 109, 110
Vaitkus, Jonas, 104, 106, 107, 109, 111
Vakhtangov, Evgeny, 82, 201, 202, 210
Vampilov, Alexander, 205
Varnas, Gintaras, 104, 112
Varnas, Saulius, 107
Varslavane, Vecella, 94
Vasilacu, Sandu, 161, 163
Vecerskis, Adolfas, 109
Vedagon Theater, Russia, 211
Vedensky, 112
Vedral, Jan, 51
Velca, Elona, 17
Versia Drama Theater, Russia, 210
Vertep, puppet theater, Ukraine, 231
Vetra, Varis, 84
Vian, Boris, 51
Victims of Duty, 16
Vidniyansky, Atilla, 239, 241, 243
Viktiuk, Roman, 207, 240
Vinnichenko, V., 238
Visa, Iulian, 185, 187, 195, 196
Visarion, Alexa, 191
Visit, The, 15
Volksstuck, 89
Volkstheater, 72, 73
Volontir, Mihai, 163
Vorosmarty, 69
Voskovec, 56
Vostry, Jaroslav, 45
Voynovich, 238
Vucans, Odums, 93
Vutkereu, Petru, 162, 163
Vysotsky, Vladimir, 212

Waiting for Godot, 14, 15, 32, 35, 69, 72, 104, 162, 163 i
Waiting For the Theater Conference, 177
Wajda, Andrzei, 1, 171, 175, 176, 178
Wallace, Neill, 191
Ward Number Six, 208
Water Hen, The, 1

We, 160
Wedekind, F., 93
Weiss, Peter, 69
Welminski, Andzej, 172
Werich, Jan, 51, 56
West Side Story, 73
Where Are We Going, Gentlemen?, 160
White, George, 209, 212
Who's Afraid of the Gray Wolf?, 235
Who's Afraid of Virginia Wolf?, 235
Wielopolie, Weilopolie, 107
Wienerfestwochen, Austria, 190
Wierszalin Association Theater,
    Poland, 177
Wififi Company, Poland, 174
Wild Duck, The, 90
Wilder, Thornton, 106, 238
Williams, Tennessee, 11, 238
Wilson, Robert, 94
Wiman, Ruta, 108, 109
Winter's Tale, The, 197
Wiseman, 209 i
Wisniewski, Janusz, 175
Witkiewicz, 1, 172, 178
Woc From Wil, 207
Wolf, Christa, 172
Wood Demon, The, 208
World and Theater, Magazine, 51, 224
World Theatre Seasons, UK, 1
Woza Albert, 190
Writer's Theater, Hungary, 68
Wyeth, Andrew, 94
Wyspianski, 171

Xarxa Theater, Spain, 111
Xhillari, Petraq, 16, 17

Yara Arts Group, USA, 234, 243
Yaremkiv, Mykola, 240
Yashin, Sergei, 207
Year In the Village, 55
You Cannot Live Like That, 206
Young Vic Theater, UK, 174
Your Sister and Your Niece, 208
Youth Studio, Albania, 15
Youth Theater, Latvia, 87
Yursky, S., 210

Z Lublina Company, Poland, 174
Zablocky, 112
Zagorskis, Rolands, 86
Zaikauskas, Linas, 107
Zajmi, Agim, 15
Zakharov, Mark, 206, 209
Zamyatin, 205
Zarina, Aija, 91
Zemgals, Gunars, 84
Zholdak, Andrey, 239, 243
Zhukov, Titus Bogdan, 164
Zilinskas, Kestutis, 104
Ziolo, Rudolf, 176
Zoo Story, 31
Zsyter, Sandor, 71
Zuderman, 105
Zvaigznite, Jekabs, 93
Zylo Kamberi, 16